# THE
# VEGAN
# TABLE

Merry Christmas Deb!

Enjoy un good health

Love,
Jen

# THE VEGAN TABLE

## 200
### UNFORGETTABLE RECIPES
### FOR ENTERTAINING EVERY GUEST
### AT EVERY OCCASION

Colleen Patrick-Goudreau

FAIR WINDS
PRESS
BEVERLY, MASSACHUSETTS

Text © 2009 Colleen Patrick-Goudreau

First published in the USA in 2009 by
Fair Winds Press, a member of
Quayside Publishing Group
100 Cummings Center
Suite 406-L
Beverly, MA 01915-6101
www.fairwindspress.com

13 12 11 10 09      2 3 4 5

ISBN-13: 978-1-59233-374-5
ISBN-10: 1-59233-374-5

**Library of Congress Cataloging-in-Publication Data available**
Patrick-Goudreau, Colleen.
  The vegan table : 200 unforgettable recipes for entertaining
every guest at every occasion / Colleen Patrick-Goudreau.
     p. cm.
  Includes index.
  ISBN-13: 978-1-59233-374-5
  ISBN-10: 1-59233-374-5
1.  Vegan cookery. 2.  Menus.  I. Title.
  TX837.P338 2009
  641.5'636--dc22

                    2008046152


Cover and book design: BradhamDesign.com
Photography:  Glenn Scott Photography; images on pages 12, 58,
              104, 126, 148, 152, 196, 245, 246, 260 and
              cover photo middle left: © 2008 Cheri M. Larsh
Food Stylist:   Jennifer Costello

Printed and bound in China

# DEDICATION

My hope is that we can all navigate through this world with the grace and integrity of those who most need our protection.

May we have the sense of humor and liveliness of the goats, the maternal instincts and protective nature of the hens, and the sassiness of the roosters. May we have the gentleness and strength of the cattle, the wisdom, serenity, and humility of the donkeys. May we appreciate the need for community as do the sheep and choose our companions as carefully as do the rabbits. May we have the faithfulness and commitment to family of the geese and the adaptability and affability of the ducks. May we have the intelligence, loyalty, and affection of the pigs and the inquisitiveness, sensitivity, and playfulness of the turkeys.

May we learn from the animals what we need to become better people.

# CONTENTS

# INTRODUCTION

## WHY VEGAN ENTERTAINING?

I have always believed that the work we do in this world should reflect our passions and skills. I never understood the notion that you have a *life* and then you have a *work life*. To me, they never should be separate.

Although I always knew that I wanted my contribution to the world to help make it better somehow, I didn't know how that desire would manifest itself. After I received my master's degree in English Literature, I was invariably asked what I would do with my degree. Having taught freshman English in graduate school, I knew that working within the confines of someone else's curriculum wasn't for me, and though literature was my first love, I wouldn't be satisfied pursuing a career in academia.

I remember saying to myself, "I don't know what it's going to look like, but I want to do something that involves writing, teaching, and animal rights." Be careful what you wish for—you just might get it.

Determined to make a life (not just a living) and led by my passion for animal rights, I built a vocation out of my activism, the foundation on which I now stand. Everything I do stems from my desire to speak for those who cannot, to raise awareness about needless suffering, and to empower people to live authentically and compassionately. Never did I imagine that cookbooks would be part of this picture.

When I was approached about writing a vegan baking cookbook, admittedly, the activist in me resisted. In fact, I flat out declined. I didn't want to write a cookbook for its own sake, and I knew it would require putting other projects aside. But because I try to demystify vegan food every chance I get, I realized that a baking cookbook was an opportunity to provide people with delicious, traditional, familiar desserts, and it was something no one had ever done before in this way. And so, *The Joy of Vegan Baking* was born.

When I was approached about writing a *second* cookbook, though flattered, I resisted again. I felt that there were a number of excellent vegan cookbooks on the market, and I wanted to be sure my contribution was unique and valuable. When the idea of writing a cookbook based on *entertaining* came along, I perked up. Here was a chance to offer ideas, tips, tools, menus, and recipes for holidays and occasions that have become meat-, egg-, and dairy-centric, and to reclaim food traditions steeped in animal exploitation. And so, *The Vegan Table* was born.

When I told friends I was writing a book about entertaining, they responded with enthusiasm but not surprise. Knowing my penchant for throwing parties, they understood that it was the perfect fit.

I grew up with a mother who entertained constantly: small dinner gatherings, festive birthdays, and large parties in the backyard that included potato sack races, horseshoes, and badminton. You name it, she hosted it. To my delight (and my husband's distress), I have taken after my mother: I am an entertaining maniac. The only difference is that animals are on the guest list, not on the menu.

When my publisher and I threw around ideas for titles of this book, the one thing I insisted on was that we not use the phrase "vegan entertaining." To me, that phrase implies that vegans employ some unique method of entertaining, when in truth, they are just normal folk who want to celebrate occasions and gather with friends, just like everyone else.

> I HAVE TAKEN AFTER MY MOTHER: I AM AN ENTERTAINING MANIAC. THE ONLY DIFFERENCE IS THAT ANIMALS ARE ON THE GUEST LIST, NOT ON THE MENU.

It would be disingenuous, however, to say there isn't something special about a gathering where no animals were harmed for the sake of our pleasure. When a sense of consciousness informs our actions, when our intentions reflect kindness and nonviolence, when our thoughts turn to someone else's needs rather than our own desires, there is no denying that something profound takes place. In the absence of suffering, there is peace. In the presence of compassion, there is joy.

*That* is "vegan entertaining."

Whether you are hosting an intimate gathering of close friends or a large celebration with an open guest list, may this book serve as a guide. May you make choices that reflect your deepest values, and may you find abundance and joy in a life lived simply so that others may simply live.

# HOW TO READ THIS COOKBOOK

I have been teaching cooking for many years and am thrilled to share these recipes with you, many of which have been developed and perfected with my students. In the process of demonstrating recipes to thousands of people, I have definitely learned that the more information you provide, the better.

Having said that, I do believe that a recipe is only a guide, and I encourage you to make modifications (short of adding animal products!). If a baked good is too sweet, reduce the sugar; if you want to use chickpea flour instead of all-purpose, be my guest. The options are endless. I can offer only so many variations.

Per serving: 73 calories; 7g fat; trace protein; 1g carbohydrate; trace dietary fiber; 0mg cholesterol; 35mg sodium.

# THERE ARE A FEW OTHER THINGS WORTH NOTING ABOUT HOW THE RECIPES ARE ORGANIZED.

## MIX-AND-MATCH MENUS

I make menu suggestions based on the recipes in each chapter, but I encourage you to draw from all chapters for menu ideas. Remember to consider the various serving sizes when doing so.

## NUTRITIONAL ANALYSIS

I'm actually not a big fan of using standard "nutritional analyses" as a way of making food choices, because I think our obsession with single nutrients simply leads to more confusion. However, I decided to include the information here because I wanted to make each recipe as comprehensive as possible. Please note that for those recipes with a range of servings (6 to 8 servings, for instance), the analysis was done on the larger number, or the smaller portion (so the 8, in this case).

Also, please keep in mind that those recipes that appear to be higher in calories and fat are often meant for special occasions. Feel free to make them lighter if you so desire.

## SENSITIVE TO ALL NEEDS

Each recipe indicates whether it is oil-free, wheat-free, or soy-free. This is not meant to imply that these ingredients are "bad" in and of themselves, but because wheat and soy tend to be common allergens, I wanted to make it easy for those avoiding or reducing these elements in their diet.

The reason I decided to indicate the absence of oil is because it reflects the way I cook. Oils such as olive and canola are indeed higher in monounsaturated fats, but they are still oils, and I encourage people to get their good fat from food itself. We *need* fat, but we don't necessarily *need* oil, and though I don't advocate counting calories or fat grams, I do encourage people to cut oil (not whole fat) when they can.

I also want to note that Earth Balance now has a soy-free version of their butter. Recipes not marked "soy-free" because of the inclusion of Earth Balance could be very easily modified using the soy-free version.

## LITERATURE, SONG, AND FILM REFERENCES

Enjoy the menu titles, many of which are titles of my favorite songs, books, and movies.

## BE PREPARED

Some recipes indicate their need for Advance Preparation (like pizza dough that has to rise). Always read through a recipe first to know what to expect.

## COMPANION COOKBOOK

Although there are certainly baked goods and other desserts in this cookbook, my first book, *The Joy of Vegan Baking*, has 150 recipes that can round out your dessert needs for every occasion or holiday!

# HAPPY ENTERTAINING!

# CHAPTER 1

COZY COUPLING:
# ROMANTIC DINNERS FOR TWO

Preparing a beautiful home-cooked meal is the perfect opportunity for romance. Devising a special menu, preparing the ingredients, eating together in a peaceful setting, and creating an intentionally romantic mood is the ultimate expression of generosity and thoughtfulness—of love.

The preparation and consumption of wholesome plant-based foods stimulate all of our senses: touch, smell, hearing, sight, and, of course, taste. This heightened awareness enables us to have a deeper sense of connection with ourselves and with those we care about.

# RECIPES

# THE INTIMACY OF FOOD

Our connection with certain foods is powerful. Not only is our sense of smell linked to our sense of taste, but smell is also intrinsically linked with the part of our brain that experiences emotional memory. This is perhaps why a particular dish can trigger a strong emotional reaction.

This is certainly a phenomenon to honor, because it elevates our appreciation of food, connects us with our past, and draws us closer to those for whom we cook and with whom we share our meals.

However, I also find that it can keep us from honoring what we say we care about most. Our relationship with food has become so romanticized, ritualized, and politicized that many of us don't realize that it also has the potential to hurt our relationship with others and with ourselves.

I often say that the way we eat is based on habit, and that's the bad news and the good news. It's the bad news because we are creatures dedicated to our habits. It's the good news because habits were meant to be broken. In fact, the earliest root of the word *habit* referred to a piece of clothing one wore, which is why we can just as easily put on new habits as shed old ones.

When we fix our gaze on what we *used* to do, we risk not seeing what we *could* do. By sanctifying the past—our old habits—we may miss out on the future—the creation of new habits.

Continuing to eat animals, a tenacious habit for many, simply because that's what we've always known is not a good enough reason to participate in something that goes against our values and supports one of the most violent industries on the planet.

## CONSUMING FEAR

Most people don't look inside a slaughterhouse because they know if they did, they might be compelled to make different choices. It is our fear of change—our attachment to old habits—that drives us to keep eating animals and their products. It is our fear of doing something different that keeps us stuck in old behavior.

This is what I mean when I say that this habit harms our relationships. Our ability to compartmentalize our emotions and justify the pain of other living creatures in favor of momentary pleasure cannot *but* affect us at the most fundamental level. How can we function as whole human beings when we consciously cut ourselves off from a part of ourselves every time we sit down to eat?

Some people even believe that the fear, pain, and violence experienced by the animals during slaughter are taken up into their flesh and fluids and then into our own bodies when we consume them. Hokey though it may sound, we cannot deny that a plant-based meal is

# FOODS FOR ROMANCE: APHRODISIACS

We all know that the saturated fat in meat, dairy, and eggs hinders blood flow, and optimum health (as well as optimum romance) is all about keeping our blood flowing—to all organs in the body. So not only is following a vegan diet the most powerful aphrodisiac there is, we can also have fun choosing certain libido-enhancing foods for their visual, tactile, olfactory, or aural traits, as well as for their internal effects. The recipes that follow were created with this in mind.

built from life-giving rather than life-taking foods. This is what I want to serve to the people I love most.

## EATING CONSCIOUSLY

I didn't stop eating animals because I didn't like the way they tasted. I stopped eating animals and their "products" because I didn't want to contribute to the violence and exploitation of another when I didn't have to. It is a powerful and empowering way to live.

The sense of peace you feel when you align your behavior with your values is tangible. It connects you with everything and everyone around you, and I can't think of a better way to deepen our participation in this world than by feeding our loved ones food that heals rather than harms.

May the dinners you create expand your heart as well as your palate, and may they draw you closer to those you love.

# CREATING A ROMANTIC DINNER

The idea is to excite—not overload—the senses. Keep the portions small, eat at a leisurely pace, and create a menu that is flavorful but not too heavy. Overeating in general can leave you feeling lethargic rather than libidinous, which can hinder a night of **AMORE**. Here are some tips to make the most of a romantic evening.

## BLITHE SPIRITS
Excessive alcohol can squelch the romance. If you choose to drink, keep the amount of alcohol to a minimum: one or two glasses of wine or champagne. If you want to skip it altogether, get the bubbly effect from sparkling juices and ciders. (See page 152 for information about vegan wine and beer.)

## IF MUSIC BE THE FOOD OF LOVE, PLAY ON
These lines open Shakespeare's *Twelfth Night*, a play brimming with romance. If you're not going to read the play to one another (though that's a great idea!), then at least take Duke Orsino's advice and strike up the tunes.

## SHAPE OF MY HEART
Whether you're making pancakes, polenta, or pie, jazz up your dish with heart shapes. Use a cookie cutter or heart-shaped cake pans, or serve dishes that feature hearts of palm, hearts of celery, romaine hearts, or artichoke hearts.

## POCKET FULL OF POSIES
Posies are little bouquets of flowers or herbs that make lovely and affordable arrangements, since you can make them as small or large as you desire. Add lavender, rosemary, and sage for additional fragrance.

## BURNING BRIGHT
Light candles in each room you'll occupy, but keep the mood high by choosing soy-based candles rather than traditional candles, which may use beeswax or stearic acid (a slaughterhouse product derived from the fat of cattle and sheep). Light a fire in the fireplace using eco-friendly logs, such as *Java Logs*, made from coffee grounds.

## POETRY IN MOTION
As an unabashed romantic with a husband who reads books of poetry from cover to cover, I admit that I'm a bit biased. Reading a poem out loud over dinner may seem sappy, but there's a reason we equate poetry with romance. Trust me.

## GONE WITH THE WIND
Although some people digest beans with no problem, it's best to err on the side of caution when planning a night of intimacy.

# SUGGESTED SEASONAL MENUS

These menus can help you create the perfect meal for two.

## 🌂 SPRING

### LAUGHTER IN THE RAIN, PAGE 18
Steamed Artichokes
Dipping Sauce for Artichokes
Spring Vegetable Risotto
Pan-Fried (or Roasted) Asparagus with Lime Juice
Not-Just-for-Breakfast Banana Split

### EASTERN GLOW, PAGE 25
Thai Curry with Veggies
Pad Thai
Honeydew Melon in Coconut Milk

## ☀ SUMMER

### RISE AND SHINE, PAGE 28
Tofu Scramble
Tempeh Bacon
Love Potions
Peach and Pecan Muffins

### IN THE HEAT OF THE NIGHT, PAGE 35
Sweet and Sour Tempeh
Basil Eggplant (Pud Makua Yow)
Dark Leafy Greens with Sesame Miso Dressing

## 🍃 AUTUMN

### THAT'S AMORE, PAGE 38
Braised Figs with Arugula
Saffron-Spiked Moroccan Stew
Red Velvet Cake with Buttercream Frosting

### INAMORATA, PAGE 44
Fennel, Orange, Walnut, and Pomegranate Salad
Sweet and Spicy Pumpkin Soup
Marvelous Mushroom Risotto

## ❄ WINTER

### BABY, IT'S COLD OUTSIDE, PAGE 47
Toasted Quinoa with Raisins and Slivered Almonds
Garlic and Greens Soup
Penne Arrabbiata

### PRELUDE TO A KISS, PAGE 50
Carrot Ginger Soup
Cashew Sour Cream
Polenta Hearts (or squares)
Roasted Red Pepper Coulis
Swiss Chard and Caramelized Onions
Chocolate Fondues

**SPRING MENU:** Laughter in the Rain

🌂 Steamed Artichokes  🌂 Dipping Sauce for Artichokes
🌂 Spring Vegetable Risotto  🌂 Pan-Fried (or Roasted) Asparagus with Lime Juice
🌂 Not-Just-for-Breakfast Banana Split

# STEAMED ARTICHOKES

*Oil-free, wheat-free, soy-free*

Artichokes, the perfect start to an intimate dinner, have been enjoyed for centuries.
The simple act of stripping an artichoke of its leaves, dipping those leaves into sauce,
and scraping off the tender flesh with your teeth is a very sensual experience.

- 4 whole artichokes
- ¼ cup (60 ml) fresh lemon juice
- 2 whole garlic cloves, peeled
- 2 bay leaves
- Dipping sauce of your choosing (see page 19)

## DIRECTIONS

If the artichokes have little thorns on their leaves, use
a pair of kitchen scissors to cut off the tips.

Turn the artichoke on its side, and using a sharp serrated knife, slice about 1 inch (2.5 cm) off the top. Pull off
any smaller leaves toward the base and on the stem. Cut
off any excess stem, leaving up to an inch (2.5 cm) on
the artichoke. Wash under cold running water, pat dry,
and rub the base of the artichoke with the lemon juice.

In a large-size pot, add a few inches (8 cm) of water
and garlic and bay leaves. Place a steaming basket in the
pot, and add the artichokes to the basket. Cover. Bring to
a boil and reduce the heat to a simmer. (Check periodically to make sure the water hasn't evaporated.)

Cook for 40 to 60 minutes, or until outer leaves
easily pull off. Serve with a dipping sauce.

**YIELD:** 2 to 4 servings

Per serving: 66 calories; trace fat; 4g protein; 15g carbohydrate; 7g dietary fiber; 0mg cholesterol; 121mg sodium.

## COMPASSIONATE COOKS' TIP

To eat an artichoke, pull off outer petals one at a time.
Dip the white fleshy end into the sauce, holding on to
the other end of the petal. Place in mouth, sauce side
down, and pull through teeth to remove soft portion of the petal. Discard remaining portion of petal.
Continue until all of the petals are removed. Then, use
a knife or spoon to scrape out and discard the inedible
fuzzy part (called the choke). The remaining bottom
of the artichoke is the heart. Cut into pieces and dip
into sauce to eat.

## DID YOU KNOW?

One hundred percent of the U.S. artichoke crop
is grown in California.

# DIPPING SAUCES FOR ARTICHOKES

*Wheat-free*

Try any of these dipping sauces for steamed artichokes.

## QUICK OPTIONS

*Garlic Aioli*, an eggless/dairy-free mayonnaise made by Wildwood Organics, is so flavorful (and garlicky!) that it alone is sufficient as your artichoke-dipping agent.

Whether it's Wildwood Garlic Aioli, NASOYA Nayonaise, Follow Your Heart Vegenaise, or Spectrum Naturals Eggless Light Mayo, all of which are vegan, you can spruce up mayonnaise by adding lemon juice, cayenne pepper, curry powder, balsamic vinegar, or fresh herbs.

Another simple option is to combine nondairy butter with some freshly squeezed lemon or lime juice.

## TANGY CREAMY DIP

- 1 1/2 cups (340 g) eggless mayonnaise (any of the above brands)
- 1 tablespoon (15 g) Dijon mustard
- 3 tablespoons (27 g) minced capers
- 3 tablespoons (30 g) minced shallots
- 1/4 cup (16 g) mixed fresh herbs (such as chives, tarragon, or parsley), finely chopped
- Lemon juice, to taste
- Salt, to taste
- Cayenne pepper, to taste

## DIRECTIONS

Mix all ingredients together until well blended.

**YIELD:** 1 1/2 cups (430 g) or 12 (2-tablespoon [36 g]) servings

Per serving: 73 calories; 7g fat; trace protein; 1g carbohydrate; trace dietary fiber; 0mg cholesterol; 35mg sodium.

## COMPASSIONATE COOKS' TIP

This dip is also fantastic for the Pan-Fried (or Roasted) Asparagus with Lime Juice on page 22.

## DID YOU KNOW?

Dilating the blood vessels, cayenne pepper increases blood flow throughout the body.

# SPRING VEGETABLE RISOTTO

*Wheat-free, soy-free*

Use this recipe as a model for many of your favorite vegetables, so long as those on the sturdy side, such as artichoke hearts, broccoli, or beets, are precooked.

- 1 bunch asparagus, tough stem ends cut off, with stalks cut into 2-inch (5 cm) pieces
- 4 carrots, peeled and julienned
- 6 cups (1410 ml) vegetable stock, plus more if needed (store-bought or homemade on page 213)
- ½ cup (120 ml) dry white wine (optional)
- 1 to 2 tablespoons (15 to 30 ml) olive oil, for sautéing
- 2 garlic cloves, minced
- 2 bunches scallions (12 to 16), white parts chopped, and ¼ cup (25 g) of thinly sliced green parts reserved
- 2 cups (390 g) Arborio rice
- 1 cup (130 g) frozen baby green peas, thawed
- Salt and pepper, to taste
- Yellow pear tomatoes, for garnish (optional)

## DIRECTIONS

Steam asparagus and carrots until tender but crisp, about 10 minutes. Transfer to a bowl and set aside until needed.

Add stock and wine to a saucepan. Heat until barely simmering. (You will typically need between 5 and 6 cups [1175 and 1410 ml] of total liquid for the risotto.)

In a large-size sauté pan, heat oil over medium heat. Add garlic and white parts of the scallions and cook, stirring, until softened, about 3 minutes. Add rice and cook, stirring constantly, for 2 minutes.

Reduce heat to medium, and add 1 cup (235 ml) simmering stock. Stir until stock is absorbed. Continue to add stock, one ladleful at a time, until almost all the liquid has been absorbed and the rice begins to soften, about 20 minutes.

Stir in peas and another cup of stock. Continue stirring constantly until the liquid has almost been absorbed and the rice begins to thicken. Stir in the steamed vegetables, adding more of the stock as needed, until the mixture is creamy, not runny, the rice is tender yet firm to the bite, and the vegetables are heated through, about 5 minutes.

Remove from heat and stir in reserved ¼ cup (25 g) scallion greens and salt and pepper. Serve at once, garnished with pear tomatoes, if desired.

**YIELD:** 2 to 4 servings

Per serving: 617 calories; 12g fat; 16g protein; 114g carbohydrate; 15g dietary fiber; 0mg cholesterol; 692mg sodium.

## COMPASSIONATE COOKS' TIP

Arborio rice works best in risotto because of its high starch content, which gives the dish it's creamy texture. You can use other types of rice, but Arborio really is best.

# PAN-FRIED (OR ROASTED) ASPARAGUS WITH LIME JUICE

*Wheat-free, soy-free*

Asparagus has frequently been considered an aphrodisiac because of its, *ahem*, shape. In fact, in nineteenth-century France, bridegrooms were required to eat several courses of asparagus because of its reputed powers to arouse.

- 1 teaspoon (5 g) nondairy, nonhydrogenated butter (such as Earth Balance), optional
- 1 tablespoon (15 ml) olive oil
- 2 garlic cloves, minced
- 1 medium-size shallot, minced
- 1 bunch fresh asparagus spears, tough ends trimmed
- Juice from ¼ lime
- Salt and pepper, to taste

## DIRECTIONS

Melt butter with olive oil in a large-size skillet over medium heat. Stir in garlic and shallot, and cook for 2 minutes. Stir in asparagus spears; cook until bright green and tender, about 5 to 7 minutes.

Squeeze lime juice over hot asparagus, and season with salt and pepper. Transfer to a serving plate and garnish with lime wedges.

**YIELD:** 2 servings

## SERVING SUGGESTIONS AND VARIATIONS

Instead of pan-frying, combine all the ingredients, coating the asparagus in oil and roast in a preheated 450-degree oven for 15 minutes.

## COMPASSIONATE COOKS' TIP

Earth Balance is now available soy-free, making this recipe easy to modify for those with allergies to soybeans, but olive oil can certainly be used instead.

Per serving: 112 calories; 7g fat; 2g protein; 8g carbohydrate; 2g dietary fiber; 0mg cholesterol; 3mg sodium.

# NOT-JUST-FOR-BREAKFAST BANANA SPLIT

*Oil-free, wheat-free*

I love this healthful variation of the typically decadent dessert. In addition to being a wonderful breakfast for two, it also makes a fantastic dessert.

- 2 ripe bananas
- 6 fresh strawberries, sliced
- 1/2 cup (75 g) fresh blueberries
- 2 containers (6 ounces, or 170 g, each) nondairy yogurt (strawberry, peach, vanilla, or blueberry)
- 1/4 cup (20 g) granola
- 4 maraschino cherries

## DIRECTIONS

Peel bananas and slice each one lengthwise. Place each banana in its own serving dish.

For each dish, place half of the strawberries and half of the blueberries on the banana slices. Spoon yogurt over the berries, and top with the remaining berries. Sprinkle with granola, and garnish with cherries, 2 per serving dish.

**YIELD:** 2 servings

## SERVING SUGGESTIONS AND VARIATIONS

After you assemble the banana split, drizzle a fruit-based sauce over it for added color and flavor. My favorite coulis (fruit sauce) is made by adding raspberries to a blender along with a sweetener (agave nectar or Sucanat, for example). Sweeten to your taste, and keep in a squeeze bottle in the fridge for drizzling on desserts or fruit.

Per serving: 233 calories; 5g fat; 4g protein; 48g carbohydrate; 6g dietary fiber; 0mg cholesterol; 13mg sodium.

## SPRINGTIME TREATS

### MAKE A GIFT BASKET

Create a special spring basket for a loved one filled with the ingredients for your favorite coffee cake or muffins, along with a recipe or a cookbook (ahem!). Festoon the basket with daffodils, or include Easter lily bulbs, the quintessential symbol of spring. For kids, include egg- or bunny-shaped cookies, carrot cake, nondairy chocolate bunnies and eggs, books and coloring books, stickers, or a stuffed animal.

### REAP WHAT YOU SOW

What better way to honor the end of winter and the promise of spring than to plant an herb or vegetable garden? Purchase organic seeds from a local nursery, and begin a process that embodies the true meaning of the season. A simple herb garden will thrive as long as you have sun, and basics such as lettuce, kale, and collards will keep you in the green stuff for many months to come.

# THAI CURRY WITH VEGGIES

*Oil-free, wheat-free, soy-free without tofu*

Making a delicious pot of curry is faster than you may think and enables you to use any variety of vegetables and any variety of curries (red, green, Massaman, or yellow). Red is the hottest; yellow is the mildest.

- 2 cans (14 ounces, or 425 ml, each) unsweetened coconut milk (use "lite" for less calories)
- Curry paste (red, green, Massaman, or yellow; see directions below for how much to use)
- 1 medium-size yellow onion, coarsely chopped
- 2 or 3 garlic cloves, minced
- 1 package (16 ounces, or 455 g) firm or extra-firm tofu, cut into ½-inch (1 cm) cubes
- 3 yellow potatoes (Yukon gold, fingerling, or yellow fin), diced
- 1 bunch cauliflower florets
- 1 can (10 ounces, or 280 g) bamboo shoots (optional)
- 1 to 2 red bell peppers, cut into long strips
- 1 bunch fresh Thai basil, coarsely chopped (optional)
- Salt, to taste
- 2 cups (330 g) cooked jasmine or basmati brown rice

Per serving: 750 calories; 55g fat; 20g protein; 58g carbohydrate; 12g dietary fiber; 0mg cholesterol; 129mg sodium.

## DIRECTIONS

Spoon out half of one of the cans, incorporating any thicker part that might be on the lid, and bring to a gentle boil over medium heat. Cook, stirring occasionally, until milk releases its sweet fragrance, about 3 minutes.

Add curry paste and cook for 3 more minutes, mashing, scraping, and stirring often to soften the paste and combine it with the coconut milk. The amount of curry paste you need to add depends on the brand you buy. The best Thai curry pastes can be found in Asian markets, but be sure to look for one without fish sauce. Follow the instructions on the package for how much to use.

Add onion and garlic, stirring gently to coat with curry paste. Sauté for 5 minutes.

Add remaining 1½ cans coconut milk, tofu, potatoes, cauliflower, and bamboo shoots (if using). Combine well, and bring to an active boil. Reduce heat to maintain a gentle boil, and simmer for 15 minutes, stirring occasionally.

Add red peppers, and stir gently. Cook for 5 more minutes, until peppers are cooked but not too soft. Add basil, and let cook for 1 more minute. Add salt to taste, remove from heat, and transfer to a serving bowl filled with rice, preferably jasmine or basmati.

**YIELD:** 2 to 4 servings

## SERVING SUGGESTIONS AND VARIATIONS

Also try button mushrooms, bok choy, peas, carrots, sweet potatoes, broccoli, or green beans.

# PAD THAI
*Wheat-free*

This is an authentic Thai recipe without the unsavory fish sauce and shrimp (though vegetarian fish sauce is available). Plus, because it's made with rice noodles, this dish is gluten-free. Although vegetables are not strictly part of traditional Pad Thai, I recommend adding broccoli or snow peas to make this dish even more nutritious.

- 8 ounces (225 g) rice noodles
- Sesame or canola oil, for sautéing tofu
- 1 package (16 ounces, or 455 g) extra-firm tofu, cubed
- Salt and pepper, to taste
- ¼ cup (64 g) creamy or crunchy natural peanut butter
- ¼ cup (50 g) granulated sugar
- ⅓ cup (80 ml) tamari soy sauce
- ⅓ cup (80 ml) lime (or lemon) juice
- ½ teaspoon red pepper flakes
- 2 or 3 garlic cloves, minced
- 2 cups (140 g) chopped broccoli or snow peas, steamed or stir-fried
- 1 bunch scallions, chopped (including green parts)
- 1 cup (50 g) bean sprouts
- Sliced lemons, for garnish (optional)
- Chopped cilantro, for garnish (optional)

## DIRECTIONS

Cook the rice noodles according to package directions, drain, and immediately return them to the pot, secured with a tight lid to keep them from drying out excessively. They will re-moisten once you add them to the sauce below.

Heat oil in a pan and sauté tofu until golden brown. Sprinkle on salt and pepper while it's cooking.

In a bowl, mix together peanut butter, sugar, tamari, lime juice, and red pepper flakes. Set aside.

In a separate large-size sauté pan, heat oil or a little water or stock and add garlic and broccoli; stir-fry for 5 to 10 minutes, until broccoli turns bright green. Add scallions and sauté for a few more minutes.

To that pan, add the cooked noodles, tofu, peanut butter mixture, and bean sprouts. Combine well, and cook just until all the ingredients are heated through. Garnish with sliced lemons and cilantro, if using. Serve immediately.

**YIELD:** 2 to 4 servings

Per serving: 387 calories; 17g fat; 18g protein; 44g carbohydrate; 4g dietary fiber; 0mg cholesterol; 1423mg sodium.

# HONEYDEW MELON IN COCONUT MILK

*Oil-free, wheat-free, soy-free*

Any tropical fruit pairs well with coconut milk, which, though fatty, is perfectly acceptable as a once-in-a-while treat.

- 1 can (14 ounces, or 425 ml) unsweetened coconut milk (lite is fine, too)
- 3 tablespoons (40 g) granulated sugar
- Juice from 1/2 lime (or to taste)
- 1 large-size honeydew melon, chilled and diced (or scooped out with a melon baller)
- Zest from 1 lime, for garnish (optional)
- Shredded coconut, for garnish (optional)

## DIRECTIONS

Fill a large-size bowl with ice and cold water.

In a smaller bowl, stir together coconut milk, sugar, and lime juice, until sugar dissolves. Place this bowl inside the larger bowl, and let chill for 10 minutes. Stir occasionally.

Divide melon among serving dishes, and add a few tablespoons of coconut mixture on top. Garnish with lime zest and shredded coconut, if desired. Serve immediately, or refrigerate for at least an hour (no more than overnight) before serving.

**YIELD:** 4 to 6 servings

## WHAT'S THE DIFFERENCE? HONEYDEW VS. CANTALOUPE

Honeydew, the American name for the White Antibes that has been grown for many years in southern France and Algeria, is round, with a smooth outer skin. Its flesh is pale green.

Cantaloupe is somewhat oblong, although not as oblong as watermelon, and has a rough outer skin. Its flesh is orange and is high in vitamin C and beta-carotene, like most orange and red fruits.

Per serving: 265 calories; 17g fat; 3g protein; 31g carbohydrate; 3g dietary fiber; 0mg cholesterol; 32mg sodium.

# TOFU SCRAMBLE

*Wheat-free, oil-free (if sautéed in water)*

Scrambled tofu makes a satisfying—and healthful—breakfast or brunch. The turmeric in this dish is essential in imparting a beautiful yellow-orange color to the final result.

- 2 tablespoons (30 ml) water or 1 tablespoon (15 ml) olive oil, for sautéing
- 1 medium-size yellow onion or 3 scallions, finely chopped
- 1 teaspoon (3 g) minced garlic
- 10 cremini mushrooms, sliced
- 1 bell pepper (red, yellow, orange, or green), diced
- 1 package (16 ounces, or 455 g) firm or extra-firm tofu, drained and rinsed
- 1 cup (30 g) spinach leaves, rinsed and patted dry
- ½ teaspoon turmeric
- 1 teaspoon (2 g) cumin
- ½ teaspoon paprika
- 2 tablespoons (25 g) nutritional yeast
- ¼ teaspoon salt (or to taste)
- Freshly ground pepper, to taste

Per serving: 178 calories; 9g fat; 15g protein; 12g carbohydrate; 5g dietary fiber; 0mg cholesterol; 152mg sodium.

## DIRECTIONS

Heat water or oil in a sauté pan. Add onion and garlic, and sauté for 2 minutes. Add mushrooms and pepper, and sauté until onions and pepper are tender and mushrooms are golden brown.

Meanwhile, using your hands, crumble tofu in a bowl to create the consistency of coarse bread crumbs. Add to sauté pan, and stir to combine.

Add spinach, turmeric, cumin, paprika, and nutritional yeast, and sauté for 5 to 8 minutes, stirring occasionally, until tofu is bright yellow and heated through. Season with salt and pepper to taste.

**YIELD:** 2 to 4 servings

## SERVING SUGGESTIONS AND VARIATIONS

* To incorporate more veggies, add 1 ½ cups (about 335 g) of any combination you prefer, such as zucchini, broccoli, tomatoes, or spinach. Throw these in at the same time you add the peppers, cooking them through before adding the tofu.
* For a Mexican scramble, add 1 cup (260 g) of your favorite salsa after the tofu is cooked, and allow it to heat through. Make a Breakfast Burrito by wrapping the scramble in a tortilla and serving with tortilla chips, avocado, and nondairy, nonhydrogenated sour cream. For an Italian twist, add fresh herbs such as basil, oregano, rosemary, or parsley and some finely chopped kalamata olives.
* You can also toss with some cut-up pieces of Tempeh Bacon (page 29), a favorite trick of tester Jill Russell.

# TEMPEH BACON

*Wheat-free*

Tempeh is a delicious, versatile soy-based food that is wonderful grilled, baked, fried, or steamed and found near the tofu in your local grocery store. It has a great nutty flavor and a satisfying chewy texture.

- 1 package (8 ounces, or 225 g) tempeh
- ¼ cup (60 ml) tamari soy sauce
- 2 teaspoons (10 ml) liquid smoke
- 3 tablespoons (45 ml) real maple syrup
- ¼ cup (60 ml) water
- Canola oil, for frying

## DIRECTIONS

Add the block of tempeh to a 3-quart (3.5 L) pot fitted with a steamer basket, and steam for about 10 minutes. Meanwhile, in a large-size bowl, combine tamari, liquid smoke, maple syrup, and water. Mix well.

Let tempeh cool before slicing into thin, bacon-size strips. Place slices in marinade, and let sit for as long as you like. The longer you marinate, the stronger the flavor. I often marinate for less than a half-hour. Shake occasionally to make sure all tempeh is coated.

After tempeh has marinated, heat oil in a skillet and fry the strips over medium-high heat until crisp. Turn and fry again until crisp on the other side. Sprinkle a little extra tamari and maple syrup on the tempeh while it's cooking. After about 5 minutes per side, the tempeh will turn brown, caramelize, and get crispier and chewier.

Remove from heat and set on a plate with a paper towel to absorb any excess oil.

**YIELD:** 10 to 14 slices

## SERVING SUGGESTIONS AND VARIATIONS

Use this tempeh bacon for a BLT, a Reuben sandwich (page 284), or on top of a Caesar salad (page 133). If you can't find tempeh, you can use tofu in its place. Cut tofu into strips, marinate, and sauté. I suggest, however, that you use tofu that has been frozen and thawed. If you have extra marinade, when you finish, simply prepare a second package of tempeh or tofu, or use it in a stir-fry.

## DID YOU KNOW?

Liquid smoke is produced by burning hardwood chips (hickory, mesquite, etc.) and condensing the smoke into a liquid form. The liquid is then scrubbed and filtered to remove all impurities. A little goes a long way, and it's a great flavoring for many dishes where you want a smoky flavor, such as Split Pea Soup (page 98). Find this in your local grocer, near the barbecue sauces and ketchups.

## COMPASSIONATE COOKS' TIP

You may slice the tempeh into strips *before* steaming it.

Per serving: 55 calories; 2g fat; 4g protein; 6g carbohydrate; trace dietary fiber; 0mg cholesterol; 291mg sodium.

TOFU SCRAMBLE
WITH TEMPEH BACON,
Pages 28-29

# LOVE POTIONS

When concocting elixirs to bewitch and beguile your beloved, the options are endless. The following beverages can allure and attract based on their color, texture, aroma, and taste.

## A STUDY IN SCARLET

The color red has long been associated with heat, passion, and love. Try combining the juice of pomegranates, raspberries, cranberries, strawberries, or cherries with sparkling mineral water, lemon or lime soda, or sparkling wine. Or adorn the base of a glass with red pears, apples, currants, grapes, watermelon, or goji berries. Serve red wine or tomato juice, or add grenadine (the sweet syrup made from pomegranate seeds) to sparkling water.

## BODY HEAT

Turn up the heat by increasing the temperature or spiciness of your beverage. For example, Mexican hot chocolate, made by adding chile powder to hot chocolate or melting Mexican/chile-laced chocolate bars in nondairy milk, is both hot and spicy. Add a touch of Kahlúa for some extra warmth. Or try warm mulled (spiced) wine or cider. They're both wonderful ways to heat things up from the inside out. Of course, hot tea, coffee, and cocoa are all simple but temperature-rising ways to cap off a meal.

## PERSUASION

Certain herbs, spices, and flowers, many of which can be found in drinks available in stores or that you prepare yourself, are said to increase the libido. Damiana, an herb that grows in Mexico and South America, has long been considered an aphrodisiac. You can find Damiana liqueur, which comes in a bottle shaped like an Incan goddess, in liquor stores. Aniseed and licorice have, for centuries, been touted for their special love powers. Add a stick of licorice to a creamy after-dinner drink, or enjoy a glass of sambuca, an Italian anise-flavored liqueur.

## POP THE CORK

Champagne, a romantic mainstay, is regarded as such more for its presentation than for any effect it has on the body. However, when using alcohol as an aphrodisiac, heed Shakespeare's words: "It provokes and it unprovokes; it provokes the desire, but it takes away the performance." Try sparkling cider for the bubbles without the booze.

# PEACH AND PECAN MUFFINS

These little gems are a perfect addition to any breakfast-in-bed tray.

- 3 cups (375 g) whole-wheat pastry flour
- 1 tablespoon (7 g) ground cinnamon
- ¼ teaspoon nutmeg
- 1 tablespoon (14 g) baking soda
- 1 teaspoon (6 g) salt
- ¾ cup (85 g) chopped raw pecans
- ½ cup (120 ml) canola oil
- 6 ounces (170 g) nondairy yogurt or nondairy sour cream
- 1 teaspoon (5 ml) vanilla extract
- 2 tablespoons (30 ml) white distilled vinegar
- ½ cup (100 g) granulated sugar
- 1 cup (225 g) packed light brown sugar (or more depending on your sweetness preference), divided
- 2 ½ cups (425 g) peeled, pitted, and chopped peaches
- Pecans or walnuts, finely ground, for sprinkling

## DIRECTIONS

Preheat oven to 400°F (200°C, or gas mark 6). Lightly grease 16 muffin cups or insert cupcake liners. In a large-size bowl, mix flour, cinnamon, nutmeg, baking soda, and salt. Add pecans, and stir.

In a separate bowl, mix oil, yogurt, vanilla, vinegar, granulated sugar, ¾ cup (170 g) brown sugar, and peaches. Stir the oil mixture into the flour mixture until just moist. Spoon into prepared muffin cups. Sprinkle remaining ¼ cup (55 g) brown sugar and finely ground pecans on top of each muffin.

Bake for 25 minutes, until a toothpick inserted into the center of a muffin comes out clean. Cool for 10 minutes before turning out muffins onto wire racks to cool completely.

**YIELD:** 16 muffins

Per serving: 257 calories; 11g fat; 4g protein; 40g carbohydrate; 4g dietary fiber; 0mg cholesterol; 376mg sodium.

## DID YOU KNOW?

In ancient Rome, the word *cinnamon* was equivalent to the current use of "sweetheart" or "darling." Remember the Song of Solomon? "I have perfumed my bed with myrrh, aloes, and cinnamon. Come, let us take our fill of love till morning."

## COMPASSIONATE COOKS' TIP

Although this recipe is great with fresh peaches, a 15-ounce (420 g) can, drained, rinsed, and chopped, will work in a pinch.

# SWEET AND SOUR TEMPEH

*Oil-free (if you don't fry the tempeh), wheat-free*

This simple and delicious dish warms as much as it satisfies. Although it's a great way to use tempeh, sautéed tofu works just as well especially if tempeh is new to you.

- 1 pound (455 g) tempeh, cubed
- Sesame oil, for sautéing (optional)
- 1 cup (235 ml) plus 3 tablespoons (45 ml) water, for sautéing, divided
- 1 medium-size yellow onion, diced
- 2 tablespoons (12 g) minced ginger
- 1 large-size red bell pepper, diced
- 1 cup (100 g) green beans, ends trimmed (optional)
- 7 ounces (200 g) apricot preserves (look for a brand that doesn't add corn syrup)
- 2 tablespoons (16 g) arrowroot powder or kudzu root starch, dissolved in ¼ cup (60 ml) cold water
- 5 tablespoons (75 ml) tamari soy sauce
- 3 tablespoons (45 ml) apple cider vinegar
- 1 tablespoon (16 g) light miso paste
- ½ to 1 teaspoon crushed red pepper flakes
- 2 to 3 teaspoons (6 to 9 g) black sesame seeds, for garnish (optional)

## DIRECTIONS

Add cubes of tempeh to a 3-quart pot fitted with a steamer basket, and steam for about 10 minutes. You can use the steamed tempeh cubes as they are or sauté them in sesame oil after steaming to add extra flavor.

Meanwhile, heat 3 tablespoons (45 ml) of the water in a sauté pan over medium heat. Add onion, ginger, bell pepper, and green beans (if using), and cook for 5 minutes, or until onion is translucent and the beans turn bright green.

Combine remaining 1 cup (235 ml) water and apricot preserves and cook for 10 minutes, stirring occasionally. Add arrowroot powder, and stir for a few minutes more. Add tamari, vinegar, miso paste, and red pepper flakes, and cook for another few minutes, stirring constantly. Add steamed tempeh and mix well. Remove from heat and garnish with black sesame seeds, if desired.

**YIELD:** 2 to 4 servings

## SERVING SUGGESTIONS AND VARIATIONS

* You can use white sesame seeds, but the black seeds add a dramatic color contrast.
* Mango or mandarin preserves can replace the apricot preserves.

## DID YOU KNOW?

The ancient Chinese considered apricots a symbol of sensuality, and these round, thin-skinned fruits were used by the Australian Aborigines as an aphrodisiac. Mangoes, peaches, and papayas also fit the sensual bill.

Per serving: 494 calories; 17g fat; 26g protein; 67g carbohydrate; 4g dietary fiber; 0mg cholesterol; 1446mg sodium.

# BASIL EGGPLANT
## (PUD MAKUA YOW)
*Wheat-free*

Basil eggplant is a simple recipe, and this version substantially reduces the unnecessary oil that usually plagues eggplant dishes. The basil and chile pepper turn the basic eggplant into something exciting. Those with a more delicate palate can make the dish without the hot peppers. Use either the long, thin Japanese eggplants or the big purple globe/Italian eggplants.

- 2 Japanese or Chinese eggplants (about 1 pound, or 455 g)
- 1 tablespoon (15 ml) sesame oil
- 2 chile peppers, chopped and seeds removed
- 2 garlic cloves, finely chopped
- 1 cup (235 ml) water
- 2 tablespoons (30 ml) tamari soy sauce
- 1 tablespoon (13 g) granulated sugar
- 1 bunch Thai basil, leaves picked from the stem and left whole
- Cooked rice, for serving

## COMPASSIONATE COOKS' TIP

Thai basil is different than Italian basil. It has small leaves, purple stems, and a subtle licorice taste. Do not use Italian basil in Thai dishes.

## DIRECTIONS

Slice eggplants into irregular shapes (cut on the diagonal) for easy turning in the pan. Eggplant sliced into disks tend to stick to the bottom of the pan, making it difficult to flip or turn.

Heat sesame oil in a nonstick pan or wok over medium heat. Add chile peppers and garlic. Cook until garlic turns golden brown, stirring constantly.

Add eggplant, gently stirring to combine with garlic and peppers. Add water and cover the pan or wok with a lid. Keep lid closed until the eggplant is cooked, 5 to 7 minutes. When eggplant turns from white to translucent, it is cooked. If, after 7 minutes, the eggplant is still not ready, add a little more water and keep lid closed until the eggplant is translucent.

Add tamari and sugar and gently stir to combine, being careful not to break up the tender eggplant. Add Thai basil, and cook for 1 minute more. Turn off heat and serve hot with rice.

**YIELD:** 2 to 4 servings

## SERVING SUGGESTIONS AND VARIATIONS

Fry some extra-firm tofu slices in a separate pan and add them when you add the tamari and sugar.

Per serving: 121 calories; 4g fat; 4g protein; 21g carbohydrate; 7g dietary fiber; 0mg cholesterol; 514mg sodium.

# DARK LEAFY GREENS WITH SESAME MISO DRESSING

*Wheat-free*

Enjoy this elegant side dish (or first course) with your loved one. What better way to express your affection than by feeding your loved one nutrient-rich greens and healthful miso?

- 1 large-size bunch greens (kale, turnip, mustard, collards, or chard)
- 2 tablespoons (16 g) raw sesame seeds
- 1 tablespoon (15 ml) toasted sesame oil
- 1 tablespoon plus 1 teaspoon (21 g) light or dark miso
- I tablespoon (15 ml) mirin
- 1 teaspoon (5 ml) freshly squeezed lemon juice
- 1 teaspoon (5 ml) tamari soy sauce

## DIRECTIONS

Wash greens, remove tough stems from leaves, and cut into bite-size pieces. Insert a steamer basket in a 3-quart (3.5 L) pot with a few inches (8 cm) of water. (The water should rise to the bottom of the steamer basket, not above. The vegetables shouldn't touch the water.) Steam greens for 5 minutes, then immediately plunge into a bowl filled with cold water. Drain, gently squeeze out excess water, and set aside.

Meanwhile, in a large-size dry sauté pan, toast sesame seeds over medium heat, stirring constantly until fragrant or beginning to pop.

Combine oil, miso, mirin, lemon juice, and tamari in a small-size bowl. Add greens to the sauté pan, turn off heat, and stir in the dressing. Toss all ingredients using nonstick tongs. Don't cook the greens but merely warm them up along with the dressing. Serve warm or at room temperature.

**YIELD:** 2 servings

Per serving: 257 calories; 11g fat; 4g protein; 40g carbohydrate; 4g dietary fiber; 0mg cholesterol; 376mg sodium.

## COMPASSIONATE COOKS' TIP

Chickpea-based miso is available for those allergic to soy, typically the main ingredient found in miso.

## DID YOU KNOW?

Miso, a traditional Japanese food, is a thick paste used for sauces, soups, and spreads, and is made by fermenting rice, barley, or soybeans with salt and a fermenting agent. The different types of miso, such as light, dark, and red, vary according to length of fermentation, proportion of salt to soybeans, and the addition of rice or barley. Light and white misos have a sweeter, milder flavor, while red and dark misos are stronger.

# BRAISED FIGS WITH ARUGULA

*Wheat-free*

One of the sexiest fruits on the planet, figs are delectable when served fresh (available June through October) with juicy pears and a little agave nectar, or warmed and sweetened with a little heat and sugar. Not to set expectations, but my wonderful tester for this recipe called it "ambrosial."

- 1 tablespoon (14 g) nondairy, nonhydrogenated butter (such as Earth Balance)
- 1 teaspoon (4 g) granulated sugar
- 1 pint (300 g) whole fresh figs (10 to 12 medium-size), halved lengthwise and stems removed
- 4 to 5 tablespoons (60 to 75 ml) balsamic vinegar
- 1 bunch baby arugula, washed and stemmed
- 1 to 2 tablespoons (15 to 30 ml) olive oil
- Juice from ½ lemon
- Salt and freshly ground black pepper, to taste

Per serving: 194 calories; 10g fat; 1g protein; 30g carbohydrate; 4g dietary fiber; 0mg cholesterol; 2mg sodium.

## DIRECTIONS

In a large-size sauté pan, melt butter and sugar. Place figs face down in the pan, and cook for 3 to 5 minutes over medium-high heat. The face of the fig will become sticky and slightly golden around the edges. Remove from heat and place figs on a plate, face up.

In the same skillet, heat balsamic vinegar until bubbly, then reduce heat and simmer for 4 to 5 minutes, until vinegar is reduced by half. Remove from heat.

In a bowl, toss arugula with olive oil to coat. Pour lemon juice over top; toss again. Sprinkle with salt and pepper to taste. Heap arugula on a plate and arrange figs over the top. Drizzle with the balsamic reduction, and sprinkle on salt. Serve warm or at room temperature.

**YIELD:** 2 or 3 servings

## SERVING SUGGESTIONS AND VARIATIONS

Although the peppery arugula is the perfect contrast to the sweet figs, I have used baby spinach leaves with much success. For another option, serve figs alone as a dessert, with vanilla nondairy ice cream and drizzled with agave nectar.

# SAFFRON-SPIKED MOROCCAN STEW

*Oil-free, wheat-free, soy-free*

This Moroccan-inspired, hearty stew is perfect over couscous or quinoa (pronounced KEEN-wah).

- 1 ½ cups (350 ml) plus 3 tablespoons (45 ml) water or vegetable stock, divided
- 1 large-size yellow onion, finely chopped
- 2 large-size red bell peppers, seeded and chopped
- 2 or 3 garlic cloves, minced
- 2 teaspoons (10 g) light brown sugar
- 1 teaspoon (2 g) ground coriander
- ½ teaspoon ground cinnamon
- ½ teaspoon ground cumin
- ¼ teaspoon ground cayenne
- 1 teaspoon (2 g) grated or minced fresh ginger
- ½ teaspoon saffron threads
- 2 medium-size sweet potatoes or garnet or jewel yams, peeled and cut into ½-inch (1 cm) cubes
- 1 can (15 ounces, or 420 g) diced tomatoes, undrained
- 2 cups (480 g) cooked chickpeas or 1 can (15 ounces, or 420 g) chickpeas, drained and rinsed
- Salt and pepper, to taste

## DIRECTIONS

Heat 3 tablespoons (45 ml) water in a soup pot over medium heat. Add onion, peppers, and garlic, and cook until the onions are translucent, 5 to 7 minutes. If the water begins to evaporate, add a little more.

Stir in brown sugar, coriander, cinnamon, cumin, cayenne, ginger, and saffron, and cook for 60 seconds, stirring constantly. Add sweet potatoes, and stir to coat. Stir in tomatoes, remaining 1 ½ cups (350 ml) water, and chickpeas. Bring to a boil, then reduce heat to low. Simmer until sweet potatoes are tender but not over-cooked, about 30 minutes. Season with salt and pepper, then serve.

**YIELD:** 2 to 4 servings

Per serving: 530 calories; 8g fat; 24g protein; 96g carbohydrate; 24g dietary fiber; 0mg cholesterol; 646mg sodium.

## FOOD LORE

Saffron, typically used in Mediterranean, North African, and Middle Eastern cuisine, is made from the dried stigmas of crocus flowers and adds a beautiful yellow-red color to food. The spice has a long and rich history that goes back thousands of years for its use as a dye, medicine, and aphrodisiac.

## COMPASSIONATE COOKS' TIP

See page 225 for the difference between yams and sweet potatoes.

# RED VELVET CAKE WITH BUTTERCREAM FROSTING

Also known as devil's food cake, this dessert is characteristically known for its deep reddish brown color.

## FOR **CAKE BATTER:**

- 3 ½ cups (440 g) unbleached all-purpose or whole-wheat pastry flour
- 1 ½ cups (300 g) granulated sugar
- 2 teaspoons (9 g) baking soda
- 1 teaspoon (6 g) salt
- 2 teaspoons (9 g) cocoa powder
- 2 cups (470 ml) nondairy milk (soy, rice, almond, hazelnut, hemp, or oat)
- ⅔ cup (155 ml) canola oil
- 3 tablespoons (45 ml) red food coloring
- 2 tablespoons (30 ml) distilled white vinegar
- 2 teaspoons (10 ml) vanilla extract
- Ground pecans, for topping (optional)

## FOR BUTTERCREAM FROSTING:

- ½ cup (112 g) nondairy, nonhydrogenated butter (such as Earth Balance), at room temperature
- 3 cups (300 g) confectioners' sugar
- 1 ½ teaspoons (8 ml) vanilla extract
- 2 tablespoons (30 ml) nondairy milk (soy, rice, almond, hazelnut, hemp, or oat) or water
- Assorted food colors (optional)

Per serving: 553 calories; 16g fat; 7g protein; 100g carbohydrate; 5g dietary fiber; 0mg cholesterol; 488mg sodium.

## DIRECTIONS

Preheat oven to 350°F (180°C, or gas mark 4). Lightly oil two 8-inch (20 cm) round cake pans.

To make the batter, in a large bowl, combine flour, sugar, baking soda, salt, and cocoa powder. Create a well in the center, and add milk, oil, food coloring, vinegar, and vanilla, and mix until thoroughly combined.

Divide cake batter evenly between prepared cake pans. Place pans in the oven spaced evenly apart. Bake for about 35 minutes, rotating 45 degrees halfway through. When the cakes pull away from the side of the pans and a toothpick inserted into the center of each comes out clean, they are ready.

Let cakes cool for 10 minutes in the pans, then run a knife around the edges to loosen them from the sides. One at a time, invert cakes onto a plate and then reinvert onto a cooling rack, rounded-sides up. Let cool completely.

To make the frosting, with an electric hand or stand mixer, cream butter until it is smooth and begins to fluff. With the mixer on low speed, add confectioners' sugar and fluff for another few minutes. Add vanilla, milk, and food coloring (if using).

Once all ingredients are well-combined, beat on high until frosting is light and fluffy, 3 to 4 minutes. Add I or 2 tablespoons more milk to achieve the right consistency. Cover the icing with plastic wrap to prevent it from drying out until ready to use. Rewhip before using.

To frost cake, place one layer, rounded-side down, on a plate or cake stand. Using a palette knife or offset spatula, spread some frosting over top of cake. Carefully set other layer on top, rounded-side down, and repeat. Cover entire cake with remaining frosting. If desired, sprinkle with pecans.

**YIELD:** 8 to 10 servings

# FENNEL, ORANGE, WALNUT, AND POMEGRANATE SALAD

*Oil-free, wheat-free, soy-free*

The colors and textures in this beautiful salad perfectly complement one another.

- 1 orange, peeled
- 1 fennel bulb, thinly sliced
- ½ small-size red onion, thinly sliced
- 1 pomegranate, seeds only
- 12 walnut halves, toasted
- 2 garlic cloves, minced
- ¼ cup (60 ml) orange or tangerine juice
- ¼ cup (60 ml) seasoned rice vinegar
- 2 teaspoons (13 g) agave nectar
- 20 mint leaves, finely chopped

## DIRECTIONS

Peel orange, separate into wedges, and slice each wedge lengthwise.

In a large-size bowl, combine fennel, red onion, orange wedges, pomegranate seeds, and walnut halves.

In a small-size bowl, whisk together garlic, orange juice, rice vinegar, agave nectar, and mint leaves. Mix well. Pour over salad ingredients and toss to combine.

Arrange on 2 serving plates.

**YIELD:** 2 servings

## SERVING SUGGESTIONS AND VARIATIONS

For a shortcut, use a can of mandarin oranges. Rinse and drain first. If pomegranates are out of season, use dried cranberries instead.

Per serving: 269 calories; 9g fat; 6g protein; 47g carbohydrate; 9g dietary fiber; 0mg cholesterol; 72mg sodium.

## COMPASSIONATE COOKS' TIP

The easiest way to extract the seeds from the whole pomegranate is to cut the fruit into quarters. Immerse the cut pomegranate in a bowl of water. Under the water, pry open the quarters one at a time. The seeds will sink to the bottom, and the fibrous pulp will float to the top. Scoop out the pulp and drain the seeds.

## FOOD LORE

Fennel was regarded as a libido enhancer by the ancient Greeks and Egyptians. Pomegranate seeds are recommended in the *Kama Sutra* (an ancient Indian lovemaking manual) as an erotic aid.

# SWEET AND SPICY PUMPKIN SOUP

*Oil-free, wheat-free, soy-free depending on milk*

This versatile recipe works well with puréed pumpkin or butternut squash. You may take the canned-pumpkin shortcut for this recipe. Just know that starting with fresh pumpkin will make the flavor that much greater.

- 3 tablespoons (45 ml) water
- 1 medium-size yellow onion, coarsely chopped
- 2 garlic cloves, finely minced
- ½ teaspoon ground turmeric
- ½ teaspoon ground ginger
- ½ teaspoon ground cumin
- ¼ teaspoon ground cinnamon
- ¼ teaspoon ground cardamom
- ⅛ teaspoon ground cayenne pepper
- 2 cups (470 ml) vegetable stock (store-bought or homemade, page 213)
- 1 can (15 ounces, or 420 g) organic pumpkin purée
- 2 tablespoons (30 ml) real maple syrup
- Juice from ½ lemon
- 2 cups (470 ml) nondairy milk (soy, rice, almond, hazelnut, hemp, or oat)
- Salt, to taste
- Parsley, for garnish (optional)

## DIRECTIONS

Heat water in a soup pot, then add onion and garlic and cook over medium heat until onion is soft, about 5 minutes.

Add turmeric, ginger, cumin, cinnamon, cardamom, and cayenne, and stir to combine. Add vegetable stock, pumpkin purée, maple syrup, and lemon juice. Simmer on low-medium heat for 15 minutes.

Stir in milk. Remove from heat, and purée soup in a blender or food processor or with a handheld immersion blender until smooth. Return soup to pan and heat over medium heat until hot—not boiling—about 5 minutes. Add salt to taste and garnish with parsley, if desired.

**YIELD:** 2 servings

## SERVING SUGGESTIONS AND VARIATIONS

For a little variety, top with a drizzle of Cashew Sour Cream on page 51.

Per serving: 390 calories; 9g fat; 16g protein; 68g carbohydrate; 9g dietary fiber; 0mg cholesterol; 1663mg sodium.

## WHAT'S THE DIFFERENCE? STOCK VS. BROTH

Although the terms stock and broth tend to be used interchangeably, there are subtle differences between the two.

Vegetable stock is generally the flavored liquid base used for soups and sauces made from a combination of onions, carrots, celery, and sometimes other vegetables, once the vegetables are discarded. Stock is typically used as an ingredient.

Vegetable broth, on the other hand, tends to refer to a finished product eaten as its own dish. Salt is often added to broth for flavor.

# MARVELOUS MUSHROOM RISOTTO

*Wheat-free, soy-free*

You can use any type of mushroom you like for this dish, but I recommend choosing a type that has a lot of flavor. Shiitake mushrooms are ideal. White mushrooms, on the other hand, would be rather bland.

- 7 to 8 cups (1645 to 1880 ml) vegetable stock (store-bought or homemade, page 213)
- 1 tablespoon (15 ml) olive oil
- 1 medium-size yellow onion, chopped
- 3 garlic cloves, finely chopped or minced
- 3 cups (210 g) sliced or coarsely chopped mushrooms (cremini, shiitake, or porcini)
- 1/4 cup (15 g dry or 30 g oil packed) chopped sun-dried tomatoes (rinse oil-packed tomatoes; soak dry tomatoes in warm water for 30 to 45 minutes to soften)
- 2 tablespoons (5 g) finely chopped fresh thyme
- 2 tablespoons (5 g) finely chopped fresh parsley
- 1 tablespoon (15 ml) truffle oil
- 2 cups (390 g) Arborio rice
- 1/2 cup (120 ml) dry white wine
- Salt and freshly ground black pepper, to taste
- 2 teaspoons (4 g) finely chopped French-cured black olives
- Fresh flat-leaf parsley, chopped, for garnish (optional)

## DIRECTIONS

Heat vegetable stock in a medium saucepan, and keep warm on the stove. Meanwhile, heat olive oil in a deep, large-size sauté pan and sauté onion, garlic, and mushrooms until golden brown, 5 to 7 minutes. Add sun-dried tomatoes, thyme, and parsley. Stir to combine, then add truffle oil. Stir to coat mushrooms.

Add rice and stir for a few moments. Add white wine, and stir as the alcohol evaporates, 1 to 2 minutes.

Add stock, ladle by ladle, waiting for the rice to absorb the liquid before adding more. Stir constantly. As the rice cooks, the risotto will start to thicken. Continue adding stock until you are happy with the consistency (you may not need all the stock). After 20 to 25 minutes, it should be creamy. Add salt and pepper to taste.

Top with chopped olives, chopped parsley (if using), and another drizzle of truffle oil, and serve right away in shallow bowls.

**YIELD:** 2-4 servings

## SERVING SUGGESTIONS AND VARIATIONS

If you can't find truffle oil, porcini oil works just as well.

Per serving: 510 calories; 6g fat; 13g protein; 94g carbohydrate; 3g dietary fiber; 0mg cholesterol; 2112mg sodium.

# TOASTED QUINOA WITH RAISINS AND SLIVERED ALMONDS

*Oil-free, wheat-free, soy-free*

Even though quinoa hails from South America, it adapts well to the flavors of India and the pilaf-cooking methods of the Middle East.

- 2 cups (350 g) quinoa
- 2 tablespoons (30 ml) water, for sautéing
- 2 shallots, minced
- 1 tablespoon (6 g) minced fresh ginger
- ½ teaspoon ground cardamom
- ½ teaspoon ground coriander
- ½ teaspoon ground cumin
- ⅛ teaspoon cayenne
- 4 cups (940 ml) vegetable stock (store-bought or homemade, page 213) or water with vegetable bouillon cube
- ½ teaspoon salt (or to taste)
- Freshly ground pepper, to taste
- ⅓ cup (50 g) raisins
- ½ cup (55 g) toasted slivered almonds
- 2 tablespoons (8 g) minced fresh parsley leaves

## DIRECTIONS

Rinse quinoa in a small-size strainer to remove the bitter coating called saponin (the plant's natural defense that keeps birds from eating it). Heat a large-size skillet over medium heat. Add quinoa and stir constantly for 5 minutes, or until moisture evaporates and quinoa is fragrant and dry.

Meanwhile, heat water in a 3-quart (3.5 L) saucepan over medium heat. Add shallots and ginger and cook, stirring constantly, until shallots are slightly softened, about 3 minutes. Add the toasted quinoa along with cardamom, coriander, cumin, and cayenne. Stir to combine.

Add stock and bring to a boil. Reduce heat to low, and season with salt and pepper to taste. Cover and cook until all water is absorbed, about 12 minutes.

Remove from heat and stir in raisins, almonds, and parsley. Serve warm or at room temperature. It will keep for a few days in the fridge.

**YIELD:** 2 to 4 servings

Per serving: 488 calories; 15g fat; 15g protein; 77g carbohydrate; 8g dietary fiber; 0mg cholesterol; 1290mg sodium.

# GARLIC AND GREENS SOUP

*Oil-free, wheat-free, soy-free*

Containing a whole head of garlic, this soup packs a punch, making the kind of robust, assertive bowlful you want on a cold winter day. Although you'll most certainly ward off vampires, cooked garlic is definitely less offensive than raw. As long as everyone's eating it, nobody will notice!

- 8 cups (1180 ml) plus 3 tablespoons (45 ml) water or vegetable stock (store-bought or homemade, page 213), divided
- 1 head garlic, separated into cloves, peeled and minced or pressed
- 1 large-size yellow onion, finely chopped
- 1 bunch kale, collard greens, bok choy, or chard, chopped into bite-size pieces
- 3 yellow potatoes, such as Yukon gold, diced
- 1 tablespoon (15 ml) seasoned rice vinegar
- Salt and pepper, to taste

## DIRECTIONS

In a large-size soup pot, heat 3 tablespoons (45 ml) of water and sauté garlic and onion until onion turns translucent, about 5 minutes.

Add kale, potatoes, and remaining 8 cups (1180 ml) water to the soup pot and bring to a boil. Simmer everything together for 25 to 30 minutes, until you can easily pierce the potatoes with a fork.

Add rice vinegar and salt and pepper to taste. Stir and serve immediately.

**YIELD:** 2 to 4 servings

## SERVING SUGGESTIONS AND VARIATIONS

For added flavor and texture, add 1 cup (155 g) *cooked* barley to the soup 5 minutes before it is finished cooking.

## COMPASSIONATE COOKS' TIP

Vegetable bouillon cubes are great to have on hand. They are economical, available in low-sodium form, and are often organic. For this recipe, add 8 cups (1880 ml) of water and a couple of bouillon cubes. (Because the garlic adds so much flavor, it would be overkill to add a number of cubes equal to the number of cups of water. I usually use 2 bouillon cubes, which is essentially the equivalent of 4 cups [940 ml] of stock.)

Per serving: 228 calories; 5g fat; 9g protein; 43g carbohydrate; 11g dietary fiber; 0mg cholesterol; 652mg sodium.

# PENNE ARRABBIATA

*Soy-free, wheat-free depending on pasta, oil-free if sautéed in water*

Although this sassy dish can easily feed a casual gathering of friends, this is my husband's favorite pasta dish, so I've included it in this chapter. Arrabbiata means "angry" in Italian, but "passionate" is probably a better translation in this case, as the heat from the red pepper flakes definitely spices things up.

- 1 pound (455 g) penne pasta (whole wheat, rice, or semolina)
- 1 to 3 tablespoons (15 to 45 ml) olive oil or water, for sautéing
- 5 garlic cloves, minced
- 1 teaspoon red pepper flakes
- 1 can (24 ounces, or 680 g) fire-roasted diced tomatoes
- Salt and pepper, to taste

## DID YOU KNOW?

Referred to as the "love-apple" by the French because of a language barrier rather than its aphrodisiac qualities, the tomato deserves inclusion as a sensual food for its juiciness and various shapes, sizes, and colors.

## DIRECTIONS

Add pasta to boiling water and cook until *al dente* ("to the teeth"). Heat oil in a large-size sauté pan. Add garlic and red pepper flakes, and sauté for about 3 minutes.

Add tomatoes, stirring to combine with the garlic and pepper flakes. Let simmer over low heat for 10 to 15 minutes.

Divide pasta among individual plates or shallow bowls, and spoon tomato mixture over it. Add salt and pepper to taste.

**YIELD:** 2 to 4 servings

## SERVING SUGGESTIONS AND VARIATIONS

* To make the dish less spicy, simply add fewer red pepper flakes. The heat level is up to you.
* You can also replace the penne pasta with angel hair or spaghetti.
* For optimum romance, slurp each piece from either end and meet in the middle. Think *Lady and the Tramp*.

Per serving: 564 calories; 12g fat; 16g protein; 98g carbohydrate; 4g dietary fiber; 0mg cholesterol; 53mg sodium.

**WINTER MENU:** Prelude to a Kiss
* Carrot Ginger Soup  * Cashew Sour Cream
* Polenta Hearts (or squares)  * Roasted Red Pepper Coulis
* Swiss Chard and Caramelized Onions  * Chocolate Fondues

# CARROT GINGER SOUP

*Oil-free, wheat-free, soy-free*

This soup is a staple in the Patrick-Goudreau household, because it is incredibly easy to make, delicious to eat, and beautiful to behold. Plus, both carrots and ginger have long been regarded for their aphrodisiac qualities.

- 2 tablespoons (30 ml) water, for sautéing
- 1 large-size or 2 small-size yellow onions, coarsely chopped
- 2 teaspoons (6 g) finely chopped garlic
- 7 or 8 carrots, peeled and cut into circles
- 2 medium-size yellow potatoes, peeled and quartered (Yukon gold is my favorite)
- 2 ½ teaspoons (5 g) finely chopped fresh ginger
- ½ teaspoon salt
- ½ teaspoon white pepper
- 4 to 5 cups (940 to 1175 ml) vegetable stock (store-bought or homemade, page 213) or water with vegetable bouillon cube

## DIRECTIONS

Heat water in a large-size saucepan over medium-high heat. Add onions and garlic and sauté until onions become translucent, about 5 minutes. Add a small amount of water if the pan gets too dry.

Add carrots, potatoes, ginger, salt, pepper, and enough stock to cover the vegetables (you may not need all the stock). Reduce heat to medium and cook until carrots and potatoes are soft and easily pierced with a fork.

Transfer to a food processor, and purée soup until creamy. Return puréed soup to a pot to heat. Season with salt as needed, adding just a pinch at first and more if necessary.

**YIELD:** 2 to 4 servings

## SERVING SUGGESTIONS AND VARIATIONS

* Try serving this soup with nondairy sour cream (see page 296 for Resources and Recommendations) or Cashew Sour Cream (page 51).
* Serve hot, garnished with a sprig of parsley.
* Always err on the side of caution. Add just a pinch of salt at first, and add more as needed.

Per serving: 145 calories; 2g fat; 3g protein; 31g carbohydrate; 5g dietary fiber; 0mg cholesterol; 1566mg sodium.

## COMPASSIONATE COOKS' TIP

To substitute dried herbs for fresh, the conversion is simple: Reduce tablespoons to teaspoons (e.g., 2 tablespoons (3 g) fresh oregano equals 2 teaspoons (2 g) dried oregano). Ginger, however, is an exception to this interchangeable rule. If a recipe calls for fresh ginger, you cannot substitute it with ground. Stick with fresh ginger for this recipe.

# CASHEW SOUR CREAM

*Oil-free, wheat-free*

Use this cream to add a little more body and richness to a dish, especially a soup or stew. A little, usually a few teaspoons, goes a long way.

- 1 ½ (220 g) raw cashews
- ¼ cup (60 ml) fresh lemon juice
- ½ to ¾ cup (120 to 175 ml) water
- Salt, to taste

## DIRECTIONS

In a blender, combine the cashews, lemon juice, and ½ cup (120 ml) of the water. Blend on low speed, gradually turning speed to maximum.

While the machine is running, gradually add more water to keep the ingredients from sinking to the bottom of the blender and until desired consistency is reached.

Continue blending until the mixture is smooth and the consistency of whipped cream. Add salt to taste.

Store in an airtight container in the refrigerator for up to 4 days. If it becomes too thick, simply thin it out with some water.

**YIELD:** 1 cup (230 g), or 16 (1-tablespoon [15 g]) servings

## SERVING SUGGESTIONS AND VARIATIONS

* For a Chipotle Cashew Sour Cream, combine the finished sour cream with ¼ cup (4 g) chopped cilantro and 1 to 2 chipotle peppers.
* The plain or chipotle variation is perfect for the Fajitas (page 265) or Three-Bean Chili (page 264).

Per serving: 75 calories; 6g fat; 2g protein; 5g carbohydrate; trace dietary fiber; 0mg cholesterol; 82mg sodium.

## COMPASSIONATE COOKS' TIP

Add more water to make a thinner cream for soup garnishes.

## DID YOU KNOW?

Both cashew and macadamia nuts are ideal for creating thick creams and sauces, either savory or sweet.

Advanced Preparation Required

# POLENTA HEARTS (OR SQUARES)

*Soy-free depending on milk, wheat-free*

You can make the polenta into any shape you want, including simple squares, but I like to add a little romance by using a heart-shaped cookie cutter.

- 4 cups (940 ml) water
- 1 ½ cups (210 g) coarse cornmeal or polenta
- ¼ cup (60 ml) nondairy milk (soy, rice, almond, hazelnut, hemp, or oat)
- 1 to 2 teaspoons (6 to 12 g) salt
- 2 to 3 tablespoons (25 to 37 g) nutritional yeast flakes
- ½ cup (55 g) finely chopped sun-dried tomatoes, oil-packed or reconstituted in water if dried
- 2 tablespoons (5 g) minced fresh basil
- 2 tablespoons (8 g) minced fresh parsley
- 1 tablespoon (15 ml) olive oil

Per serving: 469 calories; 5g fat; 16g protein; 90g carbohydrate; 14g dietary fiber; 0mg cholesterol; 1204mg sodium.

## COMPASSIONATE COOKS' TIP

Depending on how it's labeled, you will find "coarse cornmeal" or "polenta" in the bulk section of your grocery store. Do not use cornmeal flour or "fine" cornmeal.

## DIRECTIONS

Heat water to boiling in a 4-quart (4.5 L) saucepan. When the water has boiled, add polenta or cornmeal and stir frequently over low-medium heat, being careful that it does not boil over. Slowly add the nondairy milk, 1 teaspoon of salt, and nutritional yeast, and stir until the liquid is absorbed and the polenta thickens, 5 to 10 minutes. Add the sun-dried tomatoes, basil, and parsley, stir for 1 more minute, and remove from heat. Taste, and add additional salt, if necessary.

At this point, the polenta will be thick (and getting thicker). Once you remove it from the heat, you can serve it immediately. However, to form it into shapes, let it set up for an hour. To do this, pour it into a 9 x 12-inch (23 x 30.5 cm) glass or nonstick pan, and spread evenly with a rubber spatula. Chill in the refrigerator for at least 1 hour.

When ready to serve, punch out heart shapes (or cut into squares) with the cookie cutter and set aside. Heat olive oil in a nonstick skillet over medium heat. Sear the polenta hearts until golden on both sides and heated through. Serve immediately.

**YIELD:** 2 to 4 servings

## SERVING SUGGESTIONS AND VARIATIONS

* Instead of pan-frying the polenta, you can also grill them, as long as they are nice and firm. To do so, brush the squares with olive oil, and grill until seared on both sides and heated through.
* You can also serve the polenta with the Roasted Red Pepper Coulis on page 54 (as pictured at right). Just before serving, heat sauce in a saucepan, spoon ⅔ cup (160 g) of roasted red pepper sauce into a shallow bowl, and top with 2 pieces of polenta. Garnish with fresh basil if desired. Serve immediately.

# ROASTED RED PEPPER COULIS

*Oil-free, wheat-free, soy-free depending on milk*

This simple sauce creates a dramatic color contrast to polenta (see Polenta Hearts on page 52), and is a delicious sauce for any type of pasta.

- 2 roasted red bell peppers (from a jar or homemade roasted)
- ¼ cup (60 ml) nondairy milk (soy, rice, almond, hazelnut, hemp, or oat) or soy creamer
- 3 tablespoons (16 g) unsweetened shredded coconut, toasted or kept raw
- Pinch of cayenne pepper
- Salt and black pepper, to taste

## DIRECTIONS

Place all ingredients in a blender and blend until creamy. Pour into a small-size saucepan and heat over low heat until warm, approximately 5 minutes, stirring frequently. Do not boil.

**YIELD:** ½ cup (115 g), or 4 (2-tablespoon [30 g]) servings

Per serving: 183 calories; 11g fat; 5g protein; 20g carbohydrate; 8g dietary fiber; 0mg cholesterol; 18mg sodium.

## COMPASSIONATE COOKS' TIPS

To toast coconut, place shredded coconut on a dry baking sheet in the toaster oven set to 250°F (120°C) or in a dry nonstick skillet. Heat until golden brown, about 5 minutes, turning occasionally. This method also works well for nuts and seeds.

If you roast your own peppers, drain out any water from the peppers once they're roasted, cooled, and peeled. (See page 281 for instructions on how to roast your own peppers.) If you use peppers from a jar, do not use any of the water they come in or your sauce will be too runny.

## FOOD LORE

French for "strained liquid," *coulis* refers to a thick sauce made from puréed and strained vegetables or fruits.

# SWISS CHARD AND CARAMELIZED ONIONS

*Wheat-free, soy-free if using oil*

This wonderful side dish packs a punch and satisfies many taste buds with sweet onions and salty olives and capers. Dare I say this is a favorite of mine? I make it at least once a week.

- 1 tablespoon (15 ml) olive oil or (14 g) nondairy, nonhydrogenated butter (such as Earth Balance)
- 2 large-size yellow onions, sliced
- 1 tablespoon (15 g) granulated or brown sugar
- Pinch of salt
- 1 bunch Swiss chard, washed and chopped
- ¼ cup (25 g) chopped kalamata olives
- 1 tablespoon (9 g) capers, rinsed of brine or salt
- Freshly ground black pepper, to taste
- Juice of 1 lemon

## DIRECTIONS

In a large-size sauté pan (nonstick works well for this), heat oil or butter over medium-high heat and cook onions until they brown slightly and turn translucent, about 5 minutes. Stir in sugar and salt, and continue cooking until onions are brown and sweet. This may take 15 to 30 minutes, depending on how caramelized you like them. Stir occasionally. If you have trouble fitting the onions in your pan, either cook them in two separate pans or be patient. As they cook, they will shrink and fit more easily.

Stir in chard, olives, and capers, and cook until chard is wilted, 5 to 7 minutes. Season with black pepper and squeeze lemon over top.

**YIELD:** 2 servings

## SERVING SUGGESTIONS AND VARIATIONS

This makes a fantastic topping for pizza. See page 286 for pizza crust recipes or use a cornmeal crust (by Vicolo) found in the frozen section of large natural food stores. Place toppings on the crust and bake according to package directions.

Per serving: 167 calories; 8g fat; 2g protein; 24g carbohydrate; 3g dietary fiber; 0mg cholesterol; 546mg sodium.

## COMPASSIONATE COOKS' TIP

As your onions cook, you may find that they stick to the pan. Add a little extra oil or nondairy butter as needed (or use a nonstick pan).

## DID YOU KNOW?

A caper is the bud of a Mediterranean plant that, for culinary purposes, is pickled in salt or brine. Check out a gourmet grocery store that specializes in imported foods to find capers in salt. The flavor is much better than those cured in brine. Either way, rinse before using.

# CHOCOLATE FONDUES

*Oil-free, wheat-free, soy-free depending on milk*

Fondue, which comes from the French word *fonder*, or "to melt," invites intimacy, whether between two people or ten. Chocolate, the most oft-reputed aphrodisiac, is the perfect ending to a perfect meal. Below are two fondue options for you.

## CHOCOLATE CHILE FONDUE

Vary the spiciness by adding more or less chile powder.

- ½ cup (120 ml) nondairy milk (soy, rice, almond, hazelnut, hemp, or oat) or soy creamer
- 8 to 9 ounces (225 to 255 g) nondairy semisweet or dark chocolate bar or chips
- ½ to ¾ teaspoon chile powder
- ¼ teaspoon ground cinnamon

### DIRECTIONS

In a saucepan, heat milk until it begins to simmer, then add chocolate, immediately reducing heat. Stir slowly until chocolate melts, then add chile powder and cinnamon until smooth and well combined.

Transfer to a fondue pot and light a low flame, or pour into a warmed ceramic dish and serve immediately with any of the suggestions below.

**YIELD:** 2 to 4 servings

Per serving for Chocolate Chile Fondue: 316 calories; 20g fat; 4g protein; 41g carbohydrate; 1g dietary fiber; 0mg cholesterol; 15mg sodium.

## CHOCOLATE COCONUT FONDUE

If you like *Almond Joy* candy bars, you'll love this fondue.

- ½ cup (120 ml) nondairy milk (soy, rice, almond, hazelnut, hemp, or oat) or soy creamer
- 8 to 9 ounces (225 to 255 g) nondairy semisweet or dark chocolate bar or chips
- 2 to 3 tablespoons (10 to 15 g) toasted coconut
- ¼ cup (35 g) toasted almonds, roughly chopped

### DIRECTIONS

In a saucepan, heat milk until it begins to simmer, then add chocolate, immediately reducing heat. Stir slowly until chocolate melts and is smooth. Turn off heat, and add coconut and almonds. Stir to combine.

Transfer to a fondue pot and light a low flame, or pour into a warmed ceramic dish and serve immediately with any of the suggestions below.

**YIELD:** 2 to 4 servings

### SERVING SUGGESTIONS AND VARIATIONS

Dip any of these foods into your chocolate fondues: Graham cracker pieces, fresh fruit slices (apple, banana, kiwifruit, strawberry, grape, orange, berries, pineapple, mango, or papaya), dried fruit slices (banana, mango, or apricot), vegan cookies or brownies, vegan marshmallows, cake squares (lemon, vanilla, or chocolate), or pretzels.

Per serving for Chocolate Coconut Fondue: 388 calories; 26g fat; 6g protein; 45g carbohydrate; 1g dietary fiber; 0mg cholesterol; 13mg sodium.

# CHOCOLATE IS VEGAN!

Chocolate contains more than 400 different chemicals, including *phenylethylamine*, a brain chemical that some scientists believe arouses the same feelings that we experience when we are in love. Many people assume that you sacrifice chocolate for carob when you become vegan, but it's simply not true. Milk chocolate, with its addition of cow's milk, is not vegan, but by nature, chocolate is a plant-based food that comes from the tropical evergreen cacao tree, on which grows the cacao bean.

But buyer beware: some popular brands (namely, Nestlé and Hershey's) add cow's milk to their semisweet chips and dark chocolate bars. Many good brands keep their chocolate pure, so read the label first.

Here is some terminology to help you move through the delicious maze of chocolate.

### CHOCOLATE
A general term applied to products made from the cacao bean. Cacao (or *cocoa*) beans are roasted and ground, resulting in cocoa solids, which, when combined with cocoa butter, create chocolate.

### COCOA BUTTER
This is the ivory-colored, naturally occurring fat in cacao beans. Cocoa butter is the basis of white chocolate.

### COCOA POWDER
When cacao beans get fermented, dried, and roasted, their outer hulls are removed, revealing the inner cocoa nibs. These are ground to produce chocolate liquor. Most of the cocoa butter is extracted from the chocolate liquor, leaving a dry paste, which is further dried and processed to become unsweetened cocoa powder. "Dutch-processed" has been treated with an alkali to produce a dark, mellow-flavored powder.

### DARK CHOCOLATE
This is made from chocolate liquor pressed from the cacao bean during processing, with the addition of cocoa butter, sugar, vanilla, and lecithin. Semisweet, bittersweet, and extra bittersweet chocolates are all dark chocolates. Semisweet chocolate has the largest amount of sugar; extra bittersweet the least.

### BAKING CHOCOLATE
This chocolate is pure, unsweetened chocolate liquor, pressed from the cacao bean during processing. Baking chocolate, also called unsweetened or bitter chocolate, is used in many baked goods such as brownies and cakes, for icings and sauces, and in candy.

### HOT COCOA OR HOT CHOCOLATE
This is a hot drink of cocoa powder (or melted chocolate, respectively), sugar, nondairy milk, and vanilla extract. Vegan commercial brands are available, but it's just as easy to make your own using cocoa powder or chocolate chips/bars and sugar.

### LECITHIN
This is an emulsifier often added to chocolate to give it a smooth, fluid consistency. The majority of lecithin used in chocolate manufacturing is derived from soybeans.

# CHAPTER 2

FUN WITH FRIENDS:
# CASUAL MEALS FOR FOUR TO SIX

I'll be the first to admit that I'm a modern gal who loves all things domestic. There is something so basic, so fundamental, so primal about tending to our nests. The words *warmth*, *cozy*, and *calm* come to mind when I think about the mood I try to create in our home for those of us who live there and for those who come to visit. Treat your visitors to these simple but delicious dishes that will warm them from the inside out.

# RECIPES

# TASTEFUL TOUCHES

Adding little touches throughout our home makes guests feel special and appreciated. Here are a few ideas for fancying up your home a bit each season, making the most of nature's decor, and keeping the costs low.

## SPRING

In honor of the season, make flowers the focal point for an indoor or outdoor gathering. Blue hydrangeas, tulips, lilies, and irises add color and drama, especially when placed in front of a backdrop of all-white candles, plates, tablecloths, and napkins.

Set the mood inside and outside of your home, so guests feel spring in the air the moment they approach. Add water to your birdbath, plant annual spring flowers along the path to your front door, and scatter flower petals on your coffee table.

You don't have to shop for decorations. Most likely, you have everything you need. Use baskets to hold cloth napkins and flowerpots to hold utensils. Adorn tables with ceramic or stone animal figurines from your garden.

## SUMMER

During summertime, take advantage of the season's fruit. Serve fruit salad in a carved watermelon basket or pineapple boat.

Take advantage of summer flowers such as daisies, roses, and sunflowers. Add a special touch by providing leis (those wonderful flower garlands associated with Hawaii) for each of your guests.

Don't forget to decorate *above* your guests' heads, too! Hanging paper lanterns, which are appropriate indoors or outside, cast light on your guests when the sun goes down, and citronella candles suspended on tiki torches keep away uninvited flying guests.

## AUTUMN

Whether you're serving potent potables or restorative refreshments, create a cauldronlike effect by using dry ice. This works especially well for cold beverages such as sparkling pear juice, apple cider, or fruit punch, and is a fun way to serve drinks at a Halloween party.

Illuminate your home with candles. To line your outside walkways with luminaries, simply fill lunch bags (recycled, of course) with 2 cups (455 g) of sand and place a votive candle securely inside. If you have a fireplace, burn eco-friendly compressed logs instead of wood.

For another nice autumn touch, place tree branches in vases, and adorn your home with pumpkins and other gourds, which you can later use for cooking or as a treat for wildlife. Dried ears of corn and haystacks create a rustic mood, and birds will love the hay for their nests and the corn for their bellies.

## WINTER

Make living ornaments out of orange, lemon, and lime slices. Dry them on a cookie sheet in an oven turned on low overnight. Send a pretty ribbon or wire through the central hole, and adorn throughout the house or on a tree. Give as gifts by wrapping them in decorative tissue paper. Remind your recipient that the ornaments can be stored in an airtight container and reused.

Fill old-fashioned cookie tins with gingerbread men, sugar cookies, and pecan balls, and set them around the house for guests to eat or to take home as gifts. Do the same with mason jars filled with caramelized nuts or popcorn.

Strings of miniature white lights add instant elegance, especially when paired with living garlands.

## FOR ALL SEASONS

Leave a basket by the front door with a take-away gift for your guests. The surprise could be a little box of nondairy chocolates in the winter, a bulb to plant in the fall, seed packets with potting soil in the spring, or a pot of fresh herbs in the summer.

May the warmth that dwells in your home fill the hearts of those who enter.

# EDIBLE FLOWERS

Flower petals add a beautiful touch to many dishes, in terms of their color, texture, and taste. This is just a small sampling of the flowers that you can eat. For a variety of reasons, I recommend choosing organically grown flowers.

### CHRYSANTHEMUMS
Ranging in color from red and orange to white and yellow, the flavor can be anything from peppery to mildly bitter. Blanch before adding to salads.

### DANDELIONS
Imparting a sweet honeylike flavor and fragrance, the flowers, particularly the buds, are sweetest when picked young and just before eating. Leaves can be steamed, sautéed, or tossed in salads, and petals look like confetti when sprinkled over a rice dish.

### HONEYSUCKLE
The petals have a sweet honey flavor, but the berries are highly poisonous. Do not eat them!

### IMPATIENS
Although they have a mild taste, they add wonderful color to any salad and are easy to find.

### JASMINE
These intensely fragrant flowers are perfect for scenting tea.

### MARIGOLDS (CALENDULA)
Also known as "poor man's saffron," marigolds have a flavor that ranges from spicy to bitter, tangy to peppery. Add to soups, pasta, rice, or salads.

### NASTURTIUMS
A commonly used edible flower (especially in my home, since we grow them!), nasturtiums come in brilliant red, orange, and yellow colors, and have a spicy, peppery flavor similar to that of watercress. Use entire flowers to garnish platters, salads, sandwiches, or appetizers.

### PANSIES
They come in so many different colors and have a mild wintergreen flavor. Unlike with other flowers, you can eat this entire flower, stem, stamen, and petals.

### ROSES
The flavor, depending on type, color, and soil conditions, tends to be reminiscent of strawberries and tart apples. All roses are edible, but the darker varieties have a more pronounced flavor. Sprinkle on desserts or salads, freeze them in ice cubes, or float them in punches.

### VIOLETS (JOHNNY-JUMP-UPS)
Their sweet, perfumed flavors complement their colorful hues of purple, yellow, blue, or white, and enhance a salad of mixed greens. They are also wonderful additions to iced drinks and can decorate desserts. Freeze them in punches or ice cubes.

# SUGGESTED SEASONAL MENUS

Fill the bellies of your friends without spending hours in the kitchen.
Start off each menu with a salad of your choice.

## SPRING

### APRIL SHOWERS, PAGE 64
Roasted Asparagus Soup with Thyme
Creamy Miso Salad Dressing
Ratatouille with White Beans
Strawberries and Wine

### SUNSHINE DAY, PAGE 69
Olive Tapenade
Red Lentil Artichoke Stew
Pasta Primavera with Fresh Veggies and Herbs

## SUMMER

### LADIES-WHO-LUNCH, PAGE 72
Better-Than-Tuna Salad
Pasta Salad with Veggies, Pine Nuts, and
    Fresh Herbs
Balsamic Strawberries

### TEA FOR TWO (OR FOUR OR SIX!), PAGE 75
Roasted Red Pepper, Artichoke, and Pesto
    Sandwiches
Basil Pesto
Cucumber and Cream Cheese Sandwiches
Lavender Tea Cookies
Fresh Berry Parfait

## AUTUMN

### EARLY IN THE MORNING, PAGE 82
Fast and Fabulous French Toast
Golden Corn Pancakes
Herbed Scalloped Potatoes
Cocktails for Kids

### AUTUMN LEAVES, PAGE 86
Warm Spinach Salad
Butternut Squash Soup
Creamy Polenta with Mushrooms
Cauliflower with Spicy Vinaigrette
Chocolate Chocolate Chip Cookies

## WINTER

### HERE COMES THE SUN, PAGE 92
Tofu "No Egg" Benedict
Hollandaise Sauce
Home-Fried Potatoes
Apricot Whole-Wheat Muffins
Mimosas

### COME RAIN OR COME SHINE, PAGE 98
Split Pea Soup
"Honey" Mustard Salad Dressing
Penne Pasta with Fresh Veggies
Flourless Chocolate Tart

# ROASTED ASPARAGUS SOUP WITH THYME

*Wheat-free, soy-free*

This creamy and elegant soup boasts a gorgeous green color. Don't be afraid to add salt; it will bring out the flavor of the asparagus.

- 4 pounds (1820 g) asparagus, trimmed of rough, woody ends
- 2 tablespoons divided, (30 ml) olive oil, for roasting and sautéing
- 1 ½ teaspoons (9 g) salt (or to taste), divided, plus more for sprinkling
- 3 garlic cloves, minced or pressed
- 2 yellow onions, chopped
- 2 leeks, white and some green parts, chopped
- 3 carrots, peeled and finely chopped
- 1 celery stalk, chopped
- 8 cups (1880 ml) vegetable stock (store-bought or homemade, page 213)
- 1 teaspoon (1 g) dried thyme leaves
- Freshly ground black pepper, to taste
- 1 carrot, grated, for garnish (optional)
- Chopped fresh parsley, for garnish (optional)

## DIRECTIONS

Preheat oven to 450°F (230°C, or gas mark 8). Cut off asparagus tips from the stalks, and coat tips in about 1 tablespoon olive oil. Sprinkle with salt and place on a baking sheet. Roast for 15 to 20 minutes, or until soft to the bite but crispy on the outside. Reserve for garnish.

Cut remaining asparagus stalks into 1-inch (2.5 cm) pieces. Heat remaining olive oil over medium heat. Once hot, add garlic and let cook for about 1 minute before adding the onions, leeks, carrots, and celery. Cook, stirring occasionally, until vegetables are soft, about 7 minutes. Add the 1-inch asparagus stalks, stock, thyme, salt, and pepper; bring to a boil over high heat.

Reduce heat, cover, and simmer gently until the stalks are tender, stirring occasionally, 25 to 30 minutes. Let the soup cool slightly.

Transfer soup to a food processor and purée. Return to pot and add the roasted asparagus tips. Cover and heat over low heat, stirring occasionally, until the soup is heated through, about 5 minutes. Add additional salt and pepper to taste. Sprinkle with grated carrot and fresh parsley, if desired, and serve hot.

**YIELD:** 4 to 6 servings

Per serving: 135 calories; 4g fat; 5g protein; 23g carbohydrate; 6g dietary fiber; 0mg cholesterol; 1895mg sodium.

# CREAMY MISO SALAD DRESSING

*Wheat-free*

Miso is a staple in my refrigerator. It is wonderful to use in sauces and dressings or for adding a salty flavor to any dish.

- ¼ cup (60 ml) seasoned rice vinegar
- 2 tablespoons (30 ml) sesame or olive oil
- 2 tablespoons (32 g) white, yellow, or light miso paste
- 1 tablespoon (15 ml) water

## DIRECTIONS

Although you can certainly prepare this by hand, it will be creamier if made in a blender. The speed of the blender allows the oil to emulsify, resulting in a creamy dressing.

Combine all ingredients, and blend on high for 1 minute. Transfer to a container and store in the refrigerator, or serve right away, by tossing on your favorite mixed greens.

**YIELD:** ½ cup (120 ml), or 8 (2-tablespoon [30 ml]) servings

Per serving: 40 calories; 4g fat; 1g protein; 2g carbohydrate; trace dietary fiber; 0mg cholesterol; 157mg sodium.

## COMPASSIONATE COOKS' TIP

Miso, a healthful fermented paste, can be found in the refrigerated section of the grocery store. It will keep for months and months in your own refrigerator.

## FOOD LORE

According to an Assyrian creation myth, the gods drank sesame wine the night before they created the Earth. Sesame seeds are believed to be one of the first plants to be used for edible oil.

# RATATOUILLE WITH WHITE BEANS

*Oil-free if sautéed in water, wheat-free, soy-free*

This dish works best when the vegetables are in season and at their peak.
Serve it hot or cold, as an appetizer or as the centerpiece of your meal.

- 1 large-size globe eggplant, cut into ½-inch (1 cm) cubes
- 2 tablespoons (30 ml) olive oil or water, for sautéing
- 2 medium-size red onions, sliced
- 3 medium-size zucchini squash, cut into ½-inch (1 cm) cubes
- 2 red bell peppers, cut into ½-inch (1 cm) squares
- 4 garlic cloves, minced
- ¼ cup (60 ml) dry white wine
- 1 cup (235 ml) vegetable stock (store-bought or homemade, page 213)
- 4 tomatoes, seeded and roughly chopped (or 2 cans [15 ounces, or 420 g, each] fire-roasted diced tomatoes)
- 1 tablespoon (4 g) chopped fresh parsley
- 2 teaspoons (2 g) chopped fresh thyme (or ½ teaspoon dried)
- 2 teaspoons (2 g) chopped fresh marjoram (or ½ teaspoon dried marjoram or oregano)
- 2 bay leaves
- 2 cans (15 ounces, or 420 g, each) white beans, drained and rinsed (or 3 cups [515 g] beans made from scratch)
- Salt and freshly ground pepper, to taste
- ½ cup (20 g) finely chopped fresh basil
- Kalamata olives, pitted and chopped, for garnish (optional)

## DIRECTIONS

Steam eggplant cubes for 10 minutes until soft but not mushy. Heat olive oil in a large-size sauté pan. Add onions and cook, stirring, until softened, about 5 minutes. Cook them longer to create a more caramelized effect.

Add zucchini and bell peppers, and cook, stirring often, for about 5 minutes. Add steamed eggplant and cook about 5 minutes, then add garlic.

Add wine and stock. Bring to a boil over high heat, then reduce heat to medium-high and stir in tomatoes, parsley, thyme, marjoram, and bay leaves. Reduce heat, cover, and simmer gently for 15 minutes, stirring occasionally.

Add beans to skillet, stirring well to combine. Cook, uncovered, until vegetables are tender but not mushy and liquids have thickened, stirring occasionally for about 5 minutes. Season with salt to taste.

Remove skillet from heat and stir in chopped basil. Serve warm or at room temperature, garnish and pepper with chopped olives, if desired.

**YIELD:** 6 to 8 servings

Per serving: 456 calories; 5g fat; 28g protein; 79g carbohydrate; 21g dietary fiber; 0mg cholesterol; 154mg sodium.

# STRAWBERRIES AND WINE

*Oil-free, wheat-free, soy-free*

Adjust the amount of sugar based on the sweetness of the berries.
Substitute champagne for the wine for a different flavor.

- 3 cups (435 g) fresh ripe strawberries, halved, quartered lengthwise, or sliced thinly
- ¼ to ½ cup (50 to 100 g) granulated sugar (or to taste)
- 1 ½ cups (355 ml) sweet white wine

## DIRECTIONS

Place strawberries in a medium-size bowl. Dust with sugar, then pour wine over them. Cover and refrigerate for 2 to 3 hours. Overnight is fine, too.

Let strawberries stand at room temperature for 15 to 20 minutes before serving. Spoon berries into dessert cups, and distribute remaining wine over berries.

**YIELD:** 6 servings

Per serving: 127 calories; trace fat; trace protein; 22g carbohydrate; 2g dietary fiber; 0mg cholesterol; 4mg sodium.

## DID YOU KNOW?

Strawberries are highly sprayed with pesticides. Choose organic.

## COMPASSIONATE COOKS' TIP

This dish is fantastic on its own or served over vanilla nondairy ice cream, vanilla cake, or even as a filling for crepes.

## FOOD LORE

The exact origin of the word is still unknown, it is likely that "strawberry" came from the practice of placing straw around the growing plants for protection. Cultivated in the United States by Native Americans, strawberries grew wild in Italy as far back as 234 BC.

# OLIVE TAPENADE

*Wheat-free, soy-free*

From the Provençal word for capers (*tapeno*), tapenade is a traditional dish of puréed or finely chopped olives, capers, and olive oil.

- ½ cup (50 g) pitted black olives, rinsed
- 2 tablespoons (17 g) capers, rinsed and drained
- 1 garlic clove, peeled
- 1 teaspoon (1 g) chopped fresh thyme
- 2 tablespoons (30 ml) olive oil
- 1 to 2 tablespoons (15 to 30 ml) fresh lemon juice
- Fresh thyme sprigs, for garnish (optional)

## DIRECTIONS

In a food processor or blender, combine olives, capers, garlic, thyme, oil, and lemon juice. Blend until mixture becomes a coarse paste, scraping down the sides of the bowl and restarting the machine as many times as needed.

Transfer to bowl and garnish with sprigs of fresh thyme, if desired.

**YIELD:** ¾ cup (195 g), or 6 (2-tablespoon [35 g]) servings

## SERVING SUGGESTIONS AND VARIATIONS

* Serve on a toasted baguette, warmed pita triangles, or crackers, or as a dip for raw vegetables.
* Thin the tapenade with olive oil and toss with hot pasta.
* Add chopped fresh thyme, parsley, or basil, if you desire.

Per serving: 56 calories; 6g fat; trace protein; 1g carbohydrate; trace dietary fiber; 0mg cholesterol; 124mg sodium.

## FOOD LORE

The most literary of all fruit, the olive is one of the plants most cited in recorded literature, including Greek mythology, Homer's *The Odyssey*, the New and Old Testaments of the Bible, and the Koran.

# RED LENTIL ARTICHOKE STEW

*Wheat-free, oil-free, soy-free*

This aromatic, fiber-packed, tasty Middle Eastern dish is great served over brown rice or your favorite pasta.

- 1 1/2 cups (360 ml) water plus 1 tablespoon (15 ml), for sautéing
- 2 medium-size yellow onions, diced
- 2 or 3 large-size garlic cloves, pressed or minced
- 2 teaspoons (5 g) ground cumin
- 1 teaspoon (2 g) ground coriander
- 1 cup (190 g) dry red lentils, rinsed
- 1 bay leaf
- 2 tablespoons (30 ml) fresh lemon juice
- 1 can (24 ounces, or 540 g) chopped tomatoes, undrained (use fire-roasted canned tomatoes if available)
- 1 1/2 cups (450 g) quartered artichoke hearts (1 package [9 ounces, or 340 g] or 1 can [15 ounces, or 565 g], drained)
- 1/4 teaspoon crushed red pepper flakes
- Salt and ground black pepper, to taste

## DIRECTIONS

Heat 1 tablespoon (15 ml) water in a soup pot over medium heat. When hot, sauté onions until softened, about 7 minutes.

Add garlic, cumin, and coriander, and cook for 2 minutes, stirring frequently. Add more water, if necessary.

Add remaining 1 1/2 cups (360 ml) water, lentils, bay leaf, lemon juice, tomatoes and tomato liquid, artichoke hearts, and crushed red pepper, and bring to a boil.

Lower heat and simmer for 30 minutes, or until lentils are tender. Add more water if too much liquid evaporates or stew becomes too thick.

Remove and discard bay leaf and season with salt and black pepper. Serve alone or over rice or pasta.

**YIELD:** 6 servings

Per serving: 190 calories; 1g fat; 13g protein; 36g carbohydrate; 14g dietary fiber; 0mg cholesterol; 596mg sodium.

# PASTA PRIMAVERA WITH FRESH VEGGIES AND HERBS

*Soy-free, wheat-free if using rice pasta*

What better way to celebrate spring, the namesake of this dish, than with fresh spring vegetables? The veggies I selected are just one of many combinations, so visit your local farmers' market, and pick what's in season!

- 12 ounces (160 g) penne, farfalle, rigatoni, or fusili pasta

- 1 to 2 tablespoons (15 to 30 ml) olive oil

- 4 garlic cloves, minced

- 2 bell peppers (red, orange, yellow), cut into strips

- 3 to 4 carrots, peeled and cut into 1-inch (2.5 cm) strips

- 2 zucchini squash, cut into 1-inch (2.5 cm) strips

- 8 stalks asparagus, rough ends trimmed and cut into 2-inch (5 cm) pieces

- 2 cups (360 g) coarsely chopped fresh tomatoes

- 1 cup (235 ml) vegetable stock (store-bought or homemade, page 213)

- 1 bunch scallions (6 to 8), white and green parts, chopped

- 1 cup (40 g) loosely packed fresh basil leaves, chopped, plus more for sprinkling

- 2 tablespoons (8 g) minced fresh parsley, plus more for sprinkling

- ½ to 1 cup (65 to 135 g) toasted pine nuts

- 12 black, kalamata, or green olives, pitted and chopped (optional)

- Pinch of red pepper flakes (optional)

- Salt and freshly ground black pepper, to taste

## DIRECTIONS

Cook the pasta in boiling water according to package directions until al dente; drain well.

Meanwhile, in a large-size sauté pan, heat oil over medium-high heat. Add garlic and cook for about 2 minutes. Add bell pepper, carrots, squash, and asparagus. Sauté, stirring occasionally, until vegetables are tender but still crispy and beginning to brown, about 10 minutes. Reduce heat to low, and add tomatoes. Stir well to combine.

Add stock and simmer until heated through. Add scallions, basil, parsley, pine nuts, olives (if using), and red pepper flakes (if using). Turn off heat, and add pasta, tossing well to combine and adding salt to taste. Serve warm or at room temperature with freshly ground pepper and a sprinkling of minced fresh herbs.

**YIELD:** 6 servings

## SERVING SUGGESTIONS AND VARIATIONS

Roast the vegetables instead of sautéing them, then toss in a skillet with the remaining ingredients.

Per serving: 484 calories; 19g fat; 17g protein; 66g carbohydrate; 8g dietary fiber; 0mg cholesterol; 380mg sodium.

# BETTER-THAN-TUNA SALAD

*Wheat-free, soy-free*

This recipe has all the flavor of the lunchtime staple but leaves the cruelty, cholesterol, and mercury behind! Now that's a comforting thought.

- 2 cans (15 ounces or 420 g, each) chickpeas, drained and rinsed (or 3 cups [720 g] fresh beans soaked and cooked from scratch)
- ½ cup (115 g) eggless mayonnaise (see Resources and Recommendations)
- 1 medium-size red bell pepper, finely chopped
- 2 carrots, peeled and finely chopped
- 2 celery stalks, finely chopped
- 2 tablespoons (8 g) fresh parsley, finely chopped
- 1 cup (120 g) walnuts, chopped
- 1 tablespoon (15 g) Dijon mustard
- Salt and freshly ground pepper, to taste

## DIRECTIONS

Grind chickpeas in a food processor or blender down to small flaky pieces. You can make this salad with whole chickpeas, but I find ground chickpeas make it easier to add as a sandwich filling. Plus, the flakiness of the ground chickpeas really resembles tuna in texture.

In a large-size bowl, combine first eight ingredients and mix well. Season with salt and pepper, to taste.

**YIELD:** 4 to 6 servings

## DID YOU KNOW?

Many people don't realize that the tuna industry (as well as the seafood industry in general) is responsible for the death of thousands of "nontargeted" species. Thousands of sharks are killed each year in tuna fisheries, and around 100,000 albatrosses are killed by long-line fisheries every year, particularly where tuna are fished.

Because of this, many species face extinction. Although the number of dolphin deaths have decreased since new techniques have been used to catch tuna, several thousand dolphins are still killed each year, giving the "dolphin-safe" label little credence. In contrast, this Better-Than-Tuna recipe is not only dolphin-safe, but it's tuna-safe, too!

## COMPASSIONATE COOKS' TIP

Sprinkle in some kelp or dulse flakes for a "fishy" flavor.

Per serving: 384 calories; 6g fat; 20g protein; 65g carbohydrate; 19g dietary fiber; 0mg cholesterol; 76mg sodium.

# PASTA SALAD WITH VEGGIES, PINE NUTS, AND FRESH HERBS

*Wheat-free (if using a wheat-free pasta), soy-free, oil-free if omitting oil*

Pasta salads are easy to make, inexpensive, and filling. They are meant to be free-form and fast. The possibilities for variety are endless.

- 16 ounces (455 g) bowtie or penne pasta (or any dry pasta of choice)
- 1 cup (160 g) cherry tomatoes, cut in half lengthwise
- 3 bell peppers (red, orange, or yellow), seeded and diced
- 2 cucumbers, seeded and diced
- 2 to 3 carrots, peeled and diced
- 1 small-size red onion, diced
- 1 jar (16 ounces, or 455 g) artichoke hearts, drained and coarsely chopped
- 1 ½ cups (200 g) fresh or frozen corn, thawed
- ½ cup (70 g) toasted pine nuts, (see page 135)
- ¼ cup (10 g) fresh basil, finely chopped
- ¼ cup (10 g) fresh tarragon, finely chopped
- 2 tablespoons (30 ml) olive oil (optional)
- 2 to 3 tablespoons (30 to 45 ml) fresh lemon juice
- 2 tablespoons (30 ml) seasoned rice vinegar (or balsamic or red wine vinegar)
- Salt and freshly ground pepper, to taste

## DIRECTIONS

Cook pasta according to package directions. Combine tomatoes, peppers, cucumbers, carrots, onion, artichokes, corn, pine nuts, basil, and tarragon in a bowl. In a separate bowl, combine olive oil (if using), lemon juice, and vinegar.

When the pasta is finished cooking, drain and let cool completely. Add to veggie mixture. Add oil mixture and toss everything together. Add salt and pepper to taste.

**YIELD:** 6 to 10 servings

## SERVING SUGGESTIONS AND VARIATIONS

* A few slices of sun-dried tomatoes would be a wonderful addition. If you don't like raw peppers, eliminate them and replace with another crunchy vegetable, such as green beans. For some heat, add crushed red pepper flakes!
* You also can vary the herbs; dill, cilantro, and parsley are great options. Use dried if you're desperate, but fresh herbs are really the best.
* If you don't have any vinegar, this salad is just as delicious without, especially if you're using a good extra virgin olive oil. The flip side of that is true, too. If you want to omit the olive oil, you can rely on the flavor of a good vinegar.

Per serving: 312 calories; 7g fat; 11g protein; 53g carbohydrate; 7g dietary fiber; 0mg cholesterol; 62mg sodium.

# BALSAMIC STRAWBERRIES

*Oil-free, wheat-free, soy-free*

If you've never before tried this combination, you're in for a treat. The balsamic vinegar brings out the berries' beautiful color and truly enhances their flavor. They make a perfect meal-starter or dessert and can be served by themselves or with cake or vanilla nondairy ice cream.

- 16 ounces (455 g) fresh strawberries, halved or quartered lengthwise
- 2 tablespoons (30 ml) balsamic vinegar
- ¼ cup (50 g) granulated sugar
- ¼ teaspoon freshly ground black pepper (or to taste)

## DIRECTIONS

Place strawberries in a bowl. Drizzle vinegar over fruit, and sprinkle with sugar. Stir gently with a rubber spatula to combine. Cover, and let sit at room temperature for at least 1 hour but not more than 4 hours. Just before serving, grind pepper over berries.

**YIELD:** 6 servings

Per serving: 55 calories; trace fat; trace protein; 14g carbohydrate; 2g dietary fiber; 0mg cholesterol; 1mg sodium.

## DID YOU KNOW?

Strawberries top the list when it comes to produce contaminated with pesticides. Knowing which fruits and vegetables are considered the "dirty dozen" is helpful when deciding whether to use organic or conventionally grown produce. Other highly contaminated produce includes apples, bell peppers, celery, cherries, imported grapes, nectarines, peaches, pears, potatoes, red raspberries, and spinach.

## FOOD LORE

"Balsamic Vinegar of Modena" is commercial-grade vinegar that is not aged or fermented and includes such additives as caramel, coloring, and thickeners. Look for a high-quality, traditional vinegar, often labeled "Balsamico Tradizionale."

**SUMMER MENU:** Tea for Two (or Four or Six!)

● Basil Pesto  ● Roasted Red Pepper, Artichoke, and Pesto Sandwiches
● Cucumber and Cream Cheese Sandwiches
● Lavender Tea Cookies  ● Fresh Berry Parfait

# BASIL PESTO

*Wheat-free, soy-free*

The name *pesto* derives from the tradition of making this sauce in a mortar with a pestle. This recipe, for which I encourage you to use a food processor unless you have a few spare hours, proves that you absolutely don't need cheese to make a fantastic pesto. Purchase fresh basil (or grow it yourself!), and find a nice fruity olive oil.

- 3 cups (120 g) loosely packed fresh basil leaves
- ¼ cup (35 g) raw pine nuts
- 2 or 3 whole garlic cloves, peeled
- 3 tablespoons (45 ml) extra-virgin olive oil
- ¼ teaspoon salt (or to taste)

### DIRECTIONS

Combine basil, pine nuts, and garlic in a food processor, and blend until ingredients begin forming a paste, scraping down the sides of the bowl as necessary. Drizzle in a tablespoon or (15 to 30 ml) two of oil, along with the salt, and process until smooth and creamy adding additional oil, if needed. Add more salt as necessary, a little at a time.

**YIELD:** ½ cup (130 g), or 4 (2-tablespoon [35 g]) servings

## DID YOU KNOW?

In Provence, a slightly different version, known as *pistou*, is made with olive oil, basil, and garlic only. No nuts are used. *Pistou* is added to soupe au pistou, a hearty vegetable soup served in the region.

Per serving: 150 calories; 15g fat; 3g protein; 3g carbohydrate; 2g dietary fiber; 0mg cholesterol; 135mg sodium.

## COMPASSIONATE COOKS' TIP

See page 290 for Basil Pesto Pizza, page 294 for Sun-Dried Tomato and Walnut Pesto, and page 162 for Lemon-Basil Pesto.

# HOSTING AN ENGLISH-STYLE TEA PARTY

Iron your doilies and break out your tea cozies to create a traditional English-style afternoon tea, the perfect excuse to gather good friends. Here's what you need:

### THE ACCOUTREMENTS
Although "bone china" is indeed made with animal bones, everything else on the traditional tea table is animal-free, including porcelain, crystal, silver, linens, and doilies.

### THE TABLE
A vase of flowers could grace the center, but a beautiful bowl filled with lemons, pears, or small apples would also do the trick. Smaller bowls of strawberries, raspberries, and blueberries would invite nibbling as well as add color. Garnish with mint leaves.

### THE ESSENTIALS
Serve nondairy milk in a creamer, sugar cubes in a matching sugar bowl, a small bowl of jam with a small knife for spreading, lemon slices, and, of course, an English teapot, cups, and a tea strainer. (Some makers of soymilk also make a soy creamer.)

### THE TEA
English or Irish Breakfast, Earl Grey, Orange Pekoe, and Darjeeling teas are all customary. Choose a high-quality loose tea—not bagged! (See Resources and Recommendations.)

### THE AMBIANCE
In the spring, have your afternoon tea in a room that gets lots of sun and have light foods to go with the season. During summer, hold it on your patio, balcony, or porch, or in the backyard, and keep the menu light and refreshing. During colder seasons, provide a fire in your fireplace, along with some heartier fare.

### THE MENU
Sandwiches with the crusts cut off and cut into squares (or any other imaginative shape), scones, cakes, and pastries are traditionally served.

### THE PREPARATION
Since you will prepare all the food before your guests arrive, you will only need to actively serve the tea itself. Present the food buffet-style, or pass plates at a more formal table.

### THE BREWING
For black tea, the common tea served at an English tea party, the water should be boiling (212°F [100°C]). Avoid oversteeping, which may result in a bitter taste.

# ROASTED RED PEPPER, ARTICHOKE, AND PESTO SANDWICHES

*Wheat-free depending on bread, soy-free*

To quote my friend Danielle Puller, who contributed this recipe, "the combination of basil pesto, roasted red peppers, and artichokes is simply amazing!" She's right.

- Basil Pesto (see recipe, page 75)
- Eggless mayonnaise (see Resources and Recommendations, page 296)
- 16 slices bread (whole wheat, white, rice, rye, or pumpernickel)
- 2 roasted red peppers (homemade or from a jar), thinly sliced
- 1 jar (13 ounces, or 365 g) marinated artichoke hearts, drained and thinly sliced

## DIRECTIONS

To assemble the sandwiches, spread a thin layer of pesto and mayonnaise on each slice of the bread, and top with red pepper and artichoke slices. Remove crusts before cutting sandwiches into triangles or any shape desired, including those resulting from a cookie cutter! Arrange on a pretty platter.

**YIELD:** 32 servings (if cut into fourths)

Per serving: 44 calories; 1g fat; 1g protein; 7g carbohydrate; 1g dietary fiber; 0mg cholesterol; 104mg sodium.

## FOOD LORE

Traditional German pumpernickel, made from a combination of rye flour and whole rye berries, is made almost exclusively in Germany and hard to find elsewhere. American pumpernickel is made from a combination of wheat and rye flours, along with darkening agents—such as molasses or coffee—to mimic the dark color of the original German version.

# CUCUMBER AND CREAM CHEESE SANDWICHES

*Oil-free, wheat-free depending on bread*

Simplify this recipe by serving the "traditional" British cucumber sandwich, which consists of paper-thin slices of cucumber placed between two thin slices of lightly buttered (nondairy, of course) white bread, with the crusts cut off.

- 1 container (8 ounces, or 225 g) nondairy cream cheese, softened (try Tofutti brand)
- 3 tablespoons (9 g) finely chopped fresh chives
- 2 tablespoons (8 g) finely chopped fresh dill
- 2 tablespoons (12 g) finely chopped fresh mint
- 1 seedless cucumber, peeled and very thinly sliced into rounds (about 32 slices)
- 16 slices bread (whole wheat, white, rice, rye, or pumpernickel)
- ½ pound (225 g) arugula
- Salt and freshly ground black pepper, to taste

## DIRECTIONS

Mix nondairy cream cheese with chives, dill, and mint. Place cucumber slices between layers of paper towels to remove excess moisture.

Spread a thin layer of cream cheese mixture on each slice of bread. Top every other slice with cucumber and arugula, sprinkle on some salt and pepper, and assemble sandwiches.

Carefully cut crusts from each sandwich with a sharp knife. Cut sandwiches in half diagonally and cut in half again. Serve on a pretty platter.

**YIELD:** 32 servings (if cut into fourths)

Per serving: 65 calories; 2g fat; 1g protein; 10g carbohydrate; 1g dietary fiber; 0mg cholesterol; 105mg sodium.

## WHAT'S THE DIFFERENCE? HIGH TEA VS. AFTERNOON TEA

High tea sounds like the loftier of the two, but in actuality, it's just dinner. In Great Britain, when working families would return home tired and exhausted, the table would be set with various types of food and, of course, tea. You'll find none of the dainty finger sandwiches, scones, and pastries of afternoon tea. It was named "high tea" because it is served on the main, or "high," dining table rather than on low tea tables. What American hotels and tearooms call high tea is actually a misnomer.

Afternoon tea (because it was usually taken in the late afternoon) is also called "low tea" because it was usually taken in a sitting room, where low tables (like coffee tables) were placed near sofas or chairs. In England, the traditional time for tea was 4:00 or 5:00 p.m. The menu often includes three particular courses served specifically in this order:

1. Small savory sandwiches or appetizers
2. Scones served with jam
3. Pastries such as cakes, cookies, and shortbread

# LAVENDER TEA COOKIES

These elegant shortbread cookies are perfect for a tea party or any spring or summer fete. I use a $1/3$ cup measuring cup to create perfect little cookies, but you can use a biscuit cutter for larger cookies or any cookie cutter to create various shapes.

- 1 ½ cups (280 g) nondairy, nonhydrogenated butter (such as Earth Balance), at room temperature
- ⅔ cup (135 g) granulated sugar
- ¼ cup (25 g) sifted confectioners' sugar
- 3 to 4 tablespoons (15 to 20 g) finely chopped fresh lavender or 2 tablespoons (10 g) dried culinary lavender
- 2 teaspoons (4 g) grated lemon zest
- 2 ½ cups (315 g) all-purpose or whole-wheat pastry flour
- ½ cup (64 g) cornstarch
- ¼ teaspoon salt

## DIRECTIONS

In a medium-size bowl, cream butter, granulated sugar, and confectioners' sugar until light and fluffy. Add lavender and lemon zest. Stir to combine.

In a separate bowl, combine flour, cornstarch, and salt. When thoroughly mixed, add to the wet batter, and stir until well blended. You should have a thick cookie batter.

Divide dough into 2 balls, wrap in plastic wrap, and flatten to about 1 inch (2.5 cm) thick. Refrigerate until firm, about 1 hour.

When ready to prepare the cookies, preheat the oven to 325°F (170°C, or gas mark 3). On a lightly floured surface, roll the dough out to ¼-inch (6 mm) thickness. Cut into shapes with dry measuring cup, biscuit cutters, or cookie cutters. Place on ungreased baking sheets.

Bake for 18 to 20 minutes, or until the cookies begin to brown at the edges. Remove from oven, cool for a few minutes on baking sheets, then transfer to wire racks to cool completely.

**YIELD:** 2 to 3 dozen cookies (depending on size of cookie)

## COMPASSIONATE COOKS' TIP

This cookie dough freezes beautifully!

Per serving: 123 calories; 7g fat; 1g protein; 13g carbohydrate; trace dietary fiber; 0mg cholesterol; 15mg sodium.

# FRESH BERRY PARFAIT

*Oil-free, wheat-free*

This is a healthful and beautiful treat that works well for breakfast in bed, brunch, or dessert. The striking red and blue colors of this dish are a reminder of the healthful antioxidants in these berries.

- 2 pints (580 g) organic strawberries, stemmed and quartered
- 1 pint (290 g) blueberries
- 1 pint (290 g) organic raspberries
- Juice and zest from 1 lemon
- 1 container (6 ounces, or 170 g) nondairy plain or vanilla yogurt
- 2 tablespoons (30 ml) real maple syrup or agave nectar
- Sliced almonds, toasted

## DIRECTIONS

Divide strawberries among 6 wine or fluted glasses, followed by blueberries, then raspberries. Distribute lemon juice among glasses, adding some to each batch of berries.

Spoon yogurt on top and drizzle on the maple syrup or agave nectar. Garnish with almonds and lemon zest, and serve.

**YIELD:** 6 servings

## SERVING SUGGESTIONS AND VARIATIONS

Add granola in place of the sliced almonds or as another layer.

Per serving: 117 calories; 1g fat; 2g protein; 27g carbohydrate; 6g dietary fiber; 0mg cholesterol; 19mg sodium.

## DID YOU KNOW?

From the cactuslike plant, called the "agave" and native to Mexico, oozes a thick, sweet syrup similar to honey that can be used in all the same ways as its animal-derived counterpart. It's a much sexier nectar when you consider the fact that honey is fermented in and regurgitated from a bee's stomach.

# FAST AND FABULOUS FRENCH TOAST

If you need a way to use that loaf of stale Italian bread (or any bread, for that matter), French toast is the answer. Once you try this incredibly easy and delicious dish, you'll wind up asking yourself why you ever use eggs at all. You won't miss them one bit.

- 1 loaf thick Italian or sourdough bread
- 1 cup (235 ml) nondairy milk (soy, rice, almond, hazelnut, hemp, or oat)
- 1 teaspoon (2.5 g) ground cinnamon
- ¼ teaspoon ground nutmeg
- 1 teaspoon (5 ml) vanilla extract
- 4 tablespoons (65 g) nondairy, nonhydrogenated butter (such as Earth Balance)
- Real maple syrup, for drizzling
- Sifted confectioners' sugar for dusting (optional)

## DIRECTIONS

Cut bread into ½-inch (1.5 cm) slices. In a shallow bowl, whisk together milk, cinnamon, nutmeg, and vanilla with a fork. Set aside.

Melt butter in a large skillet over medium heat. Dip each slice of bread into milk mixture, then place in hot skillet. Cook until each side is golden brown. (You may need to add more nondairy butter, especially between batches.)

Remove French toast from heat, and transfer to serving plates. Drizzle with maple syrup and dust with confectioners' sugar just before serving.

**YIELD:** 8 to 9 servings

## SERVING SUGGESTIONS AND VARIATIONS

* For different flavors, mix maple syrup with raisins or ground-up toasted pecans or walnuts.
* You also can top the French toast with fresh berries or create stuffed French toast by placing bananas, strawberries, or other fruit between two slices.
* For another twist, use a loaf of cinnamon raisin bread.

## FOOD LORE

French toast, thought to have originated in medieval Europe as a way to use stale bread, has many distant cousins in many countries and under many names. In France, it is called *pain perdu* ("lost bread"); in Germany, *armer pitter* ("poor knight"); and in Portugal, *rabanadas* or *fatiasdouradas* ("gilded slices of bread").

Per serving: 62 calories; 6g fat; 1g protein; 2g carbohydrate; 1g dietary fiber; 0mg cholesterol; 16mg sodium.

# GOLDEN CORN PANCAKES

*Soy-free depending on milk*

These pancakes are a fluffy treat, and they're incredibly easy to make. Even with the unconventional corn added to our familiar pancake, with a drizzle of maple syrup, they're still appropriate for breakfast.

- 1 cup (125 g) unbleached all-purpose or whole-wheat pastry flour
- 1 tablespoon (15 g) baking powder (look for aluminum-free)
- 1 tablespoon (15 g) granulated sugar
- ¼ teaspoon salt
- 1 cup (235 ml) nondairy milk (soy, rice, almond, hazelnut, hemp, or oat)
- 2 tablespoons (30 ml) canola oil or nondairy, nonhydrogenated butter, melted
- 1 cup (130 g) fresh or frozen corn, thawed (about 1 ear)
- Additional oil or butter, for cooking (optional)

## DIRECTIONS

In a medium-size bowl, combine flour, baking powder, sugar, and salt. Make a well in the center, and add milk, oil, and corn. Stir until just combined.

Heat a nonstick griddle or sauté pan over medium-high heat. (You can add oil to the griddle/sauté pan and heat until hot, but with a nonstick pan, you don't even need it.)

Spoon batter onto the griddle to form circles about 4 inches (10 cm) in diameter. Cook pancakes for 2 minutes on one side, until bubbles appear on the surface. Slide a spatula under the pancake and flip each one over. Cook pancakes on the other side for another 2 minutes, until golden brown on each side, about 4 minutes total.

**YIELD:** 8 to 10 pancakes

Per serving: 96 calories; 3g fat; 2g protein; 15g carbohydrate; 1g dietary fiber; 0mg cholesterol; 204mg sodium.

## FOOD LORE

Varieties of pancakes are seen throughout the world (in the form of crepes, blintzes, griddle cakes, etc.), but my favourite hail from South India. Dosas are crepes made from rice and lentils and filled with such goodies as potatoes, onions, and spinach. Uttapam is similar but is more like a pancake rather than a crepe, and the goodies (onions, tomatoes, etc.) are cooked right into the batter.

# HERBED SCALLOPED POTATOES

*Wheat-free, soy-free*

I grew up eating scalloped potatoes, and whenever I eat them now, they bring me right back to my childhood. This recipe is very special to me and so easy to prepare.

- 2 pounds (910 g) yellow potatoes, peeled and thinly sliced
- 2 cups (470 ml) vegetable stock (store-bought or homemade, page 213)
- 4 garlic cloves, pressed or minced
- 2 fresh sage leaves
- 2 bay leaves
- 1 teaspoon (1.6 g) dried tarragon
- 1/2 teaspoon dried thyme
- 1/4 teaspoon dried rosemary
- 1/4 teaspoon freshly ground pepper
- Salt, to taste
- 2 tablespoons (30 ml) olive oil, divided

## DIRECTIONS

Preheat oven to 425°F (220°C, or gas mark 7). Lightly oil a 2 1/2-quart (3 L) baking dish. Arrange potatoes as flatly as possible in the dish, and set aside.

In a saucepan, combine stock, garlic, sage, bay leaves, tarragon, thyme, rosemary, and pepper. Season with salt to taste. Bring to a boil over high heat, then immediately remove pan from the stove. Cover and let stand for at least 30 minutes.

Discard sage and bay leaves, and pour herbed broth over potatoes. The liquid will not completely cover the potatoes. Drizzle tops of exposed potatoes with 1 tablespoon (15 ml) of the oil.

Bake uncovered for 20 minutes. Remove dish from oven and turn over potatoes, pressing down gently to immerse them as much as possible in the liquid. Drizzle tops of exposed potatoes with remaining 1 tablespoon (15 ml) oil.

Return to oven and bake for an additional 20 minutes, or until potatoes are tender, liquid is reduced, and top is nicely browned. Serve at once.

**YIELD:** 4 to 6 servings

## COMPASSIONATE COOKS' TIP

Make the herbed broth in advance and store it in the refrigerator for up to 3 days before completing the rest of the dish.

Per serving: 218 calories; 6g fat; 5g protein; 37g carbohydrate; 4g dietary fiber; 0mg cholesterol; 552mg sodium.

# COCKTAILS FOR KIDS

## SHIRLEY TEMPLE COCKTAIL

A Shirley Temple is a nonalcoholic mixed drink, originally made with two parts ginger ale, one part orange juice, and a small splash of grenadine syrup. Don't forget to garnish with a maraschino cherry! You can also substitute ginger ale with any other lemon-lime soft drink, and you can leave out the orange juice. An easy "recipe" would be 8 ounces (235 ml) ginger ale to 1 ounce (30 ml) grenadine.

## ROY ROGERS COCKTAIL

As children, my sister and I always ordered Shirley Temples. Until my husband told me that he ordered a similar drink with a different name, I had no idea the "Roy Rogers Cocktail" even existed. The primary difference is using cola in place of ginger ale, which is essentially a "cherry coke." The maraschino cherry is still a must; add a slice of orange or lemon, if desired.

### FOOD LORE

Ginger ales come in two varieties: golden and dry. Golden ginger ale, dark colored and strong flavored, is the older style. Dry ginger ale was developed during Prohibition when ginger ale was used as a mixer for alcoholic beverages; the strong flavor of golden ginger ale was undesirable. Dry ginger ale quickly surpassed golden ginger ale in popularity.

### DID YOU KNOW?

The "Shirley Temple" was allegedly named by the bartender of a Los Angeles restaurant, who created this concoction for the child star who wanted her own before-dinner cocktail. The "Roy Rogers" was created as a similar drink for boys.

**AUTUMN MENU:** Autumn Leaves

- Warm Spinach Salad  - Butternut Squash Soup
- Creamy Polenta with Mushrooms  - Cauliflower with Spicy Vinaigrette
- Chocolate Chocolate Chip Cookies

# WARM SPINACH SALAD

*Wheat-free, soy-free*

As a simple first course, this salad is perfect for any season but best when spinach is available locally. The warm dressing slightly wilts the spinach, and the molasses caramelizes a bit when it cooks.

- 12 to 14 ounces (335 to 395 g) baby spinach, rinsed and dried
- 1 medium-size red onion, thinly sliced
- 1 cup (110 g) pecans, toasted and coarsely chopped
- ¼ cup (60 ml) olive oil
- 1 garlic clove, pressed
- 1 cup (235 ml) balsamic vinegar
- 1 tablespoon (14 g) molasses
- ½ teaspoon ground black pepper
- 1 teaspoon (5 ml) truffle oil (optional)

## DIRECTIONS

Combine spinach, red onion, and toasted pecans in a large bowl.

In a small saucepan, warm olive oil and sauté garlic over very low heat, just to warm up the oil and allow garlic flavor to seep in. After a few minutes, add vinegar, molasses, and pepper. Whisking constantly, bring almost to a boil, remove from heat, and cool until just warm. Add truffle oil, if desired, and stir to combine.

Pour over spinach, toss to coat leaves, and serve immediately.

**YIELD:** 4 to 6 servings

## SERVING SUGGESTIONS AND VARIATIONS

Substitute brown sugar for molasses, add sautéed shiitake mushrooms, caramelize rather than toast the pecans, or use toasted pine nuts.

## FOOD LORE

Truffles are a group of highly sought-after—hence, expensive—edible species of underground fungi. The origin of the word *truffle* derives from the Latin word *tuber*, meaning "lump." Incidentally, the dessert truffle many of us are familiar with gets its name because of its resemblance to this valuable mushroom.

Per serving: 238 calories; 22g fat; 3g protein; 12g carbohydrate; 3g dietary fiber; 0mg cholesterol; 40mg sodium.

## COMPASSIONATE COOKS' TIP

Toast nuts in a toaster oven (set to 250ºF [120ºC]) or in a dry sauté pan for a few minutes, until fragrant and slightly golden.

# BUTTERNUT SQUASH SOUP

*Oil-free, wheat-free, soy-free*

Although butternut is probably my favorite autumn/winter squash, acorn or kabocha would work beautifully for this soup.

- 1 medium-size yellow onion, diced
- 1 to 2 tablespoons (15 to 30 ml) water, for sautéing
- 1-inch (2.5 cm) piece fresh ginger, minced
- 3 garlic cloves, minced
- 2 cups (450 g) peeled, seeded, and cubed butternut squash (about 1 large-size butternut squash)
- 2 medium-size yellow potatoes, peeled and cubed
- Salt and freshly ground black pepper, to taste

## DIRECTIONS

In a medium-size saucepan, cook onion in water until translucent, about 5 minutes. Add ginger and garlic and sauté for a few more minutes. Add butternut squash, potatoes, and enough water to cover the squash.

Cover and bring to a boil. Reduce heat and simmer for about 30 minutes, or until squash is soft. Add to a blender (or use an immersion blender) to process until smooth. Season with salt and pepper to taste. Serve and enjoy!

**YIELD:** 4 servings

## SERVING SUGGESTIONS AND VARIATIONS

Although I do think fresh is best, some grocery stores sell already-chopped vegetables, including butternut squash. If you'd like to take this shortcut, the option is available.

Per serving: 94 calories; trace fat; 2g protein; 22g carbohydrate; 3g dietary fiber; 0mg cholesterol; 8mg sodium.

## COMPASSIONATE COOKS' TIP

Hard squash is difficult to cut. Rather than risk cutting off your fingers, try following these simple instructions.

1. Using a sharp knife, cut the squash horizontally into two separate pieces.
2. Cut each section (the top and bottom) in half lengthwise.
3. Remove the stringy fibers and seeds from the cavity of the lower section. Stand each piece upright and cut off the thin skin, then lay the pieces flat and cut into cubes.

# CREAMY POLENTA WITH MUSHROOMS

*Wheat-free, soy-free depending on milk*

Once considered "peasant food," polenta now ranks high on the culinary ladder.

## FOR POLENTA:

- 6 cups (1410 ml) water
- 2 cups (280 g) coarse cornmeal or polenta
- 1 cup (235 ml) nondairy milk (soy, rice, almond, hazelnut, hemp, or oat)
- 1 tablespoon (14 g) nondairy, nonhydrogenated butter (such as Earth Balance)
- ¼ cup (50 g) nutritional yeast flakes
- 1 teaspoon (6 g) salt (or to taste)
- 2 tablespoons (5 g) minced fresh basil
- 2 tablespoons (8 g) minced fresh parsley
- 1 tablespoon (4 g) minced fresh thyme
- Freshly ground pepper, to taste

## FOR MUSHROOMS:

- 2 tablespoons (30 ml) olive oil
- 1 small-size yellow onion, finely chopped
- 2 pounds (910 g) assorted fresh mushrooms such as porcini, oyster, chanterelle, lobster, cremini, and shiitake, cleaned
- 1 tablespoon (15 ml) tamari soy sauce
- 4 to 5 tablespoons (60 to 75 ml) red wine, for deglazing
- 3 to 4 tablespoons (45 to 60 ml) balsamic vinegar
- 2 tablespoons (28 g) nondairy, nonhydrogenated butter (such as Earth Balance)
- 1 tablespoon (4 g) minced fresh parsley, for garnish (optional)

## DIRECTIONS

To make the polenta, heat the water to a boil. Once the water has boiled, slowly add cornmeal, and stir frequently over low-medium heat, being careful not to let it boil over. Slowly add milk, and stir until the liquid is absorbed and the polenta thickens, about 5 minutes.

Remove from heat and add butter, nutritional yeast, salt, and herbs. Season with pepper. Set mixture aside while preparing mushrooms. (Do not allow the polenta to stand for more than 30 minutes, however, as it will become overly thick.)

For mushrooms, in a large-size sauté pan, heat olive oil. Add onion, and cook for a few minutes. Add mushrooms and sauté over medium-high heat until they begin to get limp. Don't cook them too long or they will become rubbery and lose their flavor. Sprinkle with tamari and transfer to a plate or bowl.

Combine red wine and vinegar in the same sauté pan. Stir in butter, taste for seasoning, and remove from heat.

To serve, place a few spoonfuls of creamy polenta in an individual bowl, top with mushrooms, and drizzle with wine sauce. Top with chopped parsley, if desired, and serve.

**YIELD:** 4 to 6 servings

Per serving: 366 calories; 13g fat; 14g protein; 50g carbohydrate; 9g dietary fiber; 0mg cholesterol; 551mg sodium.

## COMPASSIONATE COOKS' TIP

For a special touch, replace plain balsamic vinegar with the fig version.

# CAULIFLOWER WITH SPICY VINAIGRETTE

*Wheat-free, soy-free*

This simple dish can be served as a side for a sit-down dinner or as a salad at a buffet.

- 2 large-size cauliflower heads, cut into florets
- ¼ cup (15 g) minced fresh parsley
- 3 scallions, finely chopped
- 3 garlic cloves, minced or crushed
- 2 to 3 tablespoons (30 to 45 ml) olive oil
- 2 tablespoons (30 ml) red wine vinegar
- 1 teaspoon (1.6 g) dried tarragon (or 2 teaspoons [2.6 g] minced fresh)
- A few drops hot sauce (Tabasco or other)
- 1 teaspoon (2.2 g) ground nutmeg
- 1 teaspoon (6 g) salt (or to taste)
- Freshly ground black or white pepper

## DIRECTIONS

Using a large pot with a steamer basket, steam cauliflower until tender-crisp, about 10 minutes. Meanwhile, combine parsley, scallions, garlic, olive oil, vinegar, tarragon, hot sauce, nutmeg, salt, and pepper to taste.

When cauliflower is finished cooking and still warm, place in a large bowl, and pour dressing over it. Toss until fully coated, and serve warm or room temperature.

**YIELD:** 6 to 8 servings

## SERVING SUGGESTIONS AND VARIATIONS

To add some depth of flavor and some pretty marks on the cauliflower, sear it in hot olive oil after it is steamed. To do this, add 1 teaspoon (5 ml) olive oil to a sauté pan, and let it heat up. Once it's hot, add the steamed cauliflower, and cook until golden brown sear marks appear on the florets. Transfer to a bowl, and toss with the dressing.

## COMPASSIONATE COOKS' TIP

Chop the parsley, scallions, and garlic together in the small bowl of your food processor. That way, you don't have to chop them by hand individually.

Per serving: 43 calories; trace fat; 3g protein; 9g carbohydrate; 4g dietary fiber; 0mg cholesterol; 312mg sodium.

# CHOCOLATE CHOCOLATE CHIP COOKIES

My friend Tami Wall graced me with this simple and yummy recipe.
(You can also thank Tami for the Chocolate Peanut Butter Bars in
*The Joy of Vegan Baking.*)

- 1 tablespoon (7 g) ground flaxseed (equivalent of 1 egg)
- 3 tablespoons (45 ml) water
- ³/₄ cup (170 g) nondairy, nonhydrogenated butter (such as Earth Balance)
- 1 cup (200 g) granulated sugar
- 1 teaspoon (5 ml) vanilla extract
- 1 ¼ cups (155 g) whole-wheat pastry flour
- ¹/₃ cup (40 g) unsweetened cocoa powder
- ¹/₂ teaspoon baking soda
- ¹/₂ teaspoon baking powder (look for aluminum-free)
- ¹/₄ teaspoon salt
- 1 cup (175 g) nondairy semisweet chocolate or peanut butter chips (Tami clearly loves this combination)

## DIRECTIONS

Preheat oven to 350°F (180°C, or gas mark 4). In a food processor or blender, whip flaxseed and water together until mixture reaches a thick and creamy, almost gelatinous consistency. Set aside.

In a large-size bowl, mix butter and sugar until creamy. Add "flax egg" and vanilla.

In a separate bowl, blend flour, cocoa powder, baking soda, baking powder, and salt. Add this dry mixture to the wet mixture, and mix until everything is well blended. If you need a little extra moisture, add a small amount of water or nondairy milk.

Stir in chips. Form balls and flatten slightly on an ungreased cookie sheet. Bake for 7 to 9 minutes, until the tops are no longer gooey.

**YIELD:** 12 cookies, or 6 servings

Per serving: 288 calories; 16g fat; 2g protein; 37g carbohydrate; 4g dietary fiber; 0mg cholesterol; 120mg sodium.

## COMPASSIONATE COOKS' TIP

My preferred method for forming uniform-size cookies is to scoop the cookie dough with a tablespoon (measuring spoon), and then pop it out onto the cookie sheet. Do this until all the dough is used and you'll get the same-size cookies.

# TOFU "NO EGG" BENEDICT

*Oil-free without Hollandaise sauce*

This versatile and easy-to-prepare dish is filling and delicious.

- 5 tablespoons (75 ml) water, for sautéing, divided
- 4 garlic cloves, finely chopped, divided
- 3 cups (675 g) tightly packed raw spinach leaves
- Salt and pepper, to taste
- 1 package (16 ounces, or 455 g) extra-firm tofu, drained and rinsed
- 1 teaspoon ground turmeric
- 1/2 teaspoon ground cumin
- 1/2 teaspoon salt
- 2 tablespoons (25 g) nutritional yeast
- 1/4 teaspoon chile powder
- 12 slices veggie bacon (store-bought or Tempeh Bacon, page 29)
- 6 English muffins, halved and toasted
- 2 large-size tomatoes, thinly sliced into 12 slices
- 1 recipe Hollandaise Sauce (recipe follows)
- Chopped dill, for garnish (optional)

## DIRECTIONS

Heat 3 tablespoons (45 ml) of water in a sauté pan. Sauté half of garlic over medium heat for a few minutes. Add spinach, along with a little more water, if necessary, and toss until just wilted, about 5 minutes. Add salt and pepper to taste and set aside on a separate plate, dividing the cooked spinach into 12 equal portions to prepare it for your English muffin halves.

Add tofu to a large-size bowl, and crumble using your hands. Add turmeric, cumin, salt, nutritional yeast, and chile powder. Mix well.

Using the same sauté pan you used for the garlic/spinach mixture, heat remaining 2 tablespoons water. Sauté remaining garlic for about 3 minutes. Add tofu mixture and sauté for 10 to 15 minutes, stirring occasionally until tofu is thoroughly heated and turning golden brown.

While the tofu is cooking, heat up the veggie bacon following package directions (or cook Tempeh Bacon following recipe directions); keep warm until tofu is ready.

Top each muffin half with one of the cooked spinach portions, 1 slice veggie bacon, 1 tomato slice, 2 to 3 tablespoons (30 to 45 g) of tofu mixture, 1 to 2 tablespoons (15 to 30 ml) of Hollandaise sauce, and a sprinkling of chopped dill, if desired. Repeat until you use up all muffins.

**YIELD:** 12 servings

Per serving: 169 calories; 5g fat; 11g protein; 22g carbohydrate; 2g dietary fiber; 0mg cholesterol; 523mg sodium.

# HOLLANDAISE SAUCE

*Wheat-free*

Though many recipes for this quintessential French sauce call for several yolks, our version is closer to the original, which goes as far back as the mid-1700s.

- ³/₄ cup (180 ml) unsweetened nondairy milk (soy, rice, almond, hazelnut, hemp, or oat), divided
- ½ teaspoon salt
- ¼ teaspoon chile powder or cayenne pepper
- 2 tablespoons (16 g) cornstarch
- 2 tablespoons (28 g) nondairy, nonhydrogenated butter (such as Earth Balance), melted
- 1 to 2 tablespoons (15 to 30 ml) fresh lemon juice

## FOOD LORE

The first known recipe for Hollandaise sauce came from François Marin's *Les Dons de Comus* in 1758, and it did *not* include egg yolks. My recipe, with its (nondairy) butter as the fat, cornstarch as the thickener, and chile powder or cayenne for flavor, is not far from the original recipe, which included butter, flour, bouillon, and herbs. Even Harold McGee, author of *On Food and Cooking*, admits that you don't need eggs to make delicious Hollandaise sauce.

## DIRECTIONS

In a saucepan, heat ½ cup (120 ml) milk until hot but not quite simmering. Pour into a blender pitcher with salt and chile powder.

Using the same saucepan, combine remaining ¼ cup (60 ml) milk with cornstarch, and cook over low heat. The mixture will thicken very quickly. Stir constantly with a whisk. Add the melted nondairy butter, and keep whisking. This process will take no more than a couple of minutes.

Immediately add the thick cornstarch/butter mixture to blender containing milk/spice combination, and blend well. (I say "immediately" so the butter doesn't harden.) Drizzle in lemon juice, and continue to blend. It should be thick with no oil globules. Control lemon flavor by adding just a tablespoon (15 ml), tasting it, and adding more, if desired.

Hollandaise sauce is traditionally served warm, so if you're not serving it immediately, heat it briefly in a microwave or in a small-size pot over low heat when ready to serve.

**YIELD:** ³/₄ cup (180 ml), or 6 (2-tablespoon [30 ml]) servings

## SERVING SUGGESTIONS AND VARIATIONS

Enjoy this traditional sauce on steamed vegetables and, of course, Tofu "No Egg" Benedict (page 92).

Per serving: 252 calories; 5g fat; 11g protein; 22g carbohydrate; 2g dietary fiber; 0mg cholesterol; 523mg sodium.

# HOME-FRIED POTATOES

*Wheat-free, soy-free if using oil*

Nothing says comfort like a plate of potatoes. Enjoy these as a breakfast, brunch, or side dish for a casual dinner with friends.

- 3 pounds (1365 g) creamy yellow potatoes, such as Yukon gold, quartered
- 3 tablespoons (45 ml) olive oil or (42 g) nondairy, nonhydrogenated butter (such as Earth Balance), divided
- 1 large-size yellow onion, sliced
- 2 or 3 garlic cloves, minced
- 1 teaspoon paprika
- 1 teaspoon (6 g) salt (or to taste)
- ½ teaspoon freshly ground pepper (or to taste)
- ¼ cup (15 g) fresh parsley, chopped

## DIRECTIONS

Add potatoes to a steamer basket in a 4-quart (4.5 L) pot, and steam until tender but still firm, 12 to 15 minutes. Let cool, and then cut into ½-inch (1 cm) cubes.

Meanwhile, in a large-size skillet, heat 1 tablespoon (15 ml) oil over medium-high heat. Add onion and garlic, and cook, stirring often, until it starts to brown, about 10 minutes.

Add 1 tablespoon (15 ml) oil and cubed potatoes to skillet. Add paprika, salt, and pepper. Cook, stirring occasionally, until potatoes are browned, 15 to 30 minutes. When turning the potatoes, use a flat spatula to take care that you don't mush them.

While potatoes are cooking, add remaining 1 tablespoon (15 ml) oil and chopped parsley. Combine well and serve.

**YIELD:** 4 to 6 servings

Per serving: 251 calories; 7g fat; 5g protein; 43g carbohydrate; 4g dietary fiber; 0mg cholesterol; 371mg sodium.

## FOOD LORE

"Boxty" is a traditional Irish potato pancake, or potato bread, made with flour, mashed potato, and raw potato. Traditionally made on New Year's Day and Halloween, it inspired the following rhyme: "Boxty on the griddle, boxty in the pan, if you can't make boxty, you'll never get a man."

# APRICOT WHOLE-WHEAT MUFFINS

*Soy-free depending on milk*

A healthful hearty option for breakfast or brunch, these can be made as regular-size or mini muffins.

- 1 tablespoon (7 g) ground flaxseed (equivalent of 1 egg)
- 3 tablespoons (45 ml) water
- 1 cup (125 g) whole-wheat flour
- 1 cup (125 g) whole-wheat pastry flour
- 1 teaspoon ground cinnamon
- 1 ½ teaspoons (7 g) baking powder (look for aluminum-free)
- ½ teaspoon baking soda
- ½ teaspoon salt
- ½ to ¾ cup (100 to 150 g) granulated sugar (depending on your sweetness preference)
- 1 ¼ cups (295 ml) nondairy milk (soy, rice, almond, hazelnut, hemp, or oat)
- ¼ cup (60 ml) canola oil
- 1 cup (130 g) chopped dried apricots
- ½ cup (60 g) walnuts or almonds, roughly chopped

## DIRECTIONS

Preheat oven to 425°F (220°C, or gas mark 7). Lightly oil muffin tins.

In a food processor or blender, whip flaxseed and water together, until mixture reaches a thick and creamy, almost gelatinous, consistency. Set aside.

In a large-size bowl, combine whole-wheat flour, whole-wheat pastry flour, cinnamon, baking powder, baking soda, salt, and sugar. Add milk, oil, "flax egg," apricots, and nuts, and stir quickly until just combined. Be careful not to overstir.

Spoon into prepared muffin tins and bake for 20 minutes, until lightly browned. Serve with nondairy butter, jam, or preserves.

**YIELD:** 12 muffins, or servings

Per serving: 230 calories; 9g fat; 5g protein; 36g carbohydrate; 5g dietary fiber; 0mg cholesterol; 209mg sodium.

## COMPASSIONATE COOKS' TIP

These muffins freeze well, so make extra and store them in the freezer for future enjoyment.

# MIMOSAS

This is just one variation of this simple cocktail, often served for breakfast or brunch.

- 2 cups (470 ml) chilled orange juice
- 1 ½ cups (355 ml) chilled cranberry juice
- 2 cups (470 ml) chilled champagne or sparkling wine

## DIRECTIONS

Combine orange juice and cranberry juice in a pitcher and stir to mix. Pour evenly into 6 champagne or wine glasses. Pour ⅓ cup (80 ml) champagne into each glass. Serve immediately.

**YIELD:** 6 servings

## SERVING SUGGESTIONS AND VARIATIONS

For a burst of red color, add a little grenadine and a maraschino cherry. For a tropical variation, try pineapple juice in place of orange juice

Per serving: 140 calories; trace fat; 1g protein; 20g carbohydrate; trace dietary fiber; 0mg cholesterol; 2mg sodium.

# SPLIT PEA SOUP

*\*Oil-free, wheat-free, soy-free*

This is perfect comfort food with a cooking time that offers a good excuse to relax with friends. To boot, it's filling, packed with protein, brimming with fiber, low in calories and fat, and freezes well. What more could you ask for?

- 2 cups (450 g) green split peas
- 6 to 7 cups (1410 to 1645 ml) water or vegetable stock (store-bought or homemade, page 213)
- 1 medium-size yellow onion, diced
- 2 creamy yellow potatoes (such as Yukon gold or fingerlings), diced
- 2 or 3 garlic cloves, pressed or minced
- 2 carrots, diced
- 2 celery stalks, diced
- 1 teaspoon dried marjoram
- 1 teaspoon dried basil
- ½ teaspoon dried parsley
- ¼ teaspoon ground mustard
- ¼ teaspoon black pepper
- ½ teaspoon liquid smoke, optional
- Salt and pepper, to taste

Per serving: 302 calories; 2g fat; 18g protein; 56g carbohydrate; 19g dietary fiber; 0mg cholesterol; 1202mg sodium.

## DIRECTIONS

Rinse split peas, checking for any impurities, such as stones or residue. Place all ingredients except salt and pepper in a soup pot, and bring to a simmer. Cover loosely and cook until peas are tender, 1 hour or longer. Check occasionally to make sure water has not completely evaporated. Heat should be low-medium.

The resulting soup should be thick and creamy, with the split peas quite broken down and mushy. Add salt and pepper to taste, and serve hot.

**YIELD:** 4 to 6 servings

## SERVING SUGGESTIONS AND VARIATIONS

For creamier soup, purée in a food processor or blender. This is also a great soup for a slow cooker; add all ingredients, and cook on low for 6 to 8 hours.

## COMPASSIONATE COOKS' TIP

The liquid smoke (found near the barbecue sauce in your local grocery store) takes the place of the ham(!) that people have been known to add to their soup. Because it's the smoky and salty flavor that we desire (not pig!), the liquid smoke does the job perfectly! (Yes, I needed to use that many exclamation points.)

# "HONEY" MUSTARD SALAD DRESSING

*Wheat-free, soy-free*

If I called this "Agave Mustard Dressing," I was afraid you might not know what I meant. Agave nectar comes from a succulent cactuslike plant and has the viscosity of honey and the benefit of coming from a plant—not an animal.

- 3 to 5 tablespoons (60 to 100 g) agave nectar (light or amber)
- 3 tablespoons (45 g) Dijon mustard
- 2 tablespoons (30 ml) rice wine vinegar
- 1 tablespoon (15 ml) olive oil (optional)

### DIRECTIONS

Combine all ingredients and blend or whisk until smooth. I have made this with and without the oil, and both are fantastic.

**YIELD:** ²/₃ cup (155 ml), or 5 (2-tablespoon [30 ml]) servings

Per serving: 87 calories; 3g fat; trace protein; 16g carbohydrate; 1g dietary fiber; 0mg cholesterol; 113mg sodium.

## COMPASSIONATE COOKS' TIP

Seasoned rice vinegar just means that sugar has been added to the vinegar to sweeten it. If you would like to use plain rice vinegar (or brown rice vinegar), add a little more agave nectar to the dressing.

## FOOD LORE

We have the Romans to thank for the mustard we know and love today (was there anything they *couldn't* do?). Mixing unfermented grape juice, known as *must*, with ground mustard seeds, they created this versatile condiment used for a variety of foods.

# PENNE PASTA WITH FRESH VEGGIES

*Oil-free, wheat-free depending on pasta, soy-free depending on vegetarian sausage used*

Vary this recipe by using seasonal vegetables and different types of pasta.

- 16 ounces (225 g) whole-wheat (or wheat-free) penne pasta
- 3 tablespoons (45 ml) water, for sautéing
- 1 small-size red onion, sliced
- 6 large-size garlic cloves, minced or thinly sliced
- 2 large-size red (or yellow or orange) bell peppers, seeded and cut into strips
- 2 carrots, peeled and julienned (cut into matchsticks)
- 1 large-size yellow summer squash, sliced
- 1 head broccoli, chopped into bite-size pieces
- 1 ½ cups (45 g) fresh spinach
- 2 cans (15 ounces, or 420 g, each) fire-roasted diced tomatoes
- ½ cup (50 g) kalamata olives, pitted and finely chopped
- 2 tablespoons (30 ml) balsamic vinegar
- 2 teaspoons (10 ml) tamari soy sauce
- 1 package (14 ounces, or 400 g) vegetarian Italian sausage, cut into half-moon shapes (optional)
- ½ cup (20 g) basil leaves, coarsely chopped
- Red pepper flakes (optional)

## DIRECTIONS

Bring a large pot of water to a boil. Add pasta, and stir to prevent sticking. Cook until just tender, 7 to 8 minutes. Drain well and set aside.

Meanwhile, in a large-size sauté pan (the largest one you have), heat water over medium heat. Add onion and cook, stirring often, until translucent, about 4 minutes. Stir in garlic, peppers, carrots, squash, and broccoli and cook, stirring often, until vegetables turn a bright color and are tender, about 10 minutes. To speed up the process, cover the pan while the veggies are cooking.

A few minutes before veggies are done, add spinach and stir to combine. The spinach may spill over your sauté pan, but just give it a little time. It will shrink substantially.

Stir in tomatoes, olives, vinegar, tamari, and sausage (if using), and cook for 5 minutes longer. Add penne and basil and toss until heated through. (Add red pepper flakes if you want it spicy.) Remove from heat and serve hot.

**YIELD:** 4 to 6 servings

## SERVING SUGGESTIONS AND VARIATIONS

My favorite veggie sausages are made by Tofurky and Field Roast (see Resources and Recommendations). Because these are already cooked when you buy them, you're just heating them up when you add them to a dish like this, so it's a fast process.

Per serving: 480 calories; 15g fat; 30g protein; 131g carbohydrate; 13g dietary fiber; 0mg cholesterol; 896mg sodium.

# FLOURLESS CHOCOLATE TART

*Wheat-free, soy-free depending on milk*

This is a super chocolatey treat that, despite its richness, isn't overly sweet. It all depends on the type of chocolate you use.

- 1 cup (110 g) raw pecans

- 1 cup (120 g) raw walnuts

- ³/₄ cup (150 g) granulated sugar

- 4 tablespoons (56 g) nondairy, nonhydrogenated butter (such as Earth Balance), melted

- 16 ounces (455 g) nondairy semisweet or dark chocolate chips or bar

- 2 cups (470 ml) nondairy milk (soy, rice, almond, hazelnut, hemp, or oat)

- 2 tablespoons (16 g) kudzu or cornstarch powder

- ¹/₄ cup (60 ml) water

- Sifted confectioners' sugar

## DIRECTIONS

Preheat oven to 375°F (190°C, or gas mark 5). Pulverize pecans, walnuts, and granulated sugar in a food processor. Add butter and process until a thick batter forms. Press into a 9- or 10-inch (23 or 25 cm) tart pan. Bake the crust for 10 minutes, or until golden brown.

Meanwhile, melt chocolate in a double boiler or microwave.

In a saucepan, heat milk over medium heat. It should be scalding hot but not boiling. While milk is heating up, combine kudzu and water in a bowl or measuring cup until powder completely dissolves, creating your thickener.

Add melted chocolate to milk, and whisk to thoroughly combine. Whisk in thickener, and stir well. Lower heat and simmer for 10 minutes, stirring occasionally. The chocolate mixture will slowly thicken. Pour mixture into the baked tart shell and chill for at least 2 hours or for as long as overnight.

Decorate by cutting out a stencil pattern and placing it over the tart. Dust some powdered sugar lightly over the top. Remove stencil.

**YIELD:** 6 to 8 servings

Per serving: 514 calories; 33g fat; 5g protein; 60g carbohydrate; 5g dietary fiber; 0mg cholesterol; 14mg sodium.

## DID YOU KNOW?

Baker's Chocolate is not some special chocolate that only bakers use. Baker's Chocolate was developed in 1780 by a man named John Baker, who created a block of chocolate meant for making a sweet chocolate drink. It is now the brand name for a line of baking chocolates, but unfortunately, most of their products contain milk solids, so they are not vegan.

# CHAPTER 3

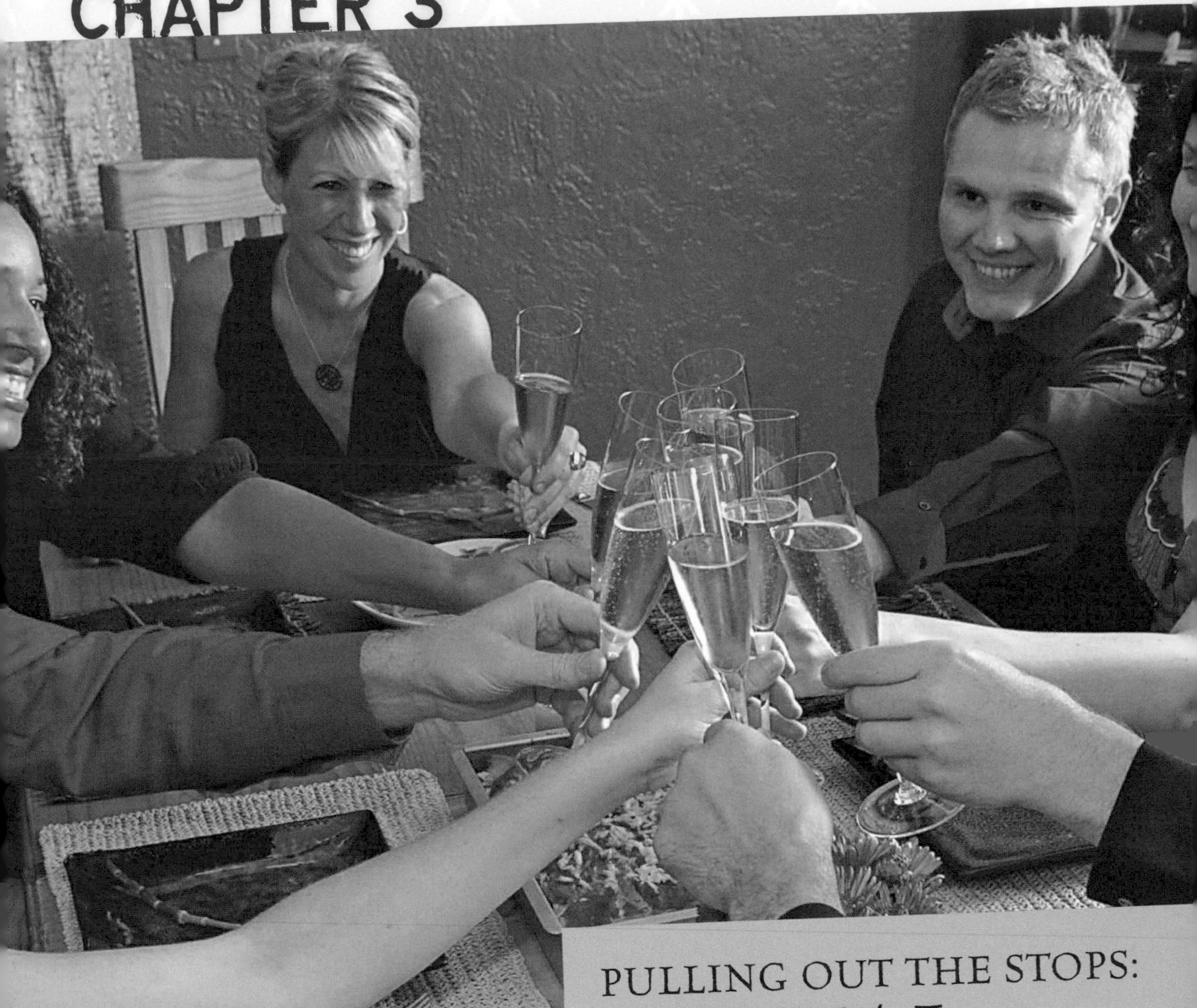

PULLING OUT THE STOPS:

# FORMAL DINING FOR SIX TO TEN

I think we tend to get overwhelmed when planning a fancy-schmancy meal because our expectations are so unrealistically high. We project these expectations onto our guests and fear that if everything isn't absolutely perfect, they will deem us inadequate.

Add to that the pressure that this *one vegan meal* represents *all* vegan meals and thus better be extraordinary, lest your guests leave with the false impression that vegan fare is mediocre or inferior.

One way to take some of the pressure off is to rethink what we have been taught about what a meal or a plate should look like.

# RECIPES

# DECONSTRUCTING OUR PLATES

The foods we choose, the way we construct our plates, and our perception of what a "complete meal" looks like are all based on what our culture and our families have taught us: Meat is the centerpiece of a meal, flanked by some token side dishes.

This is not how other cultures plate their food. Meat is not (or was not until recently) the centerpiece. Consider Mexican, Indian, Ethiopian, Thai, Chinese, Japanese, and much of Italian cuisines. They center meals around grains, vegetables, and legumes, filling their plates with what much of the Western World would call "side dishes."

So on one hand, we need to give ourselves permission to eat a meal based on vegetables and grains, rice and beans, or soup and salad. It's okay to eat only what we have been taught to call "side dishes." Having said that, it's easy to create a meal that consists of a main dish, side dishes, and salad.

## CREATING A FOCAL POINT

Reflecting back on when I ate meat, though I did enjoy my fair share, I'm not sure I ever responded with "oohs" and "aahs" when the animal carcass was brought to the table. I know some people do. What I have learned in my many years of observing people is that it's not the lifeless animal centerpiece that people are attached to as much as the notion of simply having a *centerpiece*, a *focus* on the table, a *focus* on the plate.

You can accomplish this in so many ways, using beautiful plant-based foods. In fact, a spread focused on plant-based foods is much more aesthetically pleasing than one based on animal products. Take advantage of the huge variety of colors, textures, sizes, and shapes of plant foods. Here are some suggestions for creating a focal point out of a main dish.

### STUFF IT
Stuff eggplants, bell or jalapeño peppers, mushrooms, winter or summer squash, potatoes, olives, pea pods, or corn husks.

### CONTAIN IT
In the spirit of serving food in something else, create a main dish using ramekins, custard cups, or individual bowls, or make miniature individual pot pies.

### SHAPE IT
Prepare pancakes, polenta, or tortillas, press into shapes using cookie cutters or cut into squares, and serve with a topping.

### MAINSTAY IT
Tofu, tempeh, seitan, and portobello mushrooms are all great options to serve as the main dish. They are hearty, "meaty," and protein-rich, one of the criteria by which people tend to judge main dishes.

### MOLD IT
Anything made as a loaf, patty, timbale, mold, or burger also serves as a great main-dish item.

# SUGGESTED SEASONAL MENUS

The little extra time you will spend preparing these dishes will be worth it in the end.

## SPRING

### RITES OF SPRING, PAGE 109

Fruity Spinach Salad

Pan-Grilled Portobello Mushrooms with
    Herb-Infused Marinade

Elegantly Simple Stuffed Bell Peppers

Soba Noodle Soup

Delightful Date Truffles

## SUMMER

### SUMMER SOLSTICE, PAGE 116

Magical Miso Soup with Shiitake Mushrooms

Cornmeal-Crusted Tempeh with Orange
    Ginger Sauce

Sugar Snap Peas with Toasted Sesame Seeds

Kale and Cauliflower Salad

Fruit Sushi (a.k.a. *Frushi*) with Strawberry
    Reduction Sauce

### CURRY IN A HURRY, PAGE 126

Pumpkin Curry

Yellow Split Pea Dal

Frozen Mango Lassi

## AUTUMN

### IN THE MISTY MOONLIGHT, PAGE 127

African Sweet Potato and Peanut Stew

French Onion Pie

Roasted Brussels Sprouts with Apples and Onions

Orzo Pilaf with Roasted Red Peppers and Peas

### AUTUMN SONATA, PAGE 132

Potato Leek Soup

Creamy Caesar Salad with Oil-Free Croutons

Sautéed Broccoli Rabe with Olives and Toasted
    Pine Nuts

Eggplant and Caramelized Onion "Lasagna"

## WINTER

### SUGAR AND SPICE, PAGE 137

Aloo Gobi (Curried Cauliflower and Potatoes)

Chana Masala (Curried Chickpeas)

Masoor Dal (Red Lentils)

Chai-Spiced Almond Cookies

### WINTER LIGHT, PAGE 143

Red Lentil Pâté

Roasted Beets and Fennel Bulbs in Fennel Oil

Scotch Broth (Hearty Scottish Stew)

Chocolate Cake with Coffee Ganache

# TIPS FOR STRESS-FREE ENTERTAINING

I've entertained enough to know what *not* to do, which is just as valuable as knowing what *to* do.

### START CLEAN

If you can afford to hire someone to do a pre-party scrub, you're way ahead of the game. If not, focus on the rooms your guests will occupy, and don't worry about the others. Empty the dishwasher *before* your guests come. Check labels on cleaning supplies to ensure they are nontoxic and cruelty-free (i.e., not tested on animals).

### STAY FOCUSED

Too many times, I have used a looming party date as a deadline for accomplishing house projects (decorating, gardening, etc.). Although this is fine (within reason), I have mistakenly tried to do too much *on the day of* the party, leading to a stressed-out hostess and an unhappy husband. Now I focus on the *party* on the day of the party—even if I didn't finish every project on my list.

### SHOW YOUR SEAMS

Even though I try to have everything perfect for the day of my event, I have to remember that I'm entertaining friends, who are coming to spend time with us—not to judge me on my housekeeping prowess. If the garden isn't perfect or if I forget to scrub the front porch, so be it. Friends either don't notice or don't care. (Plus, dim lighting forgives all!)

### PLAN AHEAD

A week before your party, plan what you need to do each day leading up to the event, to lessen your stress on the day of the party.

### WRITE LISTS

If you're a list-maker, then you know the benefits of transferring thoughts to paper and organizing them by their level of importance. Besides, when tasks are written down, you can more easily divvy them up among family members.

### SEEK HELP

People are always willing to help. If you forget something at the last minute, don't be shy about asking a friend to pick up an ingredient or beverage or calling a neighbor for what you need. On that same note, consider hiring help to pass out hors d'oeuvres and act as bartenders.

**SPRING MENU:** Rites of Spring

🍂 Fruity Spinach Salad 🍂 Pan-Grilled Portobello Mushrooms with
Herb-Infused Marinade 🍂 Elegantly Simple Stuffed Bell Peppers
🍂 Soba Noodle Soup 🍂 Delightful Date Truffles

# FRUITY SPINACH SALAD

*Wheat-free, soy-free, oil-free*

If it isn't obvious, I'm not a huge fan of adding oil when it's not necessary. The nuts and seeds add a natural, healthful fat, and the dressing remains light and nutritious.

- 8 cups (240 g) cleaned spinach leaves
- 3 oranges, peeled, sliced, and quartered (or 1 or 2 cans [11 ounces, or 310 g, each] mandarin oranges, drained)
- 2 cucumbers, peeled, sliced, and quartered
- ¼ cup (35 g) macadamia nuts, coarsely chopped
- ¼ cup (35 g) raw sunflower seeds
- 2 tablespoons (15 g) poppy seeds
- 1 cup (125 g) raspberries (fresh or thawed if frozen)
- ½ cup (120 ml) seasoned rice vinegar

## DIRECTIONS

In a medium-size bowl, combine spinach, oranges, cucumbers, macadamia nuts, sunflower seeds, and poppy seeds.

Blend together raspberries and vinegar, and either toss with salad, or pour into a pretty serving dish so your guests can add their own dressing.

**YIELD:** 8 servings

Per serving: 116 calories; 7g fat; 4g protein; 14g carbohydrate; 5g dietary fiber; 0mg cholesterol; 26mg sodium.

## DID YOU KNOW?

Let's dispel the myth once and for all around iron and meat consumption. Studies show very little difference in the incidence of iron deficiency between vegetarians and non-vegetarians in developed countries. In fact, the amount of iron in vegan diets tends to be higher than or at least equal to that in non-vegetarian diets because of the amount of iron-rich vegetables vegans consume, particularly vitamin C, which increases iron absorption. As with many nutrients, the key is not merely intake but absorption.

# PAN-GRILLED PORTOBELLO MUSHROOMS WITH HERB-INFUSED MARINADE

*Wheat-free*

These can be served as a main dish with a bunch of steamed spinach, chard, or collard greens, or with creamy mashed potatoes. Or add to a bun with all the fixin's!

- 8 to 12 large-size portobello mushrooms
- 1 cup (240 ml) balsamic vinegar
- 1 cup (240 ml) tamari soy sauce
- 1 cup (240 ml) water
- 2 or 3 sprigs fresh rosemary (or 1 teaspoon [1 g] dried)
- 2 or 3 sprigs fresh thyme (or 1 teaspoon [1 g] dried)
- 2 or 3 sprigs fresh marjoram or oregano (or 1 teaspoon [1 g] dried)
- Small amount of olive oil, for sautéing
- Freshly ground black pepper, to taste

Per serving: 62 calories; trace fat; 7g protein; 12g carbohydrate; 3g dietary fiber; 0mg cholesterol; 1352mg sodium.

## DIRECTIONS

Remove stems from underside of mushrooms and lightly wipe tops with a damp paper towel.

In a large-size bowl, combine vinegar, tamari, water, rosemary, thyme, and marjoram. Stir to combine. Add mushrooms and make sure each one is covered by the marinade. You may need to move them around to give the marinade a chance to coat the top mushrooms. Marinate mushrooms for as little as 30 minutes or for as long as overnight in the refrigerator.

When ready to cook, add some oil to a large-size sauté pan, and turn heat to medium. Remove mushrooms from marinade, but do not discard marinade. Put as many mushrooms as can fit in the pan, tops down. They will shrink as they cook. Cook for 3 to 5 minutes, until lightly browned. Turn and cook for 3 to 5 minutes longer.

Remove fresh herb sprigs from marinade, and pour marinade into pan, reserving some for additional batches of mushrooms. Cover and cook for 5 to 7 minutes. Flip mushrooms, and cover and cook for 5 to 7 minutes longer. When fork-tender, remove from pan, and repeat above steps with remaining mushrooms.

To serve the mushrooms hot, simply use multiple sauté pans on the stove at once. Serve 2 mushrooms per person.

**YIELD:** 4 to 6 servings

## SERVING SUGGESTIONS AND VARIATIONS

After marinating the mushrooms, cook them on the grill, about 5 minutes on each side.

# ELEGANTLY SIMPLE STUFFED BELL PEPPERS

*Wheat-free, soy-free*

Use any combination of peppers for this elegant but simple recipe. It's very versatile: the flavor will change depending on which herbs and spices you choose.

- 1 cup (235 ml) of water
- 6 bell peppers, preferably a variety of colors
- 3 tablespoons (45 ml) oil, for brushing and oiling baking dish
- Salt and pepper, to taste
- Water or vegetable stock, for sautéing
- 2 medium-size yellow onions, roughly chopped
- 4 garlic cloves, minced or pressed
- 1 can (16 ounces, or 455 g) fire-roasted diced tomatoes
- ½ cup (70 g) raw almonds, finely chopped or slivered
- 2 ½ cups (415 g) cooked long-grain brown rice
- 3 tablespoons (18 g) chopped fresh mint
- 3 tablespoons (12 g) chopped fresh parsley
- 3 tablespoons (8 g) chopped fresh basil
- 3 tablespoons (27 g) raisins
- 2 to 3 tablespoons (12 to 18 g) ground almonds
- Chopped mixed fresh herbs, for garnish (optional)

## DIRECTIONS

Preheat oven to 375°F (190°C, or gas mark 5). Boil 1 cup (235 ml) water to pour around peppers in pan.

Halve peppers lengthwise, leaving stems intact, if possible. Scoop out seeds. Brush cut sides with 1 table-spoon (15 ml) oil, place them cut side up in a shallow, lightly oiled baking dish, and sprinkle with salt and pepper. Bake for 15 minutes, until peppers are soft and easily pierced with a fork but still have their shape.

Heat a few tablespoons (45 ml) of water or stock in a large soup pot. Sauté onions and garlic for 5 minutes over medium heat, until onion becomes translucent. Add tomatoes and raw almonds, and sauté for another minute or two. Remove pan from heat and stir in rice, mint, parsley, basil, and raisins. Season well with salt and pepper, then spoon mixture into the peppers still on the baking sheet.

Pour ⅔ to 1 cup (155 to 235 ml) boiling water around the peppers, just enough to touch the base of each so they don't burn. Bake, uncovered, for 15 minutes. Sprinkle ground almonds on top. Return to oven and bake for 15 minutes longer. Serve garnished with fresh herbs, if desired.

**YIELD:** 12 servings

## SERVING SUGGESTIONS AND VARIATIONS

Try a combination of brown and wild rice, for added texture and color.

## COMPASSIONATE COOKS' TIP

When choosing peppers for this dish, look for full ones with a deep cavity to stuff.

Per serving: 259 calories; 9g fat; 7g protein; 40g carbohy-drate; 6g dietary fiber; 0mg cholesterol; 230mg sodium.

# SOBA NOODLE SOUP

*Oil-free*

If you've never had these delicious thin noodles, you're in for a treat. They're made from buckwheat flour and are a staple of Japanese cuisine.

- 6 ounces (170 g) soba noodles
- 20 shiitake mushrooms, dried or fresh
- 8 cups (1880 ml) water
- 3 tablespoons (45 ml) plus 2 teaspoons (10 ml) tamari soy sauce, divided
- 2 tablespoons (30 ml) sake or dry sherry (optional)
- 2 teaspoons (16 g) finely chopped or grated fresh ginger
- 2 teaspoons (30 ml) rice vinegar or apple cider vinegar
- 1 tablespoon (15 ml) mirin (optional)
- 2 cups (60 g) chopped spinach or kale
- 12 ounces (340 g) firm or extra-firm tofu, cut into ½-inch (1 cm) cubes
- 2 tablespoons (32 g) white (or "light") miso paste
- Sesame seeds and thinly sliced scallions, for garnish (optional)

## DIRECTIONS

Cook soba noodles in boiling water for about 5 minutes. Drain and set aside.

Combine mushrooms, water, 3 tablespoons (45 ml) of the tamari, and sake in a large pot and bring to a boil. Lower heat and simmer, covered, for 15 minutes. Add ginger, vinegar, remaining 2 teaspoons (10 ml) tamari, and mirin, if using. Cover and simmer for about 10 minutes. Remove shiitake mushrooms from the pot, thinly slice, and return them to the soup.

Add spinach and tofu, and simmer for another few minutes, until spinach is wilted but still bright green. Turn off heat.

In a small bowl, combine miso with a few tablespoons (45 ml) of the hot broth to make a smooth sauce, then stir it back into the soup. Add cooked soba noodles directly to soup or place them in individual serving bowls, and spoon the soup over them. Top individual soup servings with a sprinkling of sesame seeds and sliced scallions, if desired.

**YIELD:** 6 to 8 servings

Per serving: 203 calories; 3g fat; 12g protein; 34g carbohydrate; 3g dietary fiber; 0mg cholesterol; 1,077mg sodium.

## COMPASSIONATE COOKS' TIP

Toss the cooked noodles with sesame oil while you prepare the other ingredients. To make this soup in advance, prepare everything the day before, but do not add the soba noodles until just before you are ready to serve.

## DID YOU KNOW?

Mirin is a kind of rice wine similar to sake, but with a lower alcohol content. It has a slightly sweet taste and is a common ingredient in teriyaki sauce.

# DELIGHTFUL DATE TRUFFLES

*Soy-free, wheat-free, oil-free*

For a lighter treat after a heavy meal, these truffles will do the trick.

- 1 cup (145 g) raw almonds or walnuts
- 20 large (Medjool) dates, pitted
- 1 tablespoon (15 g) unsweetened cocoa powder
- Zest from 1 medium-size orange
- 2 tablespoons (40 g) agave nectar
- ½ teaspoon ground cinnamon
- ¼ teaspoon ground nutmeg
- ⅛ teaspoon salt
- Cocoa powder, for rolling

## DIRECTIONS

Grind almonds in a food processor until fine. Add dates, cocoa powder, orange zest, agave nectar, cinnamon, nutmeg, and salt, and process until mixture forms a ball. If mixture doesn't stick together, add more agave nectar.

Form 30 small balls out of mixture. Roll in cocoa powder, and serve on a pretty candy dish. They also store well in the refrigerator and freezer.

## YIELD: 30 servings

## SERVING SUGGESTIONS AND VARIATIONS

As with the Decadent Chocolate Truffles on page 222, you can roll these date truffles in anything from shredded coconut to ground nuts, or dip them in melted nondairy chocolate, and let them set in the fridge.

## COMPASSIONATE COOKS' TIP

A food processor makes these gems in a snap, but a blender just makes a mess. If you'd like to do this by hand, soften the dates in boiling water for about 5 minutes, then transfer them to a bowl and mash with a potato masher. Add the ground nuts and other ingredients and mix thoroughly with your hands.

Per serving: 47 calories; 3g fat; 1g protein; 6g carbohydrate; 1g dietary fiber; 0mg cholesterol; 10mg sodium.

**SUMMER MENU:** Summer Solstice

* Magical Miso Soup with Shiitake Mushrooms   * Cornmeal-Crusted Tempeh
with Orange Ginger Sauce   * Sugar Snap Peas with Toasted Sesame Seeds
   * Kale and Cauliflower Salad   * Fruit Sushi (a.k.a. *Frushi*) with Strawberry Reduction Sauce

# MAGICAL MISO SOUP WITH SHIITAKE MUSHROOMS

*\*Oil-free, wheat-free*

Miso paste is a staple in Asian cuisine. It's great as a base and flavoring for sauces and dressings. Miso is fermented soybean paste and has a thick consistency. You'll find it in the refrigerated section of Asian markets or natural foods stores.

- 8 cups (1880 ml) water, plus more for thinning miso
- 1 cup (250 g) white or "light" miso paste
- 1 cup (70 g) sliced fresh shiitake mushrooms

## DIRECTIONS

Place the water in a large saucepan or soup pot on stove. Turn heat to low-medium.

In a bowl or large-size measuring cup, combine miso paste with enough water until miso is smooth. This just thins the miso to make it easy to combine with the water already in the pot. Add this mixture to the pot, and stir or whisk to combine. If the flavor is too weak, add more miso.

Add mushrooms. Bring to a simmer, reduce the heat, and cook, uncovered, for 30 minutes. Do not boil.

**YIELD:** 8 to 10 servings

## SERVING SUGGESTIONS AND VARIATIONS

* For a heartier soup, add broccoli or tofu.
* You can also add chopped scallions or wakame, a seaweed kelp packed with nutrients.

## COMPASSIONATE COOKS' TIP

I have found that miso brands vary in terms of their flavor, so you may need more or less than 1 cup (250 g) miso paste. What works best is to first add a few tablespoons (50 g), whisk it into the water, taste it, and add more as necessary. The good thing about miso is that if you add too much, you can just add water to mellow it out. If you add too little, you can simply add more.

Red miso paste is fermented longer than the lighter version and has a stronger taste. Try half red miso, half white.

Per serving: 127 calories; 2g fat; 5g protein; 25g carbohydrate; 4g dietary fiber; 0mg cholesterol; 1006mg sodium.

# CORNMEAL-CRUSTED TEMPEH WITH ORANGE GINGER SAUCE

Tempeh is just one option for this recipe, which was modified from *The Millennium Cookbook*. Also try it with seitan, tofu, or mushrooms.

## FOR TEMPEH:

- 2 packages (8 ounces, or 225 g, each) tempeh
- ½ cup (60 g) unbleached all-purpose flour
- ½ cup (70 g) coarse cornmeal (also called polenta in the bulk section)
- 1 teaspoon (1 g) dried thyme
- 1 teaspoon (1 g) dried basil
- 1 teaspoon (1 g) dried oregano
- 1 teaspoon (2.5 g) paprika
- ½ teaspoon salt (or to taste)
- ½ teaspoon freshly ground black pepper
- 1 cup (235 ml) nondairy milk (soy, rice, almond, hazelnut, hemp, or oat)
- 2 tablespoons (30 g) Dijon mustard
- 1 tablespoon (15 ml) olive oil
- 2 cups (370 g) cooked bulgur or quinoa
- Orange segments and chopped basil, for garnish (optional)

## FOR SAUCE:

- 1 red onion, cut lengthwise into thin crescents
- 2 garlic cloves, minced
- 3 cups (705 ml) fresh orange juice
- ¼ cup (60 ml) tamari soy sauce
- ¼ teaspoon red pepper flakes, plus more to taste
- 1 tablespoon (9 g) capers, drained (optional)
- 2 tablespoons (12 g) minced fresh ginger
- 2 tablespoons (16 g) cornstarch or arrowroot, dissolved in 3 tablespoons (45 ml) water
- 1 mandarin orange, peeled and cut into quarters (or 1 can [10 ounces, or 280 g] mandarin oranges)

## DIRECTIONS

To make the tempeh, cut tempeh into 16 triangles or strips. Steam for 10 minutes, until tender. Set aside.

In a bowl, mix together flour, cornmeal, thyme, basil, oregano, paprika, salt, and pepper. In another medium-size bowl, whisk together milk and mustard. Coat tempeh in milk mixture, then dip in the crust mixture. Heat oil in a large-size sauté pan, and cook tempeh over medium-high heat until both sides are golden brown. Keep warm in a low oven.

To make the sauce, in a medium-size pan, combine onion, garlic, orange juice, tamari, pepper flakes, and capers. Simmer for 15 minutes. Add ginger, whisk in cornstarch mixture, and cook for 5 more minutes, to thicken. Remove from heat and stir in orange segments.

Spoon ⅓ cup (60 g) bulgur or quinoa onto a plate, top with some orange sauce. Add tempeh and a little more sauce. Garnish with orange segments and basil.

**YIELD:** 6 servings

Per serving: 350 calories; 7g fat; 22g protein; 54g carbohydrate; 5g dietary fiber; 0mg cholesterol; 461mg sodium.

# SUGAR SNAP PEAS WITH TOASTED SESAME SEEDS

*Wheat-free, soy-free*

A quick and delicious side dish, these sesame-coated snap peas pair especially well with an Asian-themed main course.

- 2 pounds (910 g) sugar snap peas, strings removed
- 2 teaspoons (5 g) sesame seeds (black or white)
- 2 teaspoons (10 ml) sesame oil
- ¼ teaspoon salt (or to taste)

## COMPASSIONATE COOKS' TIP

Snap peas and snow peas are my favorite veggie for this recipe, but green beans, such as French beans and runner beans, also work very well.

## DIRECTIONS

In a medium-size pot, using a steamer basket, steam peas for about 3 minutes, until crisp-tender. At the same time, toast sesame seeds, either in a toaster oven or in a nonstick pan over medium heat, until golden brown.

Now either toss steamed peas with oil or cook peas in hot oil in a large-size sauté pan until they're just brown on each side. In this process, you're simply searing the peas in oil and locking in the sesame flavor. Add salt, and toss to completely coat. This whole process takes all of 5 minutes in the pan.

Either add toasted seeds to pan at the end of the cooking time or transfer snap peas to a serving bowl, and then toss with seeds. Serve hot or at room temperature.

**YIELD:** 8 to 10 servings

## SERVING SUGGESTIONS AND VARIATIONS

Use snow peas, green beans, or wax beans as a substitute for the sugar snap peas.

Per serving: 48 calories; 1g fat; 2g protein; 7g carbohydrate; 2g dietary fiber; 0mg cholesterol; 59mg sodium.

# KALE AND CAULIFLOWER SALAD

*Oil-free, wheat-free, soy-free*

This dish is incredibly simple, fantastically nutritious, and fabulously delicious. Serve as a side or as a salad before dinner.

- 2 bunches kale (Lacinato/dinosaur or curly), leaves removed from stems and roughly chopped
- 3 tablespoons (45 ml) apple cider vinegar (or to taste)
- 3 tablespoons (45 ml) agave nectar (or to taste)
- Juice from 1 large lemon
- ½ to 1 head cauliflower, thinly sliced

## DIRECTIONS

Steam kale for 5 minutes until bright green and tender. Let cool. Alternatively, you may keep kale raw and "massage" for 5 to 7 minutes or so to tenderize.

In a large-size bowl, combine vinegar, agave nectar, and lemon juice and find the right ratio between sour vinegar/lemon juice and sweet agave nectar. This may take some tweaking and may vary according to how sour or sweet you want it, but you can't really mess up this recipe! Add kale and cauliflower and toss well to coat.

When serving, toss rigorously to ensure leaves are covered with dressing that may sink to the bottom of the bowl.

**YIELD:** 4 to 6 servings

Per serving: 24 calories; trace fat; 1g protein; 6g carbohydrate; 1g dietary fiber; 0mg cholesterol; 15mg sodium.

## DID YOU KNOW?

Calorie for calorie, dark green leafy vegetables are perhaps the most nutrient-rich foods on the planet.

They're great sources of fiber and folate, they're low in fat, they're high in protein (as percentage of their calories), and they're packed with iron, calcium, potassium, vitamins K, C, & E, as well as beta-carotene and lutein.

FRUIT SUSHI (A.K.A. FRUSHI)
WITH STRAWBERRY REDUCTION
SAUCE, Page 122

# FRUIT SUSHI (A.K.A. *FRUSHI*) WITH STRAWBERRY REDUCTION SAUCE

*Oil-free, wheat-free, soy-free*

This is a sweet, creamy variation on the traditional Japanese entrée. I recommend chilling the rice after it cooks to make it easier to mold into oblong mounds.

## FOR THE SUSHI:

- 1 cup (195 g) short-grain or other sushi rice, rinsed
- 1 cup (235 ml) water
- 1 cup unsweetened (235 ml) coconut milk (lite is fine)
- 1 to 2 tablespoons (12 to 25 g) granulated sugar
- Pinch of salt
- 4 ripe peaches or nectarines
- ¼ cup (80 g) fruit preserves
- 1 pint (290 g) fresh strawberries, thinly sliced
- 36 berries (fresh raspberries, blueberries, or blackberries)
- 48 large mint leaves or curly leaf lettuce, for garnish (optional)
- 2 tablespoons (16 g) black sesame seeds, for garnish (optional)

## FOR THE REDUCTION:

- 2 cups (340 g) diced strawberries
- ½ teaspoon black pepper
- 2 teaspoons (10 ml) orange juice
- ½ cup (120 ml) water
- 2 tablespoons (30 ml) balsamic vinegar

## DIRECTIONS

To make the sushi, add rice, water, and coconut milk to a pot, and bring to a boil. Lower heat, cover, and simmer until the liquid is absorbed and the rice is soft. (Add a small amount of extra water or coconut milk if the rice is not done but the liquid has evaporated.)

Next, stir sugar and salt in with cooked rice. Gently fluff rice with a fork to distribute evenly. Let rice cool completely.

To prepare the sauce add diced strawberries, pepper, orange juice, water, and vinegar to a pot and heat over medium heat until reduced to a syrupy consistency. Strain through a fine-mesh strainer until completely smooth. Reserve for later use.

Blanch peaches in boiling water for 60 seconds. Place in a bowl of ice water to cool, then peel off skin. Thinly slice half-moons from the fruit pit.

Create oblong mounds from the cooled rice—these become the pieces of sushi—by pressing bits of rice between the palms of your hands. Then carefully spread a thin layer of preserves on top of each mound, and top with a peach slice, a strawberry slice, and a berry.

Arrange mint leaves on a serving plate. Place the individual "frushi" rolls on the leaves and sprinkle with black sesame seeds. Drizzle with strawberry reduction sauce to finish.

**YIELD:** 36 pieces, or servings

Per serving: 59 calories; 2g fat; 1g protein; 10g carbohydrate; 1g dietary fiber; 0mg cholesterol; 3mg sodium.

# PUMPKIN CURRY

*Oil-free, wheat-free, soy-free depending on milk*

I love this dish, with its different flavors: sweet from the pumpkin and coconut, hot from the chiles and cayenne, and cool from the ginger.

- 1 ½ cups (290 g) red lentils
- 3 cups (705 ml) plus 2 tablespoons water (30 ml), for sautéing, divided
- 2 medium-size yellow onions, finely chopped
- 1 teaspoon (2 g) grated or minced fresh ginger
- 3 garlic cloves, minced or pressed
- 2 cups (470 ml) nondairy milk (soy, rice, almond, hazelnut, hemp, or oat) or 1 can (15 ounces, or 420 g) coconut milk
- 2 cans (15 ounces, or 420 g, each) pumpkin purée
- 2 teaspoons (4 g) curry powder
- ¼ teaspoon cayenne or ½ teaspoon chili powder
- ½ cup (40 g) shredded coconut
- 5 whole dried red chiles
- ½ teaspoon salt (or to taste)

## DIRECTIONS

Rinse lentils and pick out any impurities, such as stones or debris.

Heat 2 tablespoons (30 ml) water in a large saucepan. Add onions, ginger, and garlic, and cook until onions are translucent, about 6 minutes.

Add lentils, remaining 3 cups (705 ml) water, milk, pumpkin, curry powder, cayenne, coconut, and chiles, and cook over low-medium heat until lentils are mushy but still retain body and texture, 35 to 40 minutes.

Stir occasionally, and keep an eye on how quickly the liquid is evaporating. If it evaporates too quickly, you may need to add more water or milk before the lentils are cooked.

Add salt and remove whole chiles before serving. Serve over basmati or jasmine rice.

**YIELD:** 8 to 10 servings

Per serving: 177 calories; 3g fat; 11g protein; 29g carbohydrate; 13g dietary fiber; 0mg cholesterol; 123mg sodium.

# YELLOW SPLIT PEA DAL

*Oil-free, wheat-free, soy-free*

This recipe is great served with brown or basmati rice—or even quinoa—and can also be made into a soup by adding more water. Serve with Naan, a delicious flatbread (recipe included in *The Joy of Vegan Baking*).

- 3 cups (705 ml) plus 2 to 3 tablespoons (30 to 45 ml) water, for sautéing, divided
- 1 medium-size yellow onion, finely chopped
- 3 garlic cloves, pressed or minced
- 1 teaspoon (2 g) finely minced fresh ginger
- 1 teaspoon (2 g) curry powder
- 1 teaspoon (2 g) ground cumin
- ½ teaspoon ground turmeric
- ¼ teaspoon chili powder
- 2 tablespoons (32 g) tomato paste
- 1 cup (225 g) yellow split peas, uncooked
- ¼ teaspoon salt (or to taste)
- Fresh cilantro or parsley, for garnish (optional)

## DIRECTIONS

Heat 2 to 3 tablespoons (30 to 45 ml) water in a 3-quart (3.5 L) saucepan. Cook onion, garlic, and ginger until they start to soften, about 5 minutes. To prevent sticking, use more water.

Add curry powder, cumin, turmeric, and chili powder, and cook for 3 minutes, stirring frequently. Add more water, as necessary. Add tomato paste, and cook, stirring, for a minute or so, thoroughly mixing paste with other ingredients.

Add 3 cups (705 ml) water and split peas, and stir to combine. Bring to a boil, then cover and simmer for 35 to 40 minutes, until split peas are soft and broken down. Add more water, if necessary. Simmer, stirring frequently, until mixture is thick. Add salt.

Top each bowl with fresh cilantro, if desired, and serve.

**YIELD:** 6 servings

Per serving: 129 calories; 1g fat; 9g protein; 24g carbohydrate; 9g dietary fiber; 0mg cholesterol; 140mg sodium.

## COMPASSIONATE COOKS' TIP

To reduce cooking time, soak the split peas for 30 minutes or longer before cooking.

Even the smallest can of tomato paste is more than is called for in a recipe. Add leftover paste to any soup, stew, or stir-fry for extra flavor.

Advanced Preparation Required

# FROZEN MANGO LASSI

*Oil-free, wheat-free*

This is a variation on a traditional Indian beverage. Freezing the mango and nondairy yogurt results in a refreshing, creamy dessert.

- 2 medium-size ripe mangoes, peeled, seeded, and cut into chunks
- 1 cup (230 g) plain or vanilla nondairy yogurt
- Agave nectar, to taste
- ¼ teaspoon ground cardamom (optional)

## DIRECTIONS

Place cut-up mango in freezer bags or containers, and freeze for at least 24 hours. Pour yogurt into ice cube trays and freeze for at least 24 hours.

When ready to prepare, blend mango and yogurt cubes in a high-speed blender until creamy. Taste and add agave nectar to sweeten, if necessary, and cardamom, if desired.

Scoop with an ice cream scoop and serve immediately.

**YIELD:** 2 servings

## COMPASSIONATE COOKS' TIP

Although this makes a wonderful dessert, it is also healthful enough to serve as a breakfast smoothie.

Per serving: 258 calories; 2g fat; 5g protein; 58g carbohydrate; 5g dietary fiber; 0mg cholesterol; 63mg sodium.

# TOASTS FOR ALL OCCASIONS

Although the use of the word *toast*, referring to the act of honoring a person, an occasion, or a sentiment, traces back to only the eighteenth century, the custom itself is rooted in ancient civilizations.

Poisoning was a common method of dispatching enemies in ancient Greece, so a host would typically drink first to assure his guests that their wine was untainted. The Romans adopted the ritual but added a variation: they dropped a burnt piece of bread into the wine to soak up the acidity. The last person to drink from the communal cup, usually the host, would also eat the wine-soaked bread in honor of the guests or event.

Every culture partakes in the tradition of toasts in one form or another, but the Irish, with their gift for language, have made toasting an art form.

## FOR FRIENDS
"Here's a toast to the future, a toast to the past, and a toast to our friends, far and near. May the future be pleasant, the past a bright dream. May our friends remain faithful and dear."

–Anonymous

"To the old, long life and treasure; To the young, all health and pleasure."

–Ben Jonson, seventeenth-century British poet

## FOR BIRTHDAYS
"May you live to be a hundred years with one extra year to repent."

–Irish toast

"May you have the hindsight to know where you've been, the foresight to know where you are going, and the insight to know when you have gone too far."

–Anonymous

## FOR ROMANCE
"Here's to you who halves my sorrows and doubles my joys. I love you more than yesterday, less than tomorrow. May we love as long as we live, and live as long as we love."

–Anonymous

"Come in the evening, or come in the morning, Come when you are looked for, or come without warning, A thousand welcomes you will find here before you, And the oftener you come here the more I'll adore you."

–Irish toast

## FROM MY HOME TO YOURS
Please enjoy (and feel free to use) this toast/blessing that my husband and I say before our shared evening meal each night.

"May we always have a roof above us, food before us, and love between us."
Hear, hear.

**AUTUMN MENU:** In the Misty Moonlight

- African Sweet Potato and Peanut Stew    - French Onion Pie
- Roasted Brussels Sprouts with Apples and Onions
- Orzo Pilaf with Roasted Red Peppers and Peas

# AFRICAN SWEET POTATO AND PEANUT STEW

*Oil-free, wheat-free, soy-free*

If you've never had a dish that combines sweet potatoes and peanuts, you're in for a treat. Serve it over rice, quinoa, or couscous, the latter of which is a traditional North African accompaniment.

- 3 tablespoons (45 ml) water, for sautéing
- 2 medium-size yellow onions, chopped
- 3 garlic cloves, pressed or minced
- 2 red bell peppers, seeded and cut into ½-inch (1 cm) squares
- 1 tablespoon (15 g) light brown sugar
- 1 teaspoon (2 g) grated or minced fresh ginger
- 1 teaspoon (2 g) ground cumin
- 1 teaspoon (2 g) ground cinnamon
- ½ teaspoon cayenne pepper
- ½ to ¾ cup (130 to 195 g) smooth natural peanut butter (crunchy works great, too!)
- 3 sweet potatoes, peeled and cut into ½-inch (1 cm) cubes
- 1 can (15 ounces, or 420 g) red kidney beans, drained and rinsed
- 1 can (15 ounces, or 420 g) diced tomatoes or 2 fresh tomatoes, diced
- 4 cups (940 ml) vegetable stock (store-bought or homemade, page 213)
- 1 teaspoon (6 g) salt (or to taste)

- ½ to 1 cup (70 to 145 g) chopped, unsalted dry-roasted peanuts (optional)
- Chopped fresh cilantro, for garnish (optional)

## DIRECTIONS

Heat water in a large-size saucepan over medium heat. Add onions and garlic and cook until softened, about 5 minutes. Add bell pepper, cover, and cook until softened, about 5 minutes. Stir in brown sugar, ginger, cumin, cinnamon, and cayenne pepper, and cook, stirring, for 30 seconds.

Stir in peanut butter, distributing evenly throughout. Hint: To thin out peanut butter first, mix it with water in a small bowl before adding to pot. It will be easier to incorporate into the stew.

Add sweet potatoes, kidney beans, and tomatoes, and stir to coat. Add vegetable stock, bring to a boil, then reduce heat to low and simmer until sweet potatoes are soft, about 30 minutes. Taste and add salt, if necessary. Serve in individual bowls, topped with chopped nuts and cilantro, if desired.

**YIELD:** 6 to 10 servings

Per serving: 491 calories; 19g fat; 22g protein; 60g carbohydrate; 13g dietary fiber; 0mg cholesterol; 1071mg sodium.

# FRENCH ONION PIE

*Oil-free if onions sautéed in water*

This elegant yet simple dish is perfect for a casual brunch or a formal dinner. Make the pie crust from scratch using the recipe from *The Joy of Vegan Baking*, or use a premade crust that you can find in the frozen section of your grocery store. Your local natural foods store will most likely carry a healthful version.

- 2 uncooked pie shells, thawed
- 1 tablespoon (14 g) nondairy butter, oil, or water, for sautéing
- 5 large-size yellow or white onions, thinly sliced
- 4 garlic cloves, minced
- 1 teaspoon (4 g) granulated sugar
- ½ teaspoon salt, plus a little extra
- 1 ½ cups (355 ml) nondairy milk (soy, rice, almond, hazelnut, hemp, or oat)
- 15 ounces (420 g) extra-firm tofu (*not* silken)
- ½ teaspoon black pepper
- ½ teaspoon nutmeg
- 5 tablespoons (40 g) unbleached flour
- 2 tablespoons (25 g) nutritional yeast flakes (optional)

## DIRECTIONS

Preheat oven to 350°F (180°C, or gas mark 4). Bake pie shells for 10 minutes, and remove from oven. Set aside.

In a large-size sauté pan, cook onions and garlic in nondairy butter, stirring occasionally, until onions become translucent. Add sugar and a little salt to taste. Cook for 15 to 25 minutes (or longer if you'd like the onions somewhat caramelized, which happens more easily with oil than with water).

In a blender or large food processor, combine milk, tofu, remaining ½ teaspoon salt, pepper, nutmeg, flour, and nutritional yeast (if using) until mixture is smooth. In a large-size bowl, add the contents of the blender to sautéed onions.

Stir all ingredients together and distribute evenly between the 2 partially cooked pie shells. Bake for 45 minutes, or until crust is golden brown and filling sets. Serve immediately.

**YIELD:** Two 9-inch (23 cm) pies, 10 to 12 servings each

## SERVING SUGGESTIONS AND VARIATIONS

Use sautéed leeks in place of half of the onions. Choose an unsweetened version of your favorite nondairy milk. Soy, rice, and almond all come in unsweetened versions, though rice can be too thin for this recipe. See Resources and Recommendations (page 296) for suggested frozen pie crust brands.

Per serving: 111 calories; 6g fat; 4g protein; 11g carbohydrate; 2g dietary fiber; 0mg cholesterol; 146mg sodium.

# ROASTED BRUSSELS SPROUTS WITH APPLES AND ONIONS

*Wheat-free, soy-free if using only oil*

This delicious, nutritious dish can be served with or without the cider.

- 3 tablespoons (45 ml) olive oil
- 2 tablespoons (28 g) melted nondairy, nonhydrogenated butter (such as Earth Balance)
- 2 pounds (910 g) fresh Brussels sprouts, trimmed and halved
- 5 Granny Smith apples, chopped
- 2 small-size red onions, cut into 1/4-inch (6 mm) wedges
- 1 teaspoon (6 g) salt
- 1 teaspoon (2 g) ground pepper
- Juice from 1 lemon
- 1 to 2 cups (235 to 470 ml) apple cider (optional)

## DIRECTIONS

Preheat oven to 425°F (220°C, or gas mark 7). Toss sprouts, apples, and onions with oil and butter. Season with salt, pepper, and lemon juice. Place on baking sheet, making sure they don't overlap one another.

Bake, uncovered, for about 30 minutes. You'll know they are ready when the apples and onions are tender and the Brussels sprouts are brown with a bit of black on the outside. Cook longer, if necessary, until Brussels sprouts become tender, tossing periodically.

Transfer vegetables to a serving dish, cover, and serve as is or keep warm. In a small pot on the stove or in the microwave, heat apple cider, then pour over vegetables and serve.

**YIELD:** 4 to 6 servings

Per serving: 268 calories; 13g fat; 5g protein; 38g carbohydrate; 8g dietary fiber; 0mg cholesterol; 40mg sodium.

## FOOD LORE

The name *Brussels sprouts* stems from the original place of cultivation, not because of the vegetable's popularity in the capital city. During the sixteenth century, Brussels sprouts enjoyed popularity in Belgium, but enjoyment of the vegetable eventually spread throughout Europe and the rest of the world.

# ORZO PILAF WITH ROASTED RED PEPPERS AND PEAS

*Soy-free*

This pretty dish is actually much closer to a risotto than a pilaf because of its creamy texture. Its mild taste makes it especially appealing to younger taste buds.

- 2 tablespoons (30 ml) extra-virgin olive oil
- 2 garlic cloves, finely chopped
- 12 ounces (340 g) orzo
- 3 cups (705 ml) vegetable stock (store-bought or homemade, page 213)
- 1 ½ cups (200 g) frozen baby green peas, partially thawed
- 1 jar (7 ½ ounces, or 215 g) roasted red bell peppers, drained and chopped
- Salt and freshly ground black pepper, to taste

## DIRECTIONS

In a large-size, deep-sided skillet with a lid, heat oil over medium heat. Add garlic and cook, stirring, for 2 minutes. Add orzo and cook, stirring for 2 minutes longer.

Add stock, peas, red peppers, salt, and black pepper. Bring to a boil over high heat.

Reduce heat, cover, and simmer, stirring a few times, for about 15 minutes, until orzo is tender yet still firm to the bite and has absorbed the liquid. Serve at once.

**YIELD:** 6 to 8 servings

## FOOD LORE

In Italian, *orzo* means "barley," but it's actually a tiny, rice-shaped pasta slightly smaller than a pine nut. Orzo is ideal for soups and wonderful as a substitute for rice.

## DID YOU KNOW?

A pilaf (also called *pilau*) is a rice- or bulgur-based dish that originated in the Middle East and always begins by browning rice in nondairy butter or oil before cooking it in stock. Pilafs can be seasoned in a variety of ways and usually contain other ingredients, such as chopped cooked vegetables. In India, they're highly spiced with curry. You can serve pilaf as a side dish or a main dish.

Per serving: 276 calories; 6g fat; 9g protein; 47g carbohydrate; 4g dietary fiber; 0mg cholesterol; 644mg sodium.

# POTATO LEEK SOUP

*Wheat-free, soy-free, oil-free if using water for sautéing*

Paired with a green salad and homemade whole-wheat bread, this creamy soup makes a perfect fall or winter supper. Leeks give lots of iron-rich mineral nourishment, while garlic and onions add immune-boosting, heart-healthy benefits.

- 1 tablespoon (14 g) nondairy, nonhydrogenated butter (such as Earth Balance), olive oil, or water for sautéing
- 4 leeks, white and light green parts, washed and sliced into ¼-inch (6 mm) slices
- 1 medium-size yellow onion, coarsely chopped
- 4 garlic cloves, minced or pressed
- 5 large-size yellow potatoes (such as Yukon gold), peeled and cut into ½-inch (1 cm) cubes
- 7 cups (1645 ml) vegetable stock (store-bought or homemade, page 213)
- 2 tablespoons (8 g) minced fresh tarragon, plus extra for garnish (optional)
- Salt and freshly ground pepper, to taste

## DIRECTIONS

Heat nondairy butter in a large-size soup pot over medium heat. Add leeks and onion, and sauté for 5 to 7 minutes, stirring often, until onion begins to turn translucent. Add garlic and cook for 1 minute longer.

Add potatoes, vegetable stock (or water with bouillon cubes), and tarragon. Cover and bring to a boil. Reduce the heat to a simmer. Cook for 20 minutes, or until potatoes are soft when pierced with a fork.

Remove soup from heat and use an immersion blender to blend the soup in the pot, or ladle soup into a blender or food processor, adding one cup at a time. Pour soup into a large bowl or ceramic soup container, and continue until you have blended all of the soup.

Transfer blended soup back to original pot and warm over low heat until heated through. Season with salt and pepper. Serve hot, with fresh tarragon sprinkled on top, if desired.

**YIELD:** 8 servings

## SERVING SUGGESTIONS AND VARIATIONS

To leave the soup chunky, only purée half. For an easier time, roast onions and leeks before adding them to soup.

## COMPASSIONATE COOKS' TIP

Eliminate oil by sautéing in water.

Per serving: 250 calories; 5g fat; 8g protein; 45g carbohydrate; 5g dietary fiber; 0mg cholesterol; 1437mg sodium.

# CREAMY CAESAR SALAD WITH OIL-FREE CROUTONS

*Oil-free if thinned with water, wheat-free (salad); oil-free, soy-free (croutons)*

This healthful version of the traditional salad delivers all the tangy flavor and creamy texture of the original without the saturated fat, cholesterol, or potential salmonella contamination. Authentic, like the original recipe, ours does not contain anchovies.

## FOR SALAD:

- 4 ounces (115 g) firm tofu (*not* silken)
- ¼ cup (60 ml) fresh lemon juice
- 3 whole garlic cloves, peeled
- 2 to 3 tablespoons (18 to 28 g) capers, drained
- 2 tablespoons (25 g) nutritional yeast flakes
- 1 tablespoon (15 g) Dijon mustard
- ½ teaspoon ground pepper
- ¼ teaspoon salt
- Water or olive oil, as needed
- 4 heads Romaine lettuce

## FOR CROUTONS:

- 2 cups (100 g) slightly stale bread cubes
- ½ teaspoon dried oregano
- ½ teaspoon dried thyme
- ½ teaspoon dried basil
- ½ teaspoon dried tarragon
- ½ teaspoon ground paprika
- ½ teaspoon salt
- ¼ cup (60 ml) water

## DIRECTIONS

To make the salad, in a blender or food processor, blend tofu, lemon juice, garlic, capers, nutritional yeast, mustard, pepper, and salt. Add water or olive oil, as needed, to thin out. The consistency should be creamy but not so thick that you can't pour it. Tweak the flavor with the various ingredients to your liking (if you like it tangier, add more mustard; if you like it saltier, add more capers). The dressing can be stored in an airtight container and refrigerated for up to one week.

In the meantime, make the croutons. Preheat oven to 350°F (180°C, or gas mark 4). In a medium-size bowl, combine all crouton ingredients and toss well. Use water only as a means to adhere the herbs to the bread.

Spread bread cubes on a baking sheet and bake for 15 to 25 minutes, or until bread is crisp and dry. Check halfway through, and toss the bread so all sides cook evenly.

Once the croutons are finished, tear romaine lettuce into bite-size pieces, and add to a large bowl. Add the dressing and croutons, and toss to combine.

**YIELD:** 8 servings

## SERVING SUGGESTIONS AND VARIATIONS

Add sautéed tofu, tempeh, or Tempeh Bacon (page 29).

Per serving: 246 calories; 4g fat; 15g protein; 42g carbohydrate; 9g dietary fiber; 0mg cholesterol; 404mg sodium.

## FOOD LORE

Chef and restaurateur Cesar Cardini is credited with creating this salad. The dish was named for the restaurant Cardini owned and operated in Tijuana, Mexico, called Hotel Caesar.

# SAUTÉED BROCCOLI RABE WITH OLIVES AND TOASTED PINE NUTS

*Wheat-free, soy-free*

Broccoli rabe, also known as broccoli raab or rapini, is a popular Italian vegetable. Although it resembles slender, leafy broccoli, it is actually a relative of the turnip and has a slight—but satisfying—bitter flavor that perfectly complements the salty olives and hot crushed red pepper in this recipe.

- 2 tablespoons (18 g) pine nuts
- 2 bunches (about 2 pounds [910 g]) broccoli rabe, thick stems trimmed 1 inch (2.5 cm) from the bottom
- 2 tablespoons (30 ml) olive oil
- 2 garlic cloves, crushed, pressed, or minced
- 10 kalamata olives, chopped
- 1 teaspoon (1 g) crushed red pepper flakes
- Salt, to taste
- Juice from ½ lemon, lime, or orange

## DIRECTIONS

Toast pine nuts in a dry skillet over medium heat or in a toaster oven on low heat until golden brown, tossing occasionally to ensure even toasting. Remove from heat.

Meanwhile, add a steamer basket to a 3-quart (3.5 L) pot with just enough water to reach the bottom of the basket. Bring to a boil. Add broccoli rabe and cover. Steam for 2 to 3 minutes, then immediately plunge rabe into a bowl of ice water. You have just "steam blanched" the broccoli rabe. Submersing rabe in cold water will immediately stop it from continuing to cook and will enable it to maintain its bright green color. After a few minutes in the water, drain the rabe in a colander.

In a large-size skillet over medium heat, warm olive oil. Add garlic and sauté until it turns golden brown, about 2 minutes. Add drained broccoli rabe, olives, crushed red pepper, and a pinch of salt. Sauté for about 5 minutes longer, until *al dente* ("to the teeth"), which means it should be tender but still firm at the center. Before serving, sprinkle with toasted pine nuts, squeeze on the citrus juice, and give it all a toss.

**YIELD:** 6 to 8 servings

Per serving: 56 calories; 6g fat; 1g protein; 1g carbohydrate; trace dietary fiber; 0mg cholesterol; 75mg sodium.

## COMPASSIONATE COOKS' TIP

One of my favorite tools in the kitchen is a pair of tongs with nylon (nonstick) heads. I can use them in my pots and pans without worrying about scratching.

# EGGPLANT AND CARAMELIZED ONION "LASAGNA"

*Wheat-free, soy-free*

I had the pleasure of helping prepare this dish during a cooking demonstration in Umbria, Italy, where we stayed at Montali Country House, an all-vegetarian gourmet guest house. I modified this recipe to reduce the amount of prep time but none of the fantastic flavor.

- 1 pound (455 g) Italian eggplant or 2 globe eggplants, peeled and sliced into rounds
- 1 tablespoon (18 g) salt, plus more to taste
- 1 tablespoon (15 ml) olive oil, plus some for brushing and coating baking sheets
- 4 medium-size onions, thinly sliced
- 2 tablespoons (18 g) capers, rinsed, drained, and chopped
- 2 ½ tablespoons (16 g) pitted and chopped black olives
- 2 ½ tablespoons (16 g) pitted and chopped green olives
- 3 tablespoons (25 g) toasted pine nuts (see page 135)
- 3 tablespoons (27 g) raisins, soaked in water for 10 minutes and drained
- 5 tomatoes, peeled, seeded, and roughly chopped
- 5 to 7 basil leaves, roughly chopped
- 1 tablespoon (15 ml) balsamic or red wine vinegar
- Pepper, to taste

## DIRECTIONS

Preheat oven to broil. Lightly oil 2 baking sheets.

Soak eggplants for 15 minutes in water mixed with salt. Drain water and squeeze out excess from eggplants. Brush each side with olive oil and place on baking sheets. Sprinkle with salt.

Broil eggplants on a rack 4 to 6 inches (10 to 15 cm) from heat source until tops are golden brown, about 4 minutes. Turn and cook for 2 to 3 minutes longer. Transfer to a tray lined with paper towels. Pat with more paper towels to soak up excess oil. Let cool.

Meanwhile, in a large pan, sauté onions in olive oil. Cook slowly over low heat, stirring occasionally, for 20 to 25 minutes, until golden brown. When done, stir in capers, olives, toasted pine nuts, soaked raisins, peeled tomatoes, and basil, and cook for an additional minute. Add vinegar and salt and pepper, and cook for 1 more minute, or until the vinegar evaporates.

Turn the oven down to 350°F (180°C, or gas mark 4). Spread one-third of onion mixture over bottom of an ungreased 9 x 13-inch (23 x 33 cm) casserole dish. Place half of eggplants over onion mixture to completely cover. Sprinkle with salt. Spread another one-third of onion mixture, then layer remaining eggplants on top, and sprinkle with salt. Top with final third of onions and press surface gently with the back of the spoon.

Bake, uncovered, for 10 minutes. Serve hot.

**YIELD:** 8 to 10 servings

## DID YOU KNOW?

Capers are the flower buds of a bush native to the mediterranean and parts of Asia.

Per serving: 79 calories; 3g fat; 2g protein; 12g carbohydrate; 3g dietary fiber; 0mg cholesterol; 700mg sodium.

✳ Aloo Gobi (Curried Cauliflower and Potatoes)

✳ Chana Masala (Curried Chickpeas)

✳ Masoor Dal (Red Lentils) ✳ Chai-Spiced Almond Cookies

# ALOO GOBI (CURRIED CAULIFLOWER AND POTATOES)

*Wheat-free, soy-free*

If you do not have fresh chile peppers on hand, I've used 1 teaspoon (2 g) chili powder with great effect. I have also used canned tomatoes when I had no fresh tomatoes.

- 2 to 3 tablespoons (30 to 45 ml) coconut or canola oil or nondairy, nonhydrogenated butter (such as Earth Balance)
- 2 hot green chiles, stemmed, seeded, and minced
- 1 tablespoon (8 g) freshly grated ginger
- 2 teaspoons (4 g) whole cumin seeds
- 4 medium-size yellow potatoes, diced
- 1 large head cauliflower, trimmed, cored, and cut into flowerets
- ¼ to ¾ cup (60 to 180 ml) water
- 4 medium-size tomatoes, quartered (or 6 Roma tomatoes, halved)
- 1 tablespoon (6 g) ground coriander
- 2 teaspoons (4 g) ground turmeric
- 1 teaspoon (2 g) garam masala
- 2 teaspoons (10 g) brown sugar
- 1 teaspoon (6 g) salt (or to taste)
- Finely chopped fresh cilantro or flat-leaf parsley, for garnish (optional)

## DIRECTIONS

Heat oil in a large-size saucepan over medium heat. When it is hot but not smoking, add chiles, ginger, and cumin seeds, and fry until cumin seeds begin to pop, about 5 minutes. Drop in potatoes and cauliflower and cook for 4 to 5 minutes, or until vegetables pick up a few brown spots.

Add water, tomatoes, coriander, turmeric, garam masala, brown sugar, and salt. Stir well, cover, and gently cook over low heat, stirring occasionally, for 20 minutes, or until vegetables are tender. If vegetables stick to the pan, add more water. Stir gently to avoid mashing or breaking.

Serve, garnished with chopped cilantro, if desired.

**YIELD:** 8 to 10 servings

## DID YOU KNOW?

Garam masala is a blend of ground spices whose literal meaning is "hot spice." There are many variations, but most mixes include cinnamon, cumin, cloves, nutmeg, cardamom, ginger, turmeric, coriander, bay leaves, and fennel.

Per serving: 97 calories; 4g fat; 2g protein; 14g carbohydrate; 2g dietary fiber; 0mg cholesterol; 12mg sodium.

# CHANA MASALA
## (CURRIED CHICKPEAS)

*Oil-free, wheat-free, soy-free*

This wonderful dish is bursting with flavor! You can adjust the spice level to your taste.
Not only do chickpeas make a great snack and are packed with protein, but they also
have been credited with aphrodisiac qualities by Arabs and Greeks.

- 2 cups (470 ml) plus 2 tablespoons (30 ml) water, divided
- 2 large-size onions, finely chopped
- 1 teaspoon (2 g) minced fresh ginger
- 1 tablespoon (6 g) ground coriander
- 1 tablespoon (6 g) garam masala
- 1 tablespoon (7 g) ground cumin
- 1 teaspoon (2 g) ground cinnamon
- 1 teaspoon (2 g) ground cloves
- 1½ teaspoons (3 g) chili powder
- 2 tablespoons (25 g) sugar
- 1 can (6 ounces, or 170 g) tomato paste
- 4 cans (15 ounce, or 420 g, each) chickpeas, drained and rinsed (or 6 cups [1440 g] beans from scratch)
- 1 teaspoon (6 g) salt (or to taste)

### DIRECTIONS

Heat 2 tablespoons (30 ml) water in a large saucepan. Add onions and ginger, and sauté for about 5 minutes, or until onions become translucent. Add coriander, garam masala, cumin, cinnamon, cloves, chili powder, and sugar, and stir for 30 seconds. Add tomato paste, and cook for 5 minutes. Stir to combine.

Add chickpeas and remaining 2 cups (470 ml) water, and cook for 10 to 20 minutes, stirring occasionally. To vary thickness of curry, either add water or let water cook down. Add salt to taste.

**YIELD:** 8 to 10 servings

### SERVING SUGGESTIONS AND VARIATIONS

The longer the dish simmers or sits, the more the flavors mingle together. Consider making it the day before you want to serve it. Heat on the stove before serving. For information about garam masala, see page 137.

Per serving: 474 calories; 8g fat; 24g protein; 81g carbohydrate; 22g dietary fiber; 0mg cholesterol; 383mg sodium.

MASOOR DAL AND CHANA
MASALA (SERVED WITH
RICE AND PITA)

# MASOOR DAL
## (RED LENTILS)
*Wheat-free, soy-free, oil-free if using water for sautéing*

You may be surprised by how something so simple can be so delicious, but it's true. And as an added plus, red lentils cook faster than most other types, making this both a tasty and quick dish.

- 2 cups (385 g) red lentils
- 1 tablespoon (15 ml) coconut or canola oil, nondairy butter, or water, for sautéing
- 3 garlic cloves, minced
- 1 large-size yellow onion, finely chopped
- 1 teaspoon (2 g) cumin seeds
- 5 ½ cups (1.3 L) water
- 1 tablespoon (6 g) ground coriander
- ¼ teaspoon cayenne pepper (more or less depending on your taste preferences)
- 1 teaspoon (6 g) salt

### DIRECTIONS

Rinse lentils and pick out any impurities, such as stones and debris.

Heat oil in a large-size saucepan over medium heat. Add garlic, onion, and cumin seeds, and cook, stirring frequently, for about 3 minutes, or until garlic begins to turn golden brown and onion becomes translucent.

Add water, lentils, coriander, cayenne pepper, and salt, and cook over medium-low heat until beans are mushy but still retain some distinctive texture, about 25 minutes. Adjust water or cooking time to reach your desired consistency.

**YIELD:** 8 to 10 servings

Per serving: 215 calories; 2g fat; 16g protein; 35g carbohydrate; 18g dietary fiber; 0mg cholesterol; 220mg sodium.

# CHAI-SPICED ALMOND COOKIES

These versatile little balls will impress at a formal dinner party, as much as they'll delight children who can help roll them and dip them in the sugar. They also make a lovely gift or the perfect ending to an Indian-inspired meal.

- Oil for coating baking sheet
- ½ cup (1 stick, or 112 g) nondairy, nonhydrogenated butter (such as Earth Balance), at room temperature
- 1 ⅓ cups (135 g) sifted confectioners' sugar, divided
- 2 teaspoons (10 ml) vanilla extract
- 1 teaspoon (5 ml) almond extract
- 1 teaspoon (2 g) ground allspice
- 1 teaspoon (2 g) ground cardamom
- ½ teaspoon ground cinnamon
- ¼ teaspoon salt
- 1 cup (125 g) all-purpose or whole-wheat pastry flour
- ¾ to 1 cup (75 to 100 g) finely chopped toasted almonds (see page 86 for toasting nuts)

## DIRECTIONS

Preheat oven to 350°F (180°C, or gas mark 4). Lightly oil a cookie or baking sheet.

Using an electric mixer, beat nondairy butter, ⅓ cup (35 g) sugar, vanilla extract, almond extract, allspice, cardamom, cinnamon, and salt in a medium-size bowl. Add flour and beat until thoroughly combined. Stir in almonds by hand so as not to overbeat batter.

Using your hands, roll dough into tablespoon-size balls. Arrange them on prepared baking sheet. Because they don't spread much, don't worry about spacing them far apart from one another. Bake until they begin to turn golden brown, about 20 minutes. Remove from oven, and cool on sheet for 5 minutes.

Place remaining 1 cup (100 g) sugar in a large bowl. Working in batches, gently coat hot cookies in sugar. Cool cookies on a rack. Roll again in sugar, and serve.

**YIELD:** About 20 cookies, or servings

Per serving: 135 calories; 8g fat; 2g protein; 14g carbohydrate; 1g dietary fiber; 0mg cholesterol; 28mg sodium.

## DID YOU KNOW?

The word *chai* means tea in Hindi.

# RED LENTIL PÂTÉ

*Wheat-free, soy-free*

The red lentils (found in natural food or Indian stores) are seasoned with Mediterranean herbs in this recipe, quickly melting down into a savory purée.

- Oil to coat pans
- 3 tablespoons (25 g) chopped pistachio nuts or toasted sunflower seeds
- 3 cups (705 ml) plus 2 tablespoons (30 ml) water, divided
- 1 large-size yellow onion, finely chopped
- 1 cup (160 g) finely chopped shallots
- 1 teaspoon (2 g) fennel seeds, crushed in a mortar or under a chef's knife
- ½ teaspoon dried thyme leaves
- 2 garlic cloves, minced
- 1 tablespoon (16 g) tomato paste
- ¼ cup (60 ml) dry white wine or sparkling apple cider
- 1½ cups (290 g) red lentils, picked over and rinsed
- 1 bay leaf
- ½ teaspoon salt
- Freshly ground black pepper
- Mint or basil leaves, for garnish (optional)

Per serving: 65 calories; 1g fat; 4g protein; 11g carbohydrate; 3g dietary fiber; 0mg cholesterol; 56mg sodium.

## DIRECTIONS

Oil bottom and sides of 1 large or 2 small loaf pans. Sprinkle pistachio nuts on bottom of pan(s). Set aside.

In a large pot, heat 2 tablespoons (30 ml) water. Cook onion and shallots over medium-high heat, stirring frequently, until translucent, 5 to 6 minutes. Add more water, if necessary. Stir in fennel, thyme, garlic, and tomato paste and cook, stirring constantly, for about 1 minute. Add wine and cook until most of the liquid evaporates, about 1 minute. Add remaining 3 cups (705 ml) water, lentils, and bay leaf, and bring to a boil. Cover, reduce to a simmer, and cook for 20 minutes, stirring occasionally.

Add salt and pepper and continue cooking until lentils have melted into a coarse purée, 10 to 20 minutes longer. Remove bay leaf and adjust salt, to taste. Stir well, creating a smooth, thick mixture with a texture similar to that of cooked oatmeal. If purée is thin and soupy, boil it, uncovered, stirring frequently, until it thickens.

Ladle purée immediately into oiled loaf pan(s). Smooth top with a spatula. Cool to room temperature. Cover and chill for at least 2 hours. Flip pans over a platter and lift gently to reveal pâté, while keeping its shape. Garnish with mint leaves, if desired.

**YIELD:** 3 cups (675 g), or 24 (2-tablespoon [30 g]) servings

## SERVING SUGGESTIONS AND VARIATIONS

Serve with a sliced baguette, a small salad of mixed greens, olives, pickled onions, and marinated artichoke hearts.

# ROASTED BEETS AND FENNEL BULBS IN FENNEL OIL

*Wheat-free, soy-free*

Truthfully, my favorite way to prepare vegetables is to roast them, and fennel—a delightfully crunchy veggie when raw—is an example of a vegetable that becomes extra-special when roasted. Combined with the roasted beets and fennel oil, this is a fantastic side dish for any occasion.

- 6 medium-size beets, scrubbed
- ¼ cup (60 ml) olive oil, divided
- Salt and pepper, to taste
- 2 fennel bulbs, stalks removed
- 2 tablespoons (30 ml) balsamic vinegar, divided
- 1 tablespoon (6 g) fennel seeds, crushed in a mortar or spice grinder
- 1 tablespoon (3 g) thinly sliced fresh chives

## DIRECTIONS

Preheat oven to 425°F (220°C, or gas mark 7).

Remove the greens but keep the beets whole and unpeeled.

Line a large piece of aluminum foil with parchment paper. Place beets in center of parchment paper. Drizzle with 1 tablespoon (15 ml) olive oil, and season with salt and pepper. Fold aluminum foil up to enclose beets.

Cut fennel into slices or quarters, and rub just enough olive oil on the fennel to coat. Sprinkle on 1 tablespoons (15 ml) balsamic vinegar. Place on a lightly oiled baking sheet.

Place the wrapped beets and the baking sheet with fennel on the center rack of the oven. Roast the fennel for 20 to 25 minutes, tossing at least once, until the fennel is cooked through and begins to caramelize. Roast the beets until tender when pierced with the tip of a knife, 1 to 1 ½ hours.

When the beets are done, remove them from the oven, and let them cool before rubbing off their skins, which will slip off very easily. Cut beets into wedges.

In a small bowl, whisk together remaining 3 tablespoons (45 ml) olive oil, remaining 1 tablespoon (15 ml) balsamic vinegar, crushed fennel seeds, and chives, and season with salt and pepper.

Combine the fennel, beets, and fennel oil in a large bowl, toss to combine and coat, and serve.

**YIELD:** 8 servings

## SERVING SUGGESTIONS AND VARIATIONS

Truth be told, I can't resist roasting Brussels sprouts when the opportunity arises. I've roasted the sprouts along with the fennel and beets and have loved the results. The color alone is stunning.

Per serving: 107 calories; 7g fat; 2g protein; 11g carbohydrate; 4g dietary fiber; 0mg cholesterol; 79mg sodium.

# SCOTCH BROTH
# (HEARTY SCOTTISH STEW)

*Wheat-free, soy-free, oil-free*

A traditional Scottish soup served as a main winter meal and often on New Year's Eve, this recipe (modified slightly) was shared with me by Maggie Pitkethly, a huge-hearted vegetarian and owner of The Scotch Corner Pub in Boulder, Colorado, who makes sure the menu contains vegan "bangers and mash" and vegan shepherd's pie. Originally from Scotland, Maggie grew up on this hearty stew that just happens to be vegan.

- ¾ cup (150 g) pearl barley
- ¾ cup (170 g) green split peas
- ¾ cup (150 g) red lentils
- 1 large-size leek, washed well and roughly chopped
- 1 yellow onion, roughly chopped
- 2 or 3 yellow potatoes, diced
- 3 carrots, peeled and grated or shredded
- 8 to 9 cups (1880 to 2115 ml) vegetable stock, depending on thickness required (store-bought or homemade, page 213)
- 1 teaspoon (6 g) salt (or to taste)
- Freshly ground pepper, to taste
- 2 tablespoons (8 g) chopped fresh parsley, for garnish (optional)

## DIRECTIONS

Soak barley, split peas, and lentils for 1 hour in a bowl with enough water to cover. After soaking, rinse barley, peas, and lentils and add them to a large soup pot, along with leek, onion, potatoes, carrots, stock, salt, and pepper.

Bring to a boil, then reduce heat and simmer until split peas, barley, and veggies are tender.

Ladle into individual bowls, and sprinkle parsley on top of each serving, if desired.

**YIELD:** 10 to 12 servings

## SERVING SUGGESTIONS AND VARIATIONS

Other traditional veggies in Scotch Broth include turnips, cabbage, and kale.

Per serving: 303 calories; 3g fat; 13g protein; 56g carbohydrate; 11g dietary fiber; 0mg cholesterol; 1415mg sodium.

# FOOD LORE

In Scotland, the word *broth* has a very different meaning than it does in North America. It actually refers to a thick stew, not a thin, salted stock.

# COMPASSIONATE COOKS' (OR RATHER, MAGGIE'S) TIP

Maggie says that the soup is best when made the day before it's served. The flavor improves with standing.

# CHOCOLATE CAKE WITH COFFEE GANACHE

*Soy-free depending on milk (cake); *Wheat-free (glaze and ganache)*

I honestly didn't think it was possible to improve on the chocolate cake I've been making for years. I was wrong.

## FOR CAKE:

- 1 ½ cups (190 g) unbleached all-purpose flour
- ¾ cup (150 g) granulated sugar
- ½ teaspoon salt
- 1 teaspoon (5 g) baking soda
- ¼ cup (30 g) unsweetened cocoa powder
- ¾ cup (180 ml) nondairy milk (soy, rice, almond, hazelnut, hemp, or oat)
- ½ cup (120 ml) black coffee of your choice (preferably a dark espresso)
- ⅓ cup (80 ml) canola oil
- 1 tablespoon (15 ml) white distilled vinegar
- 1 teaspoon (5 ml) vanilla extract

## FOR GLAZE:

- 1 cup (320 g) apricot preserves or jam
- 2 tablespoons (30 ml) water

## FOR GANACHE:

- 2 tablespoons (15 g) unsweetened cocoa powder
- 3 tablespoons (20 g) confectioners' sugar
- 2 tablespoons (30 ml) black coffee (preferably a dark espresso)
- 2 tablespoons (28 g) nondairy, nonhydrogenated butter (such as Earth Balance)

Per serving: 436 calories; 16g fat; 8g protein; 79g carbohydrate; 9g dietary fiber; 0mg cholesterol; 316mg sodium.

## FOOD LORE

The word *ganache* is a slang French word meaning "fool," referring to the apprentice who came upon this treat by accident. (His mentor scolded him, but he was wrong. The result was delicious!)

## COMPASSIONATE COOKS' TIP

Double the recipe for a layer cake or a Bundt cake. Don't worry if you're not a coffee drinker; I've never had a cup in my life. The coffee in this recipe adds richness rather than a strong coffee flavor. It is more noticeable in the ganache.

## DIRECTIONS

To make the cake, preheat oven to 350°F (180°C, or gas mark 4). Lightly oil an 8- or 9-inch (20 or 23 cm) cake pan. A springform pan is a great option.

Combine flour, sugar, salt, baking soda, and cocoa powder in a bowl until mixed thoroughly. It may be necessary to sift the cocoa powder to make sure it is very fine. You can do this easily with a small strainer.

Make a well in the center of the dry ingredients, and add milk, coffee, oil, vinegar, and vanilla. Stir until thoroughly mixed.

Pour into the prepared pan, and bake for 30 minutes, until a toothpick inserted into center comes out clean. Cool completely.

To make the glaze, add preserves and water to a small saucepan, and heat over medium heat, stirring often. Cook until drops that cling to the spoon are very sticky and reluctant to leave, 2 to 3 minutes. Strain through a wire sieve into a small bowl, pressing hard on the solids. Set aside.

To make the ganache, combine cocoa, confectioners' sugar, coffee, and nondairy butter in a double boiler (or make a double boiler by placing a small pot in a larger one). Heat over low-medium heat until ingredients are combined and appear shiny.

Once the cake has cooled completely, spread glaze evenly over the top. Pour ganache over glaze and spread with an offset spatula, if necessary, to cover entire top. This process works well if both the glaze and the ganache are still warm. If you make them in advance and store them in the refrigerator, simply warm them over low heat and proceed.

Serve cake immediately, or store in the refrigerator until ready to serve.

**YIELD:** 8 servings

# CHAPTER 4

LET'S CELEBRATE:
# MENUS FOR SPECIAL OCCASIONS

On any given day, we have cause for celebration. A bat or bar mitzvah, an engagement, a graduation, a dog or cat adoption, and a new job are all occasions to commemorate. Mother's Day, Father's Day, or even Grandparent's Day is an opportunity for gathering friends and family, as is the turning of the seasons! Host a winter or summer solstice supper or a spring or autumn equinox affair.

# RECIPES

## SOUPS AND STEWS

## SALADS, STARTERS, AND SIDES

## MAIN EVENT

## BEVERAGES AND DESSERTS

# TAKING VEGANISM OUT OF THE BOX

In my work, I strive to take "vegan food" out of the box, encouraging people to recognize that vegan food is familiar food: vegetables, fruits, nuts, mushrooms, beans, herbs, and spices. But because meat, egg, and dairy eating are so entrenched in our culture, we need to change the lens through which we look.

I've seen some interesting reactions when non-vegans are told that an event, a menu, or a party will be vegan. I wouldn't be exaggerating when I say that some of these reactions include indignation, hostility, or even the rejection of an invitation. The most glaring instances happen around weddings. Truth be told, everyone gets kooky around weddings in general, but even more so at the thought of a vegan wedding. I have seen otherwise rational people lose perspective when it comes to the food.

The scenario goes something like this: A vegan couple is getting married. In keeping with their core beliefs and values, they plan to serve vegan-only food at the wedding. The non-vegan parents on both sides declare that the "meat-eaters will have nothing to eat" and that the couple "shouldn't impose their own personal beliefs on everyone else." I've heard everything from, "I understand that you eat this way every other day, but at your wedding, you should accommodate the guests," to "People just expect to have meat at a wedding."

I remember having this conversation with my own parents and in-laws when my husband and I were planning our wedding. I trusted that the food would speak for itself (it did) and asked our families to trust us (they did).

## SPEAK YOUR TRUTH

I knew that our families' early resistance stemmed from their misconception of "vegan food." People have been trained to think that a vegan menu consists only of tofu and brown rice, or that it's not filling or elegant. The only way I could change that perception was to show them otherwise. I needed to understand their perspective, thank them for their honesty, and calmly and articulately speak my truth.

I have seen far too many people compromise their values because of fear of asking for what they want or standing up for their own beliefs. Choosing comfort or conformity over their own ethics, many people—many vegans—relinquish their values.

On the flip side, I think we don't give people the benefit of the doubt enough. I think we underestimate our friends and family, and as long as we think we're "protecting them" from discomfort, we not only deny our own ethics and perpetuate the abuse of animals, but we also potentially deny other people their own transformations. Because how else does this occur than through honest interaction and communication with others?

# SUGGESTED SEASONAL MENUS

These recipes are perfect for a standing party or a casual sit-down meal.

## SPRING

### IT'S MY PARTY, PAGE 153
Eggless Egg Salad
No-Queso Quesadillas
Roasted Red Pepper Wraps
Pasta and Green Beans with Peanut Sauce
Peanut Butter and Jelly Cookies

### SUNNY DAY, PAGE 160
Tempeh Pâté
Cuban Black Bean Soup
Panini with Lemon-Basil Pesto
Arborio Rice with Roasted Red Peppers,
    Pine Nuts, and Basil
Blackberry Pecan Crisp

## SUMMER

### OVER THE RAINBOW, PAGE 166
Muhammara (Roasted Red Pepper and
    Walnut Spread)
Crowd-Pleasing Pasta with Tomatoes
    and Artichokes
Boston Baked Beans
Fresh Fruit Salad
Sparkling Pineapple Juice

### LET THE GOOD TIMES ROLL, PAGE 172
Homemade Hummus
Potato and Seed Spread (a.k.a. Stuffing)
Southwestern Tofu Burgers
Noodle Kugel

## AUTUMN

### AROUND THE WORLD, PAGE 176
Spring Rolls with Peanut Dipping Sauce
Caramelized Tempeh Shawarmas
English Muffin Pizzas
Quinoa Tabbouleh

### SUNRISE, SUNSET, PAGE 181
Mushroom Pecan Burgers
Oven-Baked "French-Fried" Yams
Quinoa and Corn Medley
Beet Bundt Cake

## WINTER

### COLD COMFORT FARM, PAGE 186
Autumn (or Winter) Tempeh Salad
Butternut Squash Risotto with Toasted Sage
Purple Potatoes with Cashew Cream
Warm Lentil Salad

### MAMBO ITALIANO, PAGE 191
Eggplant Caponata
Tofu Spinach Lasagna
Tuscan White Beans with Sun-Dried Tomatoes
Garlic Bread

# BLADDERS IN MY BOOZE?

Just when you thought you could explain the difference between organic and biodynamic wines, craft beers and microbreweries, enter yet one more criterion to consider when selecting the spirits: Is it vegan?

Most people assume that wine and beer are vegan. After all, they're made with plant-based ingredients: grapes and hops, respectively. However, what many people don't realize is that some beverages are fined (filtered) using animal products. Examples include gelatin (the boiled bones and tissue of slaughterhouse animals), isinglass (obtained from the swim bladders of fish), chitosan (derived from the exoskeleton of crustaceans such as crabs and shrimp), casein (from cow's milk), and egg albumen (from chickens). Although it is possible that minute amounts of these animal products wind up in the wine or beer, typically they are not found in the finished product.

If a label does not say "Suitable for vegans," follow this general guide for choosing beer or wine:

### BEER

- Many traditional British beers, including Guinness, use animal products.

- German purity laws forbid the use of ingredients other than water, grain (barley or wheat), hops, and yeast. So, generally, German beers are vegan. The same goes for Belgian beers.

- Generally, animal products are not used to make beer in the United States, except for a few brewers who adhere to traditional British (or cask-treated) processes.

### WINE

- All kosher wines are vegan.

- Some wine makers (particularly small, artisanal ones) boast on the label that their wine is unfiltered, which means it's vegan.

- Not all organic wines are vegan.

Although it may seem daunting to have to contemplate even your beverage options, it's important to keep in mind that being vegan is about reducing suffering, not trying to attain vegan purity. There is no such thing. When we have the opportunity to make compassionate choices, it's important to do so, but if we focus on what we *can* do—and there is much—it feels a lot less overwhelming.

# EGGLESS EGG SALAD

*Wheat-free (as salad, not sandwich)*

This recipe is perfect for anytime but makes an ideal accompaniment to a traditional English tea in place of an egg salad sandwich. And it's great for kids too!

- 1 ½ pounds (685 g) extra-firm tofu
- ½ cup (115 g) eggless mayonnaise
- 2 red bell peppers, finely chopped
- 4 or 5 scallions, white and green parts, finely chopped
- 2 carrots, peeled and finely chopped
- 3 celery stalks, finely chopped
- 2 tablespoons (8 g) finely chopped fresh parsley
- 4 teaspoons (20 g) pickle relish
- 1 ½ tablespoons (17 g) prepared Dijon mustard
- ¾ teaspoon turmeric
- ½ teaspoon salt (or to taste)
- Black pepper, to taste
- 10 slices good-quality bread

## DIRECTIONS

In a large bowl, mash tofu with a fork, potato masher, or your hands. Add mayonnaise, bell peppers, scallions, carrots, celery, parsley, relish, mustard, turmeric, salt, and pepper, and combine well.

Spread a few tablespoons of tofu mixture on bottom bread slices. Top with remaining slices of bread.

Carefully cut crusts off sandwiches with a sharp knife. Cut in half diagonally, then cut in half again so you're left with small, triangle-shaped finger sandwiches. (Throw the crusts out to the grateful birds.)

**YIELD:** 10 servings (one-half sandwich each)

## SERVING SUGGESTIONS AND VARIATIONS

Serve on crackers as an appetizer or party dish. Served as a side salad, this is great for picnics and BBQs.

Per serving: 202 calories; 12g fat; 12g protein; 12g carbohydrate; 5g dietary fiber; 0mg cholesterol; 310mg sodium.

## COMPASSIONATE COOKS' TIP

Serve these sandwiches as part of your afternoon tea menu (see page 75).

# NO-QUESO QUESADILLAS

*Oil-free, soy-free, wheat-free if using corn tortillas*

If the combination of Middle Eastern hummus and Mexican tortillas seems strange, just trust me. The result is absolutely delightful and comes out as an incredibly fast meal, snack, or appetizer. Kids of all ages love it!

- 1 ½ recipes Homemade Hummus (page 172)
- 8 (10-inch, or 25-cm) flour tortillas (corn is fine, too, but they're usually smaller)
- ½ cup (50 g) chopped scallion
- ½ to 1 cup (130 to 260 g) salsa

Per serving (including hummus): 175 calories; 3g fat; 7g protein; 32g carbohydrate; 5g dietary fiber; 0mg cholesterol; 161mg sodium.

## WHAT'S THE DIFFERENCE? SALSAS VS. PICO DE GALLO

- Salsa roja, "red sauce," usually consists of cooked tomatoes, chile peppers, garlic, onion, and tomato.
- Salsa verde, or "green sauce," is made with tomatillos.
- Pico de gallo is made with fresh tomato, onion, and chilies. Lemon juice is often added.

## DIRECTIONS

Spread 3 heaping tablespoons (45 g) hummus on a tortilla and place (hummus side up) in a large-size nonstick skillet over medium heat.

Sprinkle with chopped scallion and spread on a thin layer of salsa.

Top with a second tortilla, and cook until bottom tortilla is warm and turning golden brown, 3 to 5 minutes. Turn over and cook second side for another few minutes, until golden brown. (This process becomes a lot quicker once the pan is hot, so stay close to the stove! The first one always takes the longest because the pan isn't totally hot.) Either cut in half or into pizza-shaped triangles to serve as finger food. Repeat with remaining tortillas.

Alternatively, spread hummus on half of tortilla, place tortilla in pan, add other toppings to the hummus in a thin layer, and fold empty half on top of filled side. (Just be careful not to overload it, which makes it too difficult to flip.) Let it get golden brown on bottom, then carefully turn over to brown other side. Remove from pan and serve hot.

**YIELD:** 4 to 8 servings

## SERVING SUGGESTIONS AND VARIATIONS

* Hearty Mexican-style: Add pinto or black beans when you add the salsa.
* Greek-style: Instead of salsa and scallions, add spinach, thinly sliced red onions, kalamata olives, and nondairy yogurt.
* Italian-style: Instead of salsa and scallions, add roasted red peppers, parsley, and oregano.

# ROASTED RED PEPPER WRAPS

*Oil-free, soy-free*

The simplicity astounds! This is the perfect quick appetizer for parties. Ask my good friend Pam Webb, who brings them to every party she attends.

- 2 (10-inch, or 25-cm) flour tortillas or 2 whole-grain flat breads (such as lavash)
- 1 cup (225 g) hummus (store-bought or homemade, page 172)
- 1 cup (55 g) shredded lettuce
- 2 roasted red peppers, sliced
- 2 carrots, peeled and grated
- 2 avocadoes, peeled and sliced
- ¾ cup (35 g) alfalfa sprouts
- Salt and freshly ground pepper, to taste

## DIRECTIONS

Place each tortilla on a clean work surface. Spread equal amounts of hummus in a horizontal line about 1 inch (2.5 cm) from the bottom. Arrange lettuce, red peppers, carrots, avocado, and sprouts on top of hummus.

Season with salt and pepper, and roll up as if rolling sushi or a burrito, tucking in the sides as you go.

Cut in half and serve as a sandwich, or roll tightly and cut into thick slices to be served on a platter. Cut diagonally for a pretty presentation.

**YIELD:** 4 halves, or 16 slices

## SERVING SUGGESTIONS AND VARIATIONS

Add any other veggies you like; consider this version a simple foundation on which you can build.

## DID YOU KNOW?

Lavash is a popular flatbread that hails from Armenia and used also in Turkey, Georgia, and Iran. It dries out pretty quickly but can be perked up with a little water.

Per serving: (one half, including hummus): 158 calories; 6g fat; 6g protein; 21g carbohydrate; 6g dietary fiber; 0mg cholesterol; 15mg sodium.

# PASTA AND GREEN BEANS WITH PEANUT SAUCE

*Oil-free, wheat-free depending on noodles*

Although I feature this peanut sauce to accompany a stir-fry, it was worth repeating for this dish, as it's perfect for a children's party. Kids love peanut butter, and they love long noodles covered in peanut butter even more!

- 8 ounces (225 g) long pasta (udon, rice noodles, angel hair, or spaghetti all work well)
- 8 ounces (225 g) fresh green beans, ends trimmed
- 7 tablespoons (105 ml) water, divided
- ½-inch (1 cm) piece fresh ginger, minced
- 2 garlic cloves, minced
- ¼ cup (65 g) natural peanut butter
- 2 teaspoons (10 ml) fresh lemon juice
- 2 tablespoons (30 ml) tamari soy sauce
- 2 tablespoons (30 ml) nondairy milk (soy, rice, almond, hazelnut, hemp, or oat)

## DIRECTIONS

Bring a large pot of water to a boil. Cook pasta until al dente. Drain well, and transfer to a large bowl.

Meanwhile, steam, grill, or roast green beans for 7 to 10 minutes, until soft but still crisp.

To make peanut sauce, heat 2 tablespoons (30 ml) water in a small sauté pan over medium heat. When hot, add ginger and garlic. Cook for a minute or two, then stir in peanut butter and remaining 5 tablespoons (75 ml) water. Stir until smooth. Add lemon juice, tamari, and milk, and stir well. To thin out, add more water.

Add peanut sauce to pasta, and toss to coat. If finished product is too sticky, add a splash of oil or water, and toss again. Serve warm or at room temperature.

**YIELD:** 4 servings

## SERVING SUGGESTIONS AND VARIATIONS

Instead of green beans, try snow peas, broccoli, carrots, or asparagus or sauté some extra-firm tofu and add to pasta along with veggies.

Per serving: 340 calories; 10g fat; 14g protein; 49g carbohydrate; 4g dietary fiber; 0mg cholesterol; 594mg sodium.

## KID-TESTED

I just had to include this comment from one of my fabulous testers. Chessa wrote that her two-year-old son, Silas, "is a lunatic for this recipe! He's never shown much interest in green beans, but tonight my mom and I had to keep giving him the ones off our plate! He loved the pasta, too. We will definitely be making this again."

# PEANUT BUTTER AND JELLY COOKIES

These cookies are perfect for a children's party, a treat to send with your kids to school, or for those of us who still love this classic combination.

- 1/3 cup (75 g) nondairy, nonhydrogenated butter (such as Earth Balance)
- 1/2 cup (115 g) packed light brown sugar
- 1/2 cup (130 g) natural peanut butter, creamy or chunky
- 2 tablespoons (30 ml) nondairy milk plus extra, if necessary (soy, rice, almond, hazelnut, hemp, or oat)
- 1 teaspoon (5 ml) vanilla extract
- 1 1/4 cups (160 g) all-purpose or whole-wheat pastry flour
- 3/4 teaspoon baking powder (look for aluminum-free)
- 2 to 3 tablespoons (40 to 60 g) strawberry (or any flavor you prefer) preserves or jam

## DIRECTIONS

Preheat oven to 375°F (190°C, or gas mark 5). Line cookie sheet with parchment paper.

In a large bowl, beat butter, brown sugar, peanut butter, milk, and vanilla extract until creamy. In a smaller bowl, combine flour and baking powder. Add dry ingredients to wet ingredients, and mix until combined. Test batter to make sure you can roll it into balls. If you need extra moisture, add a small amount (1 teaspoon [5 ml]) nondairy milk.

Roll batter into 1-inch (2.5 cm) balls, and place 2 inches (5 cm) apart on cookie sheet. Use your thumb to make a well in the center of each cookie, flattening each ball as you go but keeping it intact. (The sides may crack as you press into the center. I find it works well to hold the dough ball with one hand while you press into the center with the other, and then patch as needed.)

Using a 1/4-teaspoon measuring spoon to measure your preserves, fill well in each cookie with preserves. Bake for 10 to 11 minutes. Remove from oven, and let cool on pan for 2 minutes before transferring cookies to a cooling rack.

**YIELD:** 2 to 2 1/2 dozen cookies

## COMPASSIONATE COOKS' TIP

Almond butter can be used in place of peanut butter.

Per serving (one cookie): 74 calories; 4g fat; 2g protein; 8g carbohydrate; trace dietary fiber; 0mg cholesterol; 34mg sodium.

**SPRING MENU:** Sunny Day

🍃 Tempeh Pâté  🍃 Cuban Black Bean Soup  🍃 Panini with Lemon-Basil Pesto
🍃 Arborio Rice with Roasted Red Peppers, Pine Nuts, and Basil
🍃 Blackberry Pecan Crisp

# TEMPEH PÂTÉ

*Wheat-free*

The texture of mashed tempeh is perfect as a *pâté*, which incidentally has nothing to do with duck or goose livers but simply means "paste" in French. The geese and ducks thank you for leaving them off your menu.

- 1 package (8 ounces, or 225 g) tempeh
- ½ cup (115 g) eggless mayonnaise (or more to taste)
- ½ cup (50 g) finely chopped scallions
- ¼ cup (16 g) finely chopped fresh dill
- ½ teaspoon minced fresh ginger
- 2 to 4 tablespoons (30 to 60 ml) tamari soy sauce

## DIRECTIONS

Cut tempeh into 4 squares, and add to steamer basket. Steam for 10 minutes, until its nutty aroma fills the air and it turns a lighter color. Transfer to a bowl, and let cool.

Add steamed tempeh to a food processor, and process to a pastelike consistency. Add mayonnaise, scallions, dill, ginger, and 2 tablespoons (30 ml) tamari. Mix well. Taste and add additional tamari or mayo, as needed.

Serve on crackers or crispy bread.

**YIELD:** 1 ¾ cups (400 g), or 14 (2-tablespoon [30 g]) servings

## FOOD LORE

Pâté simply means "paste," but many people associate it with foie gras, a product made from the unnaturally fattened livers of ducks and geese. Producers force-feed the birds until they're grossly enlarged. Foie gras production is illegal in many countries.

Per serving: 57 calories; 3g fat; 4g protein; 3g carbohydrate; trace dietary fiber; 0mg cholesterol; 289mg sodium.

# CUBAN BLACK BEAN SOUP

*Oil-free, wheat-free, soy-free*

This complex-tasting dish will have your guests wondering how many hours you toiled in the kitchen. Keep them guessing. Only you will know it took no time at all!

- 2 tablespoons (30 ml) water, for sautéing

- 2 medium-size yellow onions, chopped

- 3 garlic cloves, minced

- 2 red bell peppers, chopped, plus 1 finely diced, for garnish (optional)

- 4 cans (15 ounces, or 420 g, each) black beans, rinsed and drained (or 6 cups [1030 g] from scratch)

- 3 medium-size ripe bananas, peeled and sliced

- 1 tablespoon (6 g) ground cumin

- 1 teaspoon (2 g) ground ginger

- 2 tablespoons (30 ml) hot pepper sauce (or to taste)

- 2 cans (15 ounces, or 420 g, each) lite coconut milk

- 4 cups (940 ml) vegetable stock (store-bought or homemade, page 213)

- Salt, to taste

- ½ cup (115 g) nondairy sour cream or Cashew Sour Cream (page 51), for garnish (optional)

## DIRECTIONS

Place water in a soup pot, and heat over medium-high heat. Add onions, garlic, and chopped red pepper. Cook until onion is transparent, about 5 minutes.

Stir in black beans. Add bananas, cumin, ginger, and hot pepper sauce. Stir and cook until fruit softens. Pour in coconut milk and vegetable stock. Bring to a boil over medium heat. Reduce heat to low, and simmer until liquid reduces, about 45 minutes.

Place soup, in batches, into a blender or use an immersion blender in the soup pot and blend until smooth. Season to taste with salt.

Serve hot, garnished with dollop of nondairy sour cream and sprinkled with finely diced red bell pepper, if desired.

**YIELD:** 6 to 8 servings

Per serving: 386 calories; 14g fat; 16g protein; 51g carbohydrate; 14g dietary fiber; 0mg cholesterol; 1319mg sodium.

## COMPASSIONATE COOKS' TIP

Rinse and drain the beans first or your soup will be too thin.

# PANINI WITH LEMON-BASIL PESTO

*Soy-free*

Fortunately, you don't need a panini maker to create this delicious hot sandwich.
To mimic the appearance of a sandwich pressed in one, place a baking sheet, with a
heavy can on top, on top of the sandwich as it cooks in the skillet. You can also use a
tabletop or indoor grill.

## FOR PESTO:

- 2 cups (80 g) loosely packed fresh basil leaves
- 2 whole garlic cloves, peeled
- ¼ cup (35 g) pine nuts
- Salt, to taste
- 2 tablespoons (30 ml) olive oil
- 1 to 2 teaspoons (5 to 10 ml) fresh lemon juice (or to taste)

## FOR PANINI:

- 2 medium-size roasted red bell peppers, cut lengthwise into slices
- 3 zucchini squash, sliced and roasted or grilled
- 1 medium-size red onion, sliced
- 1 or 2 medium-size tomatoes, sliced
- 1 ripe avocado, peeled and sliced
- 8 large slices Italian bread, such as ciabatta
- 2 tablespoons (30 ml) balsamic vinegar
- Salt and pepper, to taste (optional)
- Olive oil, for brushing

## DIRECTIONS

To make the pesto, combine basil, garlic, pine nuts, and salt in food processor or blender. Mix until smooth. Add oil and lemon juice; process until smooth. If not using immediately, store tightly covered in refrigerator for up to 2 days.

To make panini, divide bell peppers, squash, onion, tomatoes, and avocado evenly among 4 slices of bread. Drizzle each with vinegar, spread on some pesto (about 2 tablespoons [30 g]), and sprinkle on salt and pepper, if desired.

Top each with remaining bread slices, lightly brush outside with a little olive oil, and press in a panini maker or place on tabletop grill. Press until lightly browned and hot. You also could cook the lightly oiled sandwiches in a skillet instead of grilling them. Serve immediately.

**YIELD:** 4 panini, or servings

Per serving: 359 calories; 21g fat; 9g protein; 38g carbohydrate; 7g dietary fiber; 0mg cholesterol; 251mg sodium.

# ARBORIO RICE WITH ROASTED RED PEPPERS, PINE NUTS, AND BASIL

*Wheat-free, soy-free*

This is a simple, delicious way to use Arborio rice, instead of using it in risotto—though the results are pretty similar. This tasty dish comes alive with the freshness from the herbs, the sweetness from the roasted peppers, and the crunch from the pine nuts!

- 4 cups (940 ml) vegetable stock or water
- 1 ½ cups (285 g) Arborio rice
- 2 tablespoons (30 ml) olive oil
- 4 large garlic cloves, finely chopped
- 3 roasted red bell peppers, sliced lengthwise
- ¼ cup (25 g) pitted black olives, preferably kalamata
- ¼ cup (25 g) pitted green olives
- ½ cup (20 g) packed chopped fresh basil
- ¼ cup (15 g) packed chopped fresh parsley
- Salt and freshly ground pepper, to taste
- ½ cup (65 g) toasted pine nuts (see page 135)
- Cherry tomatoes, for garnish (optional)

## DIRECTIONS

Bring stock to a boil in a large-size pot. Add rice, and boil until tender but firm to the bite (al dente), 12 to 15 minutes, stirring a few times. Drain well and set aside.

Meanwhile, heat oil in a large-size skillet over medium heat. Add garlic and cook, stirring constantly, for 2 minutes. Add bell peppers and black and green olives and cook, stirring constantly, for 2 minutes. Add cooked rice, basil, parsley, salt, and pepper. Cook, tossing and stirring to combine, for 2 minutes. Remove from heat. Toss in pine nuts.

Serve warm or at room temperature, garnished with the cherry tomatoes, if desired.

**YIELD:** 8 servings

Per serving: 304 calories; 11g fat; 8g protein; 45g carbohydrate; 3g dietary fiber; 0mg cholesterol; 895mg sodium.

## COMPASSIONATE COOKS' TIP

You can store this dish in the fridge in a covered container for up to 3 days. However, by the third day, the nuts will have lost some of their crunch. Serve at room temperature or reheat over low heat.

# BLACKBERRY PECAN CRISP

In season from May to August, blackberries are rich in vitamins A and C and are best when eaten right off the vine. Short of that, store them in the fridge for no more than two days. Alternatively, store them in your belly, by means of this delicious crisp!

- 4 cups (580 g) fresh blackberries, rinsed
- 4 tablespoons (30 g) all-purpose or whole wheat pastry flour, divided
- 4 tablespoons (56 g) nondairy, nonhydrogenated butter (such as Earth Balance), divided (1 tablespoon [14 g] cut into bits, 3 tablespoons [42 g] melted)
- ¼ cup (20 g) rolled oats
- ½ cup (55 g) pecans
- Pinch of salt
- 2 tablespoons (30 g) light brown sugar
- 2 tablespoon s (25 g) granulated sugar
- 1 teaspoon (5 ml) vanilla extract
- Vanilla nondairy ice cream, for accompaniment

## DIRECTIONS

Preheat oven to 350°F (180°C, or gas mark 4).

Gently toss blackberries in 1 tablespoon (8 g) flour. Place in a glass baking dish. Dot with 1 tablespoon (14 g) chopped nondairy butter.

In a food processor or mixing bowl, combine oats, pecans (roughly chop pecans first if you're not using a food processor), remaining 3 tablespoons (22 g) flour, salt, brown sugar, granulated sugar, remaining 3 table-spoons (42 g) melted nondairy butter, and vanilla.

Sprinkle topping over fruit, and bake for 15 to 20 minutes, or until crispy and golden brown on top.

Serve warm with vanilla nondairy ice cream.

**YIELD:** 8 servings

## SERVING SUGGESTIONS AND VARIATIONS

Blackberries pair beautifully with peaches. Add 1 cup (170 g) sliced peaches to the blackberries for added color and flavor.

Per serving: 179 calories; 11g fat; 2g protein; 21g carbohy-drate; 5g dietary fiber; 0mg cholesterol; 18mg sodium.

**SUMMER MENU:** Over the Rainbow

● Muhammara (Roasted Red Pepper and Walnut Spread)
● Crowd-Pleasing Pasta with Tomatoes and Artichokes
● Boston Baked Beans ● Fresh Fruit Salad ● Sparkling Pineapple Juice

# MUHAMMARA (ROASTED RED PEPPER AND WALNUT SPREAD)

*\*Soy-free, oil-free, wheat-free depending on bread*

This may very well be my favorite spread. Although I've modified it somewhat over the years, this recipe first came to me by way of my friend Laurie Judd Young, and I've been impressing people with it ever since.

- 2 to 3 whole roasted red bell peppers (fresh or from a jar)
- ²/₃ cup (75 g) bread crumbs (see below to make your own)
- 1 cup (120 g) walnuts, raw or toasted
- 4 large whole garlic cloves, peeled
- ¹/₂ teaspoon salt
- 1 tablespoon (15 ml) fresh lemon juice
- 2 teaspoons (13 g) agave nectar
- 1 teaspoon (2 g) ground cumin
- ¹/₄ teaspoon red pepper flakes (or more to taste)

## DIRECTIONS

In a blender or food processor, combine peppers, bread crumbs, walnuts, garlic cloves, salt, lemon juice, agave nectar, cumin, and red pepper flakes. Purée to a smooth consistency. Scrape down the sides of blender to make sure all ingredients are thoroughly combined. Season to taste, tweaking as necessary.

**YIELD:** 1 cup (225 g), or 8 (2-tablespoon [30 g]) servings

## SERVING SUGGESTIONS AND VARIATIONS

Most recipes for muhammara call for olive oil; I don't think it's necessary, but feel free to drizzle some in while puréeing the ingredients. Serve with pita triangles, fresh bread, crackers, chips, carrots, mushrooms, cucumber, or other raw veggies. Make it the day before serving to allow the flavors to mingle.

## COMPASSIONATE COOKS' TIPS

- See page 281 for directions on roasting your own peppers.
- To make bread crumbs: In a 300°F (150°C, or gas mark 2) oven, cook some bread until crispy but not browned. Let cool. Add to food processor until it is reduced to crumbs. Add Italian herbs such as dried oregano, thyme, basil, marjoram, rosemary, and black pepper.

Per serving: 151 calories; 9g fat; 5g protein; 13g carbohydrate; 2g dietary fiber; 0mg cholesterol; 213mg sodium.

# CROWD-PLEASING PASTA WITH TOMATOES AND ARTICHOKES

*Soy-free*

An easy dish for feeding a large crowd, this recipe comes from my wonderful mother-in-law, Mary Jane Goudreau, who has been making it for years. It's a perfect example of a familiar dish that many people would prepare without calling it "vegan."

- 16 ounces (455 g) penne or whole-wheat penne pasta
- 2 tablespoons (30 ml) olive oil
- 3 garlic cloves, finely chopped
- 1 can (26 ounces, or 735 g) diced tomatoes
- 2 tablespoons (32 g) tomato paste
- 1 can (15 ounces, or 420 g) artichokes (with or without olive oil)
- 1 tablespoon (3 g) chopped fresh basil
- ½ cup (50 g) sliced black olives
- Salt and pepper, to taste

## DIRECTIONS

Cook penne in boiling water until al dente. Drain right before serving.

In a large sauté pan, heat oil. Cook garlic for 2 to 3 minutes. Do not brown. Add canned tomatoes and tomato paste. Heat to near boiling.

Add artichokes, basil, and black olives. Season with salt and pepper.

Serve penne in a large bowl, pouring sauce over all and mixing together. Or serve penne in individual bowls with sauce on the side, so each person can take as much as desired.

**YIELD:** 6 servings

## SERVING SUGGESTIONS AND VARIATIONS

* Serve with a green salad and a loaf of Italian or Mediterranean bread.
* Replace the can of diced tomatoes, tomato paste, and basil with a 26-ounce (735 g) jar of tomato sauce.

Per serving: 379 calories; 7g fat; 12g protein; 67g carbohydrate; 5g dietary fiber; 0mg cholesterol; 185mg sodium.

## DID YOU KNOW?

There are over 350 different shapes of pasta. Other suggestions for this dish besides penne would be farfalle, fusilli, gemelli, rotini, and ziti.

# BOSTON BAKED BEANS

*Oil-free if using water for sautéing, wheat-free, soy-free*

This traditional favorite provides hearty fare any time of the year.

- 1 tablespoon (15 ml) canola oil or 2 tablespoons (30 ml) water
- 1 large-size onion, finely chopped
- 3 cans (15 ounces, or 420 g, each) navy beans, drained and rinsed
- 1/3 cup (115 g) molasses
- 2 tablespoons (30 g) light or dark brown sugar
- 1 teaspoon (3 g) dry mustard
- 1 teaspoon (2 g) ground ginger
- Dash of liquid smoke (optional)
- 1/2 teaspoon salt (or to taste)
- 1/4 cup (60 ml) water

## DIRECTIONS

Preheat oven to 350°F (180°C, or gas mark 4).

Heat oil in a sauté pan until hot. Add onion, stirring and sautéing until softened and browning, 5 to 7 minutes.

In a 2- or 3-quart (2 or 3.5 L) baking dish, combine beans, cooked onions, molasses, brown sugar, dry mustard, ginger, liquid smoke (if using), salt, and water. Cover and bake for 30 to 40 minutes.

**YIELD:** 6 to 8 servings

Per serving: 212 calories; 2g fat; 9g protein; 40g carbohydrate; 6g dietary fiber; 0mg cholesterol; 141mg sodium.

## DID YOU KNOW?

The navy bean was used as standard provision in the U.S. Navy. Go legumes!

## FOOD LORE

In colonial days, a favorite Boston food was beans baked in molasses for several hours. Back then, Boston was awash in molasses, being part of the "triangular trade" in which slaves in the Caribbean grew sugar cane to be shipped to Boston, to be made into rum, to be sent to West Africa to buy more slaves to send to the West Indies. The Great Molasses Flood of 1919 occurred when a tank, holding molasses intended for rum, exploded, killing twenty-one people.

# FRESH FRUIT SALAD

*Oil-free, wheat-free*

Simple as can be, this salad delights with fresh fruit, a little sweetener, and vanilla, which will be the mystery ingredient that will baffle your friends.

- 2 pints (580 g) organic strawberries, halved
- 1 pint (290 g) fresh blueberries
- 1 cup (145 g) organic raspberries
- 2 kiwifruit, peeled and sliced
- 2 bananas, sliced
- 2 cups (300 g) seedless grapes, halved
- 1 container (8 ounces, or 225 g) plain or vanilla nondairy yogurt
- 2 teaspoons (10 ml) lemon juice
- 1 teaspoon (4 g) granulated sugar
- 1 teaspoon (5 ml) vanilla extract

## DIRECTIONS

In a large salad bowl, combine strawberries, blueberries, raspberries, kiwifruit, bananas, and grapes.

In a small bowl, combine yogurt, lemon juice, sugar, and vanilla, and mix well. Add to fruit bowl and stir gently to combine, using a rubber spatula.

**YIELD:** 8 servings

Per serving: 140 calories; 1g fat; 3g protein; 33g carbohydrate; 6g dietary fiber; 0mg cholesterol; 22mg sodium.

## TESTING ON HUMANS

Keep in mind that unless you're very close with the friends coming over to enjoy your gourmet meal and they know you'll be testing on them, I highly recommend serving dishes that you have made at least once. It is always a good idea to know whether something works before trying it on your guests.

And remember these words of wisdom: First, many of these dishes may take a little extra time in the kitchen, but they are worth the effort. Second, it is your intentions that guests appreciate. They do not expect perfection—and neither should you.

# SPARKLING PINEAPPLE JUICE

*Oil-free, wheat-free, soy-free*

There are so many fancy juices and sparkling sodas on the market these days, but here's a quick one to make on your own.

- 20 ounces (570 ml) pineapple juice
- ½ cup (120 ml) sparkling mineral water
- 4 pineapple chunks
- ½ cup (75 g) blueberries
- Mint sprigs

## DIRECTIONS

Combine juice, mineral water, and pineapple chunks in a blender, and blend until smooth. Pour into chilled glasses, and add a few blueberries and a mint sprig.

**YIELD:** 4 servings

Per serving: 168 calories; trace fat; 2g protein; 43g carbohydrate; 2g dietary fiber; 0mg cholesterol; 5mg sodium.

## FOOD LORE

Native to Brazil and Paraguay, the pineapple reached the Caribbean where Columbus discovered it in the Indies and brought it back with him to Spain. Introduced to Hawaii in 1813, pineapples are produced worldwide primarily by Thailand, Brazil, and the Philippines.

## COMPASSIONATE COOKS' TIP

If you're not serving this right away or if you'll serve it over the course of a few hours, blend everything except the mineral water. When you pour the drink into individual glasses, top each with some sparkling water. That way, each serving stays fresh and bubbly.

# HOMEMADE HUMMUS

*Oil-free if using water for thinning, wheat-free, soy-free*

Hummus is one of the easiest spreads to make from scratch, and it is
a heap cheaper than the store-bought stuff.

- 2 cans (15 ounces, or 420 g, each) chickpeas, drained and rinsed
- Juice from ½ lemon (or more as needed)
- 2 tablespoons (30 g) tahini (sesame seed butter)
- 2 or 3 whole garlic cloves, peeled
- ½ teaspoon cumin
- Water or olive oil, for thinning out spread
- Salt, to taste
- Paprika, for garnish (optional)

## DIRECTIONS

Place chickpeas in a food processor or blender with
lemon juice, tahini, garlic, and cumin. Process until very
smooth, 1 to 2 minutes. Add a little water, olive oil, or
lemon juice to thin out, if desired. Salt to taste. Scrape
into a serving bowl and sprinkle with paprika, if desired.

**YIELD:** 2 cups (450 g), or 16 (2-tablespoon [30 g])
servings

## SERVING SUGGESTIONS AND VARIATIONS

* Add roasted garlic instead of raw. Add ¼ roasted red
  pepper. For extra spice, add minced jalapeño pepper or
  a pinch of cayenne.
* Garnish the plate or bowl of hummus with whole chickpeas and parsley.
* Serve as a dip for flat bread (such as pita) or for fresh
  vegetables such as tomatoes, cucumbers, carrots, and
  celery. It also goes surprisingly well with tortilla chips
  and as the replacement for cheese in No-Queso Quesadillas (page 154).

Per serving: 206 calories; 4g fat; 11g protein; 33g carbohydrate; 9g dietary fiber; 0mg cholesterol; 15mg sodium.

## FOOD LORE

One of the oldest known prepared foods, hummus has
been used in Middle Eastern and Mediterranean cuisine
for thousands of years. Plato and Socrates even sang
its praises! In Arabic, the word *hummus* simply means
"chickpea," a healthful legume and one of the earliest
crops cultivated in Mesopotamia.

# POTATO AND SEED SPREAD (A.K.A. STUFFING)

*Oil-free, wheat-free depending on flour*

This recipe, for which my friend Alka Chandna is famous, is a versatile one. It can be served as a spread for crackers or bread, a stuffing to round out a hearty meal, or a filling for knishes or pierogi. One of my brilliant testers suggested adding curry powder and ginger, making it perfect to prepare as an East Indian pakora. As a dressing or stuffing, it reminds me of one my nanny used to make. As a filling, it reminds me of the pierogi my mom regularly served.

- ½ cup (75 g) raw sunflower seeds
- ¼ cup (36 g) raw sesame seeds
- 2 cups (250 g) flour (see note below)
- ½ cup (100 g) nutritional yeast flakes
- ½ teaspoon dried thyme
- ½ teaspoon dried basil
- ½ teaspoon dried oregano
- ½ teaspoon dried savory
- ½ teaspoon salt
- 1 teaspoon (2 g) freshly ground pepper
- 2 large-size potatoes, peeled and boiled or steamed
- 1 medium-size yellow onion, coarsely chopped
- 3 tablespoons (45 ml) freshly squeezed lemon juice
- 3 tablespoons (45 ml) tamari soy sauce
- 1 ½ cups (355 ml) very hot water

## DIRECTIONS

Preheat oven to 350°F (180°C, or gas mark 4). Lightly oil one 9 x 9-inch (23 x 23 cm) pan.

Using a coffee or seed grinder (every kitchen needs this tool to grind flaxseed to get your omega-3 fatty acids!), grind the sunflower and sesame seeds into a coarse powder.

Transfer to a large-size bowl, and add flour, nutritional yeast, thyme, basil, oregano, savory, salt, and pepper.

In the large bowl of your food processor, purée potatoes, onion, lemon juice, and tamari until smooth.

Combine potato mixture, dry ingredients, and hot water. Mix well and pour into prepared pan. Bake for 50 minutes.

**YIELD:** 20 servings

## SERVING SUGGESTIONS AND VARIATIONS

Alka's original recipe calls for a combination of brown rice flour and soy flour, and they work well. Frankly, I've tried it with a number of different flours, including whole-wheat pastry flour (regular whole wheat would make it too dense), oat flour, and all-purpose flour, and they all work well.

Per serving: 113 calories; 3g fat; 6g protein; 16g carbohydrate; 3g dietary fiber; 0mg cholesterol; 206mg sodium.

# SOUTHWESTERN TOFU BURGERS

*Oil-free if broiled*

I created this recipe in order to replicate a favorite store-bought tofu burger of mine, and I'm thrilled to have fulfilled my quest! This version is much less expensive and contains less fat.

- 1 package (16 ounces, or 455 g) extra-firm tofu, frozen and thawed
- 2 tablespoons (14 g) ground flaxseed
- 6 tablespoons (90 ml) water, plus extra for binding
- 1 1/2 cups (165 g) bread crumbs or cracker meal
- 1 red bell pepper, finely diced
- 1 cup (130 g) corn kernels (roasted corn kernels are fantastic)
- 1/4 cup (65 g) vegetarian refried beans
- 3 tablespoons (48 g) tomato paste
- 1 teaspoon (2 g) cumin
- 2 teaspoons (4 g) chili powder
- 1 teaspoon (2 g) onion powder
- 1/2 teaspoon smoked paprika
- 1/4 teaspoon cayenne pepper
- Salt, to taste
- Canola oil, for frying

## DIRECTIONS

Squeeze out water from thawed tofu, and crumble into large-size bowl. Leave some large chunks, but crumble enough so it will bind well with other ingredients.

Combine ground flaxseed and 6 tablespoons (90 ml) water in a small food processor bowl or blender, and blend until thick and viscous. Scrape down the sides at least once while blending, to make sure seeds and water thoroughly mix. I usually blend for 2 minutes.

Add flaxseed mixture to tofu, along with bread crumbs, bell pepper, corn, refried beans, tomato paste, cumin, chili powder, onion powder, paprika, cayenne, and salt. Combine everything using a wooden spoon, and then your hands, to feel the consistency. Make sure spices are thoroughly combined and that you can create patties from the mixture. Taste and add salt, as necessary. Add water to help bind the patties, as needed.

Using your hands, form mixture into patties. In a sauté pan lightly coated with oil, fry over medium heat for 5 to 7 minutes on each side, until lightly browned and crispy. Be careful to keep patties intact.

**YIELD:** 10 to 12 servings

## SERVING SUGGESTIONS AND VARIATIONS

For an oil-free version, broil burgers in oven for 3 minutes on each side.

## DID YOU KNOW?

The key to creating a chewy, satisfying tofu burger is using tofu frozen for at least 48 hours and thawed for 6-8 hours. Squeeze out water and use in any recipe.

Per serving: 114 calories; 3g fat; 6g protein; 16g carbohydrate; 2g dietary fiber; 0mg cholesterol; 178mg sodium.

# NOODLE KUGEL

*Wheat-free depending on pasta*

Sometimes translated as "pudding" or "casserole," kugel is traditional Jewish fare, served as a side dish or dessert. There are savory kugels and sweet kugels—such as the one featured here—and a huge variation within each.

Note, however, that the recipe below is not kosher for Passover. To make it kosher, replace graham cracker crumbs with matzoh cake meal and use a rice- or quinoa-based pasta. Some Jewish people do not eat rice or quinoa during Passover, so be sure to double-check before you bring this dish to a Passover meal.

- 8 ounces (225 g) eggless egg noodles
- ½ cup (112 g) nondairy, nonhydrogenated butter (such as Earth Balance), melted
- ¾ cup (175 g) nondairy sour cream
- ¾ cup (185 g) unsweetened applesauce
- 12 ounces (340 g) firm tofu, crumbled (not silken)
- ¾ cup (150 g) granulated sugar
- 1 teaspoon (5 ml) vanilla extract
- ¼ cup (35 g) raisins
- ¼ cup (30 g) graham cracker crumbs (optional)
- 1 teaspoon (2 g) ground cinnamon (or to taste)

## DIRECTIONS

Preheat oven to 350°F (180°C, or gas mark 4). Lightly oil a 9 x 13-inch (23 x 33 cm) or 9 x 9-inch (23 x 23 cm) baking dish.

Bring a large pot of water to a boil. Cook noodles in boiling water until al dente, about 7 minutes. Drain.

In a large bowl, combine melted butter, sour cream, applesauce, crumbled tofu, sugar, and vanilla. Stir in cooked noodles and raisins.

Spread graham cracker crumbs on bottom of prepared dish, if desired. Pour noodle mixture over crumbs. Sprinkle top with cinnamon.

Bake uncovered for 35 to 40 minutes.

**YIELD:** 12 servings

Per serving: 325 calories; 14g fat; 8g protein; 43g carbohydrate; 2g dietary fiber; 0mg cholesterol; 151mg sodium.

## DID YOU KNOW?

Although much pasta is vegan, not all of it is kosher. If you're looking for kosher pasta, try a brand such as DeBoles Organic Eggless Ribbon Style Pasta, made with Jerusalem artichoke flour. Check out www.deboles.com for a list of products and a store locator.

## COMPASSIONATE COOKS' TIP

If you cannot find graham cracker crumbs, buy graham crackers and crumble them into a meal.

# SPRING ROLLS WITH PEANUT DIPPING SAUCE

*Oil-free, wheat-free*

These fresh spring rolls make great appetizers, finger food, or a light meal and should not be made too far in advance—four to five hours at most.

- 3 ounces (85 g) "bean thread" (also called "cellophane") noodles
- 1 package (16 ounces, or 455 g) extra-firm tofu, cut into long, thin strips
- 10 rice paper wrappers
- ½ cup (55 g) peeled and julienned carrots
- ½ to 1 cup (60 to 120 g) julienned seeded cucumber
- 24 mint leaves, whole or chopped
- 24 basil leaves, whole or chopped

## DIRECTIONS

Cook noodles in boiling water 3-5 minutes. Transfer to colander and rinse with cold water. Drain well and set aside. You can use tofu as is or sauté it in sesame oil.

Fill a large bowl with warm water and place next to rolling area, along with filling ingredients. If the noodles have become sticky, rinse briefly under cold water and drain well before beginning. Work on 2 wrappers at a time. Dip each in warm water for a few seconds, then set on a clean, dry work surface. Let sit for about 1 minute to become more pliable.

Lay a small handful of noodles across bottom third of each wrapper, leaving a little space empty at each end. Add remaining filling ingredients on top of noodles. Roll wrapper firmly and tightly over filling, tucking in ends as you roll. Cover your finished rolls with a barely damp towel as you roll more. Cut in half and serve with dipping sauce.

**YIELD:** 20 rolls, or servings

Per serving: 37 calories; 1g fat; 2g protein; 4g carbohydrate; 1g dietary fiber; 0mg cholesterol; 84mg sodium.

## PEANUT DIPPING SAUCE
*Oil-free, wheat-free*

- ½ cup (130 g) natural peanut butter
- ¼ cup (60 ml) water
- 3 tablespoons (25 g) crushed toasted peanuts (not necessary if you use chunky peanut butter)
- 2 to 3 tablespoons (30 to 45 ml) tamari soy sauce
- 2 tablespoons (30 ml) lime juice
- 1 garlic clove, minced
- 1 tablespoon (6 g) minced ginger

## DIRECTIONS

Blend all ingredients, tweaking to find right balance of flavors and right consistency for dipping.

**YIELD:** 1 ½ cups (340 g), or 24 (2-tablespoon [30 g]) servings

Per serving: 82 calories; 7g fat; 4g protein; 3g carbohydrate; 1g dietary fiber; 0mg cholesterol; 302mg sodium.

# CARAMELIZED TEMPEH SHAWARMAS

Think of shawarmas as Middle Eastern burritos. Fill them with whatever yummy ingredients you like. Meatless "chicken" works fantastically, and purists won't know the difference—though the chickens will.

## FOR THE FILLING:

- 1 package (8 ounces, or 225 g) tempeh
- Olive or canola oil, for sautéing
- 2 tablespoons (30 ml) tamari soy sauce (or more, as needed)
- 2 tablespoons (30 ml) real maple syrup (or more, as needed)
- 2 tomatoes, chopped
- 2 cucumbers, peeled and diced
- 1 red onion, thinly sliced
- 3 tablespoons (12 g) minced fresh parsley

## FOR THE SAUCE:

- ¼ cup (60 g) tahini
- 2 whole garlic cloves, peeled
- 3 tablespoons (45 ml) lemon juice
- ¼ cup (60 ml) water (or as needed)
- Salt, to taste
- Lavash bread or large tortillas
- Hot sauce or any red chile paste

## DIRECTIONS

To make the filling, cut the block of tempeh into strips. Steam for 10 minutes. (Don't skip this step. It tenderizes the tempeh.) In a sauté pan filled with just enough oil to coat pan, fry tempeh until it turns golden brown. Flip to brown on both sides. Add tamari and maple syrup, and continue to cook. As tempeh becomes sticky and caramelized, add more tamari or maple syrup, as needed.

Meanwhile, in a bowl, combine tomatoes, cucumbers, onion, and parsley.

To make the sauce, in a food processor or blender, combine tahini, garlic cloves, lemon juice, and enough water to make a smooth sauce, and blend until smooth, adding more water as needed to thin out, and adding salt or more lemon juice to taste. Sauce should be thick but pourable.

Cut lavash into thirds (one third for each shawarma) or use large tortillas. In a hot skillet or over flame of gas stove burner, slightly warm one lavash or tortilla for a few seconds to soften. Lay lavash on a flat surface and layer ingredients as you would for a burrito.

Starting one-third of the way from each edge, spread a thin layer of hot sauce, add tempeh and tomato/onion/cucumber mix, then drizzle on tahini sauce. Roll up like a burrito, tucking in the sides as you go, and place in a hot skillet, seam side down. Cook for a minute or so, rolling until all sides become lightly browned. Serve warm or at room temperature.

**YIELD:** 4 servings

Per serving: 287 calories; 13g fat; 17g protein; 32g carbohydrate; 4g dietary fiber; 0mg cholesterol; 536mg sodium.

# ENGLISH MUFFIN PIZZAS

*Oil-free*

Growing up, we made these every Friday night, with each person in the family requiring a unique, personal variation: a little more sauce, a little less oregano, sauce before cheese, cheese before sauce. These easy-to-make treats are a fun addition to any party—for children or adults.

- 12 English muffin halves (6 English muffins)
- 1 package (10 ounces, or 280 g) nondairy mozzarella cheese (such as Follow Your Heart brand), grated
- 1 jar (25 ounces, or 700 g) pasta or pizza sauce
- Toppings such as vegetarian pepperoni, fresh tomato slices, red onion, mushrooms, or bell peppers
- 2 tablespoons (6 g) dried oregano

## DIRECTIONS

Preheat oven to 425°F (220°C, or gas mark 7).

In toaster, toast muffin halves until golden brown. Once toasted, place on cookie sheet or baking pan.

In my family, there was a great debate over whether to add cheese before sauce, or vice versa. You will have to work that out within your own family.

Distribute cheese evenly on top of muffin halves. Add sauce and any other toppings you desire. Sprinkle on oregano, and bake for 8 to 9 minutes, until cheese melts. If you can watch very closely, you can bake pizzas under a broiler, which takes only 2 to 3 minutes.

Cut into quarters for appetizers or leave whole for a meal.

**YIELD:** 12 servings

Per serving (excluding toppings): 355 calories; 15g fat; 10g protein; 53g carbohydrate; 1g dietary fiber; 0mg cholesterol; 2391mg sodium.

## FOOD LORE

Though English muffins and crumpets are related, neither should be confused with an American muffin, which is a sweet-tasting cake. English muffins feel and taste more like bread, are baked on both sides, and must be split in two before they can be toasted. Crumpets, with their distinctive holes on the top, are more pancake-like and cooked only on one side.

# QUINOA TABBOULEH

*Wheat-free, soy-free*

Tabbouleh is traditionally made with bulgur wheat (peeled and crushed wheat), but this version takes advantage of the fabulously nutritious supergrain quinoa.

- 1 cup (175 g) quinoa
- 2 ½ cups (590 ml) water or stock
- 4 scallions, finely chopped
- 1 cucumber (peeling optional), seeded, and finely diced
- 2 large-size tomatoes, finely diced
- 2 garlic cloves, minced or pressed
- ½ cup (30 g) finely chopped flat-leaf parsley
- ¼ cup (25 g) finely chopped fresh mint
- ⅓ cup (80 ml) fresh lemon juice (or to taste)
- 1 teaspoon (6 g) salt (or to taste)
- ¼ cup (60 ml) olive oil
- ¼ teaspoon freshly ground pepper

## DIRECTIONS

Rinse quinoa using small strainer, to remove a natural substance called saponin, which protects the plant from birds and tends to have a bitter taste. It is easily rinsed off before cooking.

In a medium-size pot, add quinoa to water and bring to a boil. Lower heat and simmer for 10 to 15 minutes. When all water is absorbed, quinoa is done. Simmer for a few more minutes, if necessary. If excess water remains, turn off heat and let water soak into the grain. If you still have excess water after that, drain off. Let cool.

In large mixing bowl, combine scallions, cucumber, tomatoes, garlic, parsley, mint, lemon juice, salt, and olive oil. Once quinoa cools, add to bowl, mixing well and tweaking salt, lemon juice, and oil to get right consistency and desired taste.

**YIELD:** 4 to 6 servings

## SERVING SUGGESTIONS AND VARIATIONS

Add any or all of these vegetables: finely chopped celery, green or red bell peppers, or chopped olives. Also try adding 1 cup (240 g) cooked chickpeas or a pinch of cinnamon. Serve this wonderful summer salad or side dish with pita bread or crackers.

Per serving: 212 calories; 11g fat; 5g protein; 26g carbohydrate; 3g dietary fiber; 0mg cholesterol; 372mg sodium.

## DID YOU KNOW?

Nutritionally, quinoa is considered a super grain. A complete protein, it contains 11 grams of protein per ½ cup (95 g), offers more iron than other grains, and contains high levels of potassium and riboflavin, as well as B6, niacin, and thiamin. For variety and fantastic color, look for black or red quinoa.

# HOST A CONSCIOUSNESS-RAISING FILM NIGHT

Many sophisticated films explore our relationship with and exploitation of nonhuman animals. Some of these classic films entertain as they educate, some inspire deep discussion, and some require tissues on hand at all times. Popcorn is optional.

### TIES THAT BIND

Two beautiful films that illustrate the bond between humans and animals are *Umberto D.*, by the great Italian neorealist director Vittorio De Sica, which tells the story of a man whose devotion to his dog saves his life, and *Princess Mononoke*, the Japanese anime masterpiece by Hayao Miyazaki, which centers around a strong and fearless princess whose beloved companions are the wolves who raised her.

### STRONG AND SENSITIVE

The depiction of the "sensitive criminal" is characterized in Elia Kazan's *On the Waterfront* and Jim Jarmusch's *Ghost Dog: The Way of the Samurai*, both of which feature loner protagonists who find solace only in the homing pigeons they raise. This idea is epitomized in John Frankenheimer's *Birdman of Alcatraz*, which dramatizes the true story of convict Robert Stroud, who finds redemption through his relationship with birds.

### PARALLELS OF EXPLOITATION

Three classic French films explore the links between human and animal exploitation. *Au Hasard Balthazar* is an exquisite film by Robert Bresson, whose titular main character, a donkey, is as much a victim of human cruelty as is his human counterpart, Marie. In *Eyes without a Face (Les Yeux sans Visage)*, young women kidnapped by a mad surgeon become research subjects, much like the animals he keeps in his basement. *Fantastic Planet (La Planete Sauvage)* is a smart, animated science-fiction film that takes place on a planet inhabited by a race of giants who keep humans as pets.

### WHAT GOES AROUND COMES AROUND

Our violence toward animals affects us both psychically and socially, and is explored in a number of fine films. The main character in Charles Burnett's 1977 treasure, *Killer of Sheep*, is numb with despair from working in a slaughterhouse. The violent world of dog fighting devastates many lives in *Amores Perros*. Finally, humans get a taste of their own medicine in *28 Days Later*, when research chimpanzees infected with "rage" are released from a laboratory, causing an outbreak of this deadly and contagious virus.

Advanced Preparation Required

# MUSHROOM PECAN BURGERS

*Wheat-free*

Even self-described mushroom haters are surprised by how much they love these burgers! Because there's no use trying to improve perfection, I just had to include this recipe, a slightly modified version of Dreena Burton's from *The Everyday Vegan*.

- 1 1/2 pounds (685 g) cremini mushrooms
- 1/2 cup (30 g) fresh parsley
- 2 tablespoons (30 ml) olive oil, divided
- 2 large-size yellow onions, finely chopped
- 3 large-size garlic cloves, minced
- 1 1/2 to 2 cups (165 to 220 g) bread crumbs or cracker meal
- 3 tablespoons (45 g) tahini
- 2 tablespoons (30 g) hoisin sauce
- 3/4 cup (85 g) toasted pecans or walnuts, chopped
- 3 tablespoons (45 ml) tamari soy sauce
- 1 teaspoon (2 g) dried oregano
- 1/2 teaspoon dried sage
- salt and ground pepper, to taste

## DIRECTIONS

In a food processor, mince mushrooms and parsley. Remove and set aside.

In a sauté pan over medium heat, warm 1 tablespoon (15 ml) olive oil and cook onions and garlic for 5 to 6 minutes. Transfer onion mixture to a large-size bowl, and combine with minced mushrooms and parsley, bread crumbs, tahini, hoisin sauce, chopped nuts, tamari, oregano, sage, salt, and pepper.

Place mixture in refrigerator for at least half an hour. Mixture will be soft, but you should be able to form patties. Add additional bread crumbs or tahini, if needed.

Create patties using your hands. In a sauté pan, warm remaining 1 tablespoon (15 ml) oil, and fry patties over medium heat for 3 to 5 minutes on each side, until lightly browned and crispy. Be careful to keep patties intact.

**YIELD:** 10 to 12 servings

## SERVING SUGGESTIONS AND VARIATIONS

Instead of making patties, put mixture into 5 x 9 x 2-inch (13 x 23 x 5 cm) loaf pan and bake at 350°F (180°C, or gas mark 4) for 20 to 25 minutes.

## DID YOU KNOW?

Hoisin sauce is a sauce used in Chinese cuisine. Traditionally, hoisin sauce is made using sweet potato, but commercial brands usually contain fermented soybeans, garlic, vinegar, and chile peppers.

Per serving: 183 calories; 9g fat; 6g protein; 21g carbohydrate; 2g dietary fiber; 0mg cholesterol; 505mg sodium.

# OVEN-BAKED "FRENCH FRIED" YAMS

*Wheat-free, soy-free*

A delicious and colorful alternative to traditional french fries, these goodies add color and flavor to any meal.

- 4 garnet or jewel yams
- 2 tablespoons (30 ml) olive oil
- 1 teaspoon (2 g) paprika
- 1 teaspoon dried parsley
- ½ teaspoon garlic powder
- ½ teaspoon pepper (or lemon pepper)
- ¼ teaspoon chili powder (optional)
- ¼ teaspoon salt

## DIRECTIONS

Preheat oven to 400°F (200°C, or gas mark 6).
    Cut potatoes into 2-inch (5 cm) "french fries." No need to peel. Make sure they are uniform size.
    In a bowl, toss potatoes with olive oil, paprika, parsley, garlic powder, pepper, chili powder (if using), and salt. Arrange fries on baking sheet in a single layer, evenly spaced.
    Bake for 45 minutes, turning once or twice, until fries are crispy on the outside and tender on the inside. Yams contain more water than yellow potatoes do, so don't expect super crispy "fries." They will be soft but oh-so-delicious.

**YIELD:** 4 to 6 servings

Per serving: 129 calories; 5g fat; 1g protein; 23g carbohydrate; 3g dietary fiber; 0mg cholesterol; 120mg sodium

## DID YOU KNOW?

See page 225 to learn the difference between yams and sweet potatoes.

# QUINOA AND CORN MEDLEY

*Oil-free if omitting drizzle of oil, wheat-free, soy-free*

Quinoa is a highly nutritious grain that was a staple of the ancient Incan diet. It has a wonderful nutty flavor and a light, fluffy texture.

- 4 cups (940 ml) water or vegetable stock (store-bought or homemade, page 213), plus 2 tablespoons (30 ml) water, for sautéing
- 2 cups (350 g) quinoa, well rinsed in fine strainer
- 1 cup (150 g) diced bell pepper
- 2 cups (260 g) corn kernels (organic frozen, canned, or fresh)
- 2 or 3 garlic cloves, pressed or minced
- 1 cup (100 g) finely chopped scallions
- ¼ cup (15 g) freshly chopped parsley
- ¼ cup (60 ml) lemon juice
- ½ teaspoon salt (or to taste)
- Freshly ground pepper, to taste
- Olive oil, for drizzling (optional)

## DIRECTIONS

Add 4 cups (940 ml) water and rinsed quinoa to a saucepan, and bring to a boil. Reduce heat to low, and simmer for 10 to 12 minutes, or until tender. Drain off excess water, if necessary, and transfer to a bowl. Fluff with a fork.

Meanwhile, in a sauté pan, heat remaining 2 table-spoons (30 ml) water and cook pepper for 3 minutes, or until it begins to soften. Add corn and garlic, and sauté for 3 minutes longer. Add scallions and sauté for 2 more minutes.

Add sautéed vegetables, parsley, lemon juice, salt, and pepper to cooked quinoa, and toss well to combine. Season to taste, and add a drizzle of olive oil, if desired. Serve warm or at room temperature.

**YIELD:** 6 to 8 servings

## SERVING SUGGESTIONS AND VARIATIONS

* Instead of buying vegetable stock in a can or vacuum-packed box, try using vegetable bouillon cubes, which you can add to any cooking grain, soup, or stew. Check a health food store for different brands. Look for natural ingredients.
* In terms of color contrast, it's lovely to serve this on a plate with steamed or roasted green vegetables, such as Brussels sprouts, broccoli, green beans, or asparagus.

## FOOD LORE

The incas referred to quinoa as the "mother of all grains."

Per serving: 287 calories; 5g fat; 10g protein; 53g carbohydrate; 6g dietary fiber; 0mg cholesterol; 965mg sodium.

# BEET BUNDT CAKE

*Soy-free*

All I can say is TRUST ME. We use vegetables in other desserts (think carrot cake, zucchini bread, and pumpkin pie), so why not beets? No one would ever guess that the incredible moisture and beautiful color of this cake comes from an earthy root vegetable!

- ½ cup (120 ml) canola oil
- 1 ½ cups (340 g) packed dark brown sugar
- 2 cups (450 g) puréed cooked (boiled or steamed) red beets (about 3 medium-size beets)
- ½ cup (90 g) nondairy semisweet chocolate chips, melted
- 1 teaspoon (5 ml) vanilla extract
- 2 cups (250 g) all-purpose flour
- 2 teaspoons (9 g) baking powder (look for aluminum-free)
- ¼ teaspoon salt
- Confectioners' sugar, for dusting

## DIRECTIONS

Preheat oven to 375°F (190°C, or gas mark 5), and lightly oil a Bundt pan.

In a mixing bowl, cream together oil and brown sugar. Add beets, melted chocolate chips, and vanilla, and mix well.

In a separate bowl, combine flour, baking powder, and salt. Add to wet beet mixture, and stir until just combined.

Pour into prepared Bundt pan, and bake for 45 minutes, or until a toothpick inserted near the center comes out clean.

Cool in pan for 10 minutes before removing to a wire rack. Cool completely. Before serving, dust with confectioners' sugar and top with blueberries, if desired.

**YIELD:** 16 servings

Per serving: 228 calories; 9g fat; 2g protein; 37g carbohydrate; 1g dietary fiber; 0mg cholesterol; 117mg sodium.

## COMPASSIONATE COOKS' TIP

Reserve ¼ cup (55 g) of the puréed beets (or purée a fourth beet) to create a red/pink frosting or ganache, using confectioners' sugar and nondairy butter such as Earth Balance. For a ganache, use the water in which you cooked the beets to thin out the topping. For frosting, fluff up using a hand mixer.

## DID YOU KNOW?

Many bakers use beets to add dramatic color to their recipes, as in the Red Velvet Cake with Buttercream Frosting (page 42).

# AUTUMN (OR WINTER) TEMPEH SALAD

*Wheat-free, oil-free*

This simple but sophisticated dish will delight your guests as they cozy up to a warm fire. It's also a great main or side dish for a Thanksgiving feast.

- 1 butternut squash or any other winter squash, cut into 1-inch (2.5 cm) cubes
- 1 package (8 ounces, or 225 g) tempeh
- 2 tablespoons (30 ml) sesame or olive oil (optional)
- 2 celery stalks, diced
- 1 small-size red onion, finely diced
- 3 to 4 tablespoons (45 to 60 ml) tamari soy sauce (or more as needed)
- 1/4 cup (15 g) chopped fresh parsley
- 2 to 3 tablespoons (20 to 30 g) raisins or any dried fruit (dried apricot would be a nice touch)
- 1 teaspoon (1 g) dried basil
- 1 teaspoon (1 g) dried rosemary
- 1 teaspoon (1 g) dried sage
- 1 teaspoon (1 g) dried thyme
- Freshly ground pepper, to taste

Per serving: 279 calories; 8g fat; 12g protein; 47g carbohydrate; 6g dietary fiber; 0mg cholesterol; 699mg sodium.

### DIRECTIONS

Steam or roast squash until tender (see tip below). It is done when a fork can easily pierce it, but it should not be so soft that it's falling apart. Transfer to a bowl to cool.

While squash is cooling, cut tempeh into 1/2-inch (1 cm) cubes and steam for 10 to 12 minutes, until its nutty aroma fills the air and it turns a lighter color. At this point, you can use the steamed tempeh as is or fry it in sesame or olive oil for added flavor and texture.

Transfer tempeh to bowl with squash, and let cool. (If you have a large enough steamer, steam the squash and tempeh together, to save time.)

Add celery, onion, tamari, parsley, raisins, basil, rosemary, sage, thyme, and pepper, and gently toss. Taste, and add more tamari, if necessary. Serve immediately, or refrigerate until ready to serve.

**YIELD:** 4 to 6 servings

### COMPASSIONATE COOKS' TIP

To roast squash, preheat oven to 425°F (220°C, or gas mark 7). In a bowl, toss cut-up squash with enough olive oil to coat. Add some salt and pepper. Arrange squash in a single layer on a nonstick baking sheet (or one lightly coated with oil). Bake for 30 minutes. Stir gently, and bake for 10 to 15 minutes longer, until tender and slightly browned.

# BUTTERNUT SQUASH RISOTTO WITH TOASTED SAGE

*Wheat-free*

Nothing says "comfort" more than a plate of creamy risotto. It requires a little attention on the stove, but it's worth every minute. And it's even better the next day!

- 7 cups (1645 ml) vegetable broth, or half water, half broth (store-bought or homemade, page 213)
- 2 ½ to 3 cups (565 to 675 g) butternut squash (about 1 medium), peeled and cut into 1-inch (2.5 cm) cubes
- 2 tablespoons (30 ml) olive oil
- 2 tablespoons (20 g) minced garlic
- 2 tablespoons (5 g) minced fresh sage
- 2 cups (390 g) Arborio rice
- ½ cup (120 ml) white wine (optional)
- Salt and freshly ground black pepper, to taste
- Fresh flat-leaf parsley or sage, minced, for garnish (optional)

Per serving: 337 calories; 6g fat; 5g protein; 62g carbohydrate; 1g dietary fiber; 0mg cholesterol; 1182mg sodium.

## DIRECTIONS

In a large-size saucepan, heat broth at a gentle simmer. Add squash, and allow it to cook until it is easily pierced with a fork. Do not overcook or it will be mushy. (Alternatively, you can heat the broth up alone and roast or steam the squash separately. The idea is to cook the squash before adding it to the rice.)

Warm olive oil in a large-size sauté pan over low-medium heat. Add garlic and sage and sauté for a few minutes until garlic turns golden brown.

Add rice to the pan (do not rinse first) and stir until rice is less opaque, about 3 minutes. Add while wine, if using, and cook until it evaporates, just a few minutes.

Add about 1 cup (235 ml) simmering broth to rice (without adding the squash), and stir until broth is absorbed. Continue adding broth, one ladleful at a time, until rice kernels are al dente in the center and creamy on the outside, 20 to 25 minutes.

Finally, when broth is almost gone from the original saucepan and rice is the perfect texture, add cooked squash along with the last addition of broth. Season with salt and pepper to taste, sprinkle with parsley, if desired, and serve right away.

**YIELD:** 4 to 6 servings

## SERVING SUGGESTIONS AND VARIATIONS

For a nutty flavor, add 1 cup (145 g) peeled, cooked, and coarsely chopped chestnuts along with the last addition of broth.

# PURPLE POTATOES WITH CASHEW CREAM

*Wheat-free, soy-free if using only oil*

These little gems were on our wedding menu in 2001 and people are STILL talking about them.

- 30 small-size purple potatoes
- Olive oil, for roasting and frying
- Salt and pepper, to taste
- 1 tablespoon (14 g) nondairy butter (such as Earth Balance)
- 1 yellow onion, chopped
- 3 garlic cloves, minced
- 1 teaspoon (5 g) granulated or brown sugar
- 4 large-size sage leaves
- ½ cup (60 g) walnuts, toasted
- 1 cup (125 g) unsalted raw cashews, toasted (see page 86)
- 1 tablespoon (12 g) nutritional yeast flakes
- 1 cup (235 ml) vegetable stock (store-bought or homemade, page 213), non-tomato-based (to preserve cream color), if available

## DIRECTIONS

Preheat oven to 425°F (220°C, or gas mark 7).

Wash potatoes under running water, then dry with a towel. Roast or bake them.

**To roast:** Toss whole potatoes with enough olive oil to coat lightly. Season with salt and pepper. Arrange in an even layer on a lightly oiled baking pan. Roast for 20 to 30 minutes, or until tender, moving them around occasionally. Let cool on a towel-lined plate to soak up excess oil.

**To bake:** Using a small fork, pierce potatoes in several places so steam can escape. (Since you will later cut the potatoes in half, consider making the piercing marks where you'll be cutting.) Place potatoes on oven rack or baking sheet. Bake for 40 minutes, or until tender when pierced with a fork.

Meanwhile, in a large sauté pan, warm nondairy butter (or olive oil) and cook onion and garlic over medium-high heat until they begin to brown slightly, about 5 minutes. Stir in sugar and a pinch of salt, and continue cooking until onion turns brown and sweet, 20 to 25 minutes.

While potatoes and onions cook, heat up 1 tablespoon (15 ml) olive oil in a small sauté pan, and fry sage leaves until crispy, 30 to 60 seconds. Set them on a towel-lined plate to soak up extra oil, then place them with toasted walnuts in a blender. Pulse to a coarse crumble. Add salt to taste. Transfer to a bowl, and set aside.

When onions are ready, add to a high-speed blender with cashews, nutritional yeast, and vegetable stock. Blend on high until the mixture is creamy. This could take several minutes, so be patient. Add more cashews or stock as necessary, to get the right consistency. You want it to be creamy and thick. Add salt to taste.

Once potatoes have cooled, cut in half without tearing skin. Scoop out center with a melon baller, leaving ¼-inch (6 mm) walls. Cut a small slice off the bottom of each potato to help it sit level.

Spoon cashew mixture into halved potatoes, sprinkle with walnut/sage mixture, and set on pretty plates to serve. Serve warm or at room temperature.

**YIELD:** 60 potato halves, or servings

Per serving: 61 calories; 2g fat; 2g protein; 9g carbohydrate; 1g dietary fiber; 0mg cholesterol; 30mg sodium.

# WARM LENTIL SALAD

*Oil-free, wheat-free, soy-free*

I attribute this recipe to one of my dear friends, Antonia Fokken, who brought this dish to a girls' night I hosted a few years ago.

- 1 ¼ cups (240 g) small French lentils du Puy (or brown lentils if these aren't available)
- 3 ¼ cups (765 ml) vegetable stock (or water with bouillon cube or powder or homemade, page 213)
- 2 sprigs fresh thyme or 1 teaspoon (1 g) dried
- 2 bay leaves
- 2 tablespoons (30 ml) water, for sautéing
- 1 yellow onion, coarsely chopped
- 2 carrots, peeled and finely chopped
- ¼ cup (60 ml) red wine vinegar
- 2 tablespoons (30 g) Dijon mustard
- ¼ cup (15 g) finely chopped fresh flat-leaf or curly Italian parsley
- Salt and pepper, to taste

## DIRECTIONS

Combine lentils, stock, thyme, and bay leaves in a medium-size saucepan. Cover, and simmer over low-medium heat until lentils are tender, about 45 minutes. (Check after 30 minutes to make sure water hasn't evaporated.) Drain any liquid that remains after lentils are done.

Remove from heat, and discard bay leaves and thyme sprigs. Transfer lentils to a mixing bowl. You can either let mixture cool to room temperature or add remaining ingredients while lentils are still warm.

Meanwhile, heat water (or stock) in a large-size sauté pan over medium heat. Add onion and carrots, and cook until carrots are soft, about 10 minutes.

Add onion mixture to cooked lentils, and gently stir to combine. Stir in the vinegar, mustard, and parsley. Add salt and pepper to taste. Serve immediately, or store in the refrigerator and serve the next day. You can certainly serve this dish right out of the fridge, but it's so lovely when it's warm.

**YIELD:** 8 servings

## FOOD LORE

The small French green lentils called for in this recipe are the same as *lentilles du Puy*. These choice lentils were originally grown in the volcanic soils of Puy in France, which gives them their unique nutty flavor. Now they're also grown in North America and Italy. Also known as "poor man's caviar," they are considered the finest lentils due to their subtle, earthy flavor and their ability to hold their form.

Per serving: 188 calories; 2g fat; 12g protein; 32g carbohydrate; 12g dietary fiber; 0mg cholesterol; 719mg sodium.

✳ Eggplant Caponata  ✳ Tofu Spinach Lasagna
✳ Tuscan White Beans with Sun-Dried Tomatoes
✳ Garlic Bread

# EGGPLANT CAPONATA

*Oil-free if using water for sautéing, wheat-free, soy-free*

Thanks to my good friend Kristin Schwarz (and her mom), I can share this classic Sicilian recipe with you, which can be eaten warm, as a side dish, or at room temperature on crackers or bread.

- 1 large-size Italian globe eggplant, peeled and diced (about 5 cups [410 g])
- 2 teaspoons (10 ml) olive oil or water, for sautéing
- 1 large-size yellow onion, finely chopped
- 3 celery stalks, finely diced
- 1 can (6 ounces, or 170 g) tomato paste
- 1 tablespoon (12 g) granulated sugar
- ¼ cup (35 g) capers, drained
- ¼ cup (60 ml) red wine vinegar
- 3 cups (705 ml) water
- ½ teaspoon salt
- ¼ teaspoon red pepper flakes

## DIRECTIONS

In a pot with a steamer basket, steam eggplant until soft, 10 to 15 minutes.

Meanwhile, heat olive oil in a soup pot. Sauté onion and celery for about 10 minutes. Add eggplant and sauté for a few minutes longer.

Add tomato paste, sugar, capers, vinegar, water, salt, and red pepper flakes. Bring to a boil, then reduce heat and simmer, uncovered, for 30 minutes, or until thick and flavorful.

Remove from heat, let cool, and serve with crackers or crispy bread.

**YIELD:** 8 servings

Per serving: 58 calories; 1g fat; 2g protein; 11g carbohydrate; 3g dietary fiber; 0mg cholesterol; 355mg sodium.

## COMPASSIONATE COOKS' TIP

Caponata can be served hot, but it is much better when it has a chance to mellow. Let it come to room temperature before serving as an appetizer or side dish.

# TOFU SPINACH LASAGNA

*Oil-free, wheat-free if using rice lasagna noodles*

The tofu "ricotta" has a wonderful creamy texture and boasts all the familiarity of the traditional lasagna, with which most of us grew up.

- ½ to 1 pound (225 to 455 g) lasagna noodles
- 2 packages (10 ounces, or 280 g, each) frozen, chopped spinach, thawed and drained
- 1 package (16 ounces, or 455 g) firm tofu (not silken)
- 1 tablespoon (13 g) granulated sugar (optional)
- ¼ cup (60 ml) nondairy milk (such as rice, oat, soy, almond, or hazelnut), or as needed
- ½ teaspoon garlic powder or 2 peeled garlic cloves
- Juice from ½ lemon (about 2 tablespoons [30 ml])
- 2 tablespoons (5 g) minced fresh basil (about 20 leaves)
- 1 teaspoon (6 g) salt (or to taste)
- 4 to 6 cups (980 to 1470 g) tomato or pasta sauce of your choice

Per serving: 270 calories; 3g fat; 13g protein; 50g carbohydrate; 6g dietary fiber; 0mg cholesterol; 1155mg sodium.

## DIRECTIONS

Preheat oven to 350°F (180°C, or gas mark 4).

Cook lasagna noodles according to package directions or use "no-boil" lasagna noodles. Drain and set aside.

Squeeze as much water from spinach as possible and set aside. (If using fresh spinach, blanch first.)

Place tofu, sugar (if using), milk, garlic powder, lemon juice, basil, and salt in a blender or food processor and blend until smooth. The tofu "ricotta" should be creamy but still have body.

Transfer to large-size bowl, and stir in spinach. Continue tasting until you get amount of salt just right.

Cover bottom of 9 x 13-inch (23 x 33 cm) baking dish with a thin layer of tomato sauce, then a layer of noodles (use about one-third of noodles). Follow with half the tofu filling. Continue in the same order, using half the remaining tomato sauce and noodles, and all remaining tofu filling. End with remaining noodles, covered by remaining tomato sauce. Bake for 40 to 45 minutes, until hot and bubbling.

**YIELD:** 8 to 10 servings

## SERVING SUGGESTIONS AND VARIATIONS

Add meatless meat crumbles to your tomato sauce for more texture and body. For more cheesiness, add shredded nondairy mozzarella cheese to each layer.

This recipe is also great for making stuffed shells. To do so, stuff pasta shells with the tofu ricotta from this recipe, place them in a baking dish, pour on tomato sauce, and bake in a 350°F (180°C, or gas mark 4) oven for 20 to 30 minutes.

# TUSCAN WHITE BEANS WITH SUN-DRIED TOMATOES

*Wheat-free, soy-free*

When my husband and I visited Florence, Italy, recently, we ordered this favorite dish of ours every night. Variations (in olive oil, in red sauce, and with garlic) appear on every restaurant menu, and I was determined to replicate it at home.

- 1 cup (55 g or 110 g oil-packed or reconstituted) chopped sun-dried tomatoes
- 1 tablespoon (15 ml) olive oil
- 1 large-size yellow onion, chopped
- 3 zucchini or summer squash, thinly sliced
- 3 garlic cloves, minced
- 3 cups (90 g) fresh spinach
- 3 cans (15 ounces, or 420 g, each) small white beans, rinsed and drained (or 4 cups [690 g] cooked beans, if making beans from scratch)
- 1 cup (235 ml) water
- 1/2 teaspoon ground sage
- Salt and freshly ground black pepper, to taste
- 1/4 teaspoon dried red pepper flakes
- 1/3 cup (13 g) chopped fresh basil

## DIRECTIONS

If using dried tomatoes, soak in a bowl of warm water for 30 to 45 minutes until softened. Drain off water and chop tomatoes coarsely. (Or, use sun-dried tomatoes jarred in liquid and proceed directly to chopping.)

Heat oil in a large-size sauté pan over medium-high heat. Add onion and cook, stirring, until soft and translucent, about 5 minutes.

Add squash and cook for 5 minutes longer. Add garlic, spinach, beans, tomatoes, water, sage, salt, black pepper, and red pepper flakes, stirring to combine. Salt to taste, and cook for 10 minutes longer. Stir in basil, and serve right away.

**YIELD:** 4 to 6 servings

## SERVING SUGGESTIONS AND VARIATIONS

This dish is perfect on its own as a first course, or over pasta or polenta. Note that even once the beans are cooked, they will soak up a lot of liquid. If you want more of a broth, add more water. Just make sure it gets heated and incorporated into the dish before serving.

## COMPASSIONATE COOKS' TIP

Whereas cannellini beans are simply white kidney beans and have a lot of body and texture, I prefer smaller, more tender white beans, such as great Northern or navy beans, for this dish.

Per serving: 397 calories; 4g fat; 23g protein; 74g carbohydrate; 17g dietary fiber; 0mg cholesterol; 852mg sodium.

# GARLIC BREAD

*Soy-free if omitting cheese*

It doesn't get any better than garlic and bread. This bread is perfect for a daytime party or a nighttime soiree.

- 1 baguette (long loaf of French bread)
- 4 or 5 garlic cloves, minced
- 2 tablespoons (8 g) minced fresh parsley
- 1/4 cup (60 ml) extra-virgin olive oil
- 1/8 teaspoon cayenne pepper
- 1/4 teaspoon salt (or to taste)
- Freshly ground black pepper, to taste
- 1/2 cup (60 g) nondairy cheese, shredded (optional)

## DIRECTIONS

Preheat oven to 350°F (180°C, or gas mark 4). Cut baguette in half lengthwise.

In a small-size bowl, combine garlic, parsley, olive oil, cayenne pepper, and salt. Grind some fresh pepper into the bowl.

Spread mixture evenly on each side of baguette, using the back of a spoon. Place the bread, face up, on a baking sheet, and bake for 10 minutes.

If you want to add cheese, take bread out of oven after 10 minutes, sprinkle on cheese, turn oven up to broil, and pop bread back in for 2 minutes, until sides are golden brown and cheese is melted.

Remove from oven and let cool. Using a serrated knife, cut bread into single servings, on an angle, for a pretty presentation.

**YIELD:** 24 pieces, or servings

## SERVING SUGGESTIONS AND VARIATIONS

If you don't want spicy garlic bread, eliminate cayenne and use paprika instead.

Per serving: 79 calories; 3g fat; 2g protein; 11g carbohydrate; 1g dietary fiber; 0mg cholesterol; 154mg sodium.

## FOOD LORE

According to French food laws, "bread" is defined as a product that contains only four ingredients: water, flour, yeast, and salt. Bakers who stray from this must use a name other than "bread" to refer to their product.

# CHAPTER 5

HONORING TRADITION:
FEASTS
FOR THE
HOLIDAYS

A misconception about veganism is the implication that vegans cannot eat foods that reflect our values *and* honor tradition, as if these two components are mutually exclusive. Food-related traditions, particularly those involving animals, are likely to be so revered, that they leave little room for anything or anyone else. Vegans are accused of flying in the face of tradition and of committing cultural blasphemy against certain practices that are justified simply because they are culturally embedded and sanctified by tradition.

# RECIPES

# EMBRACING OUR ETHICS

However much we romanticize the idea of tradition, our attachment to it is not as tenacious as we think. The truth is, we cherry-pick from the lot and decide which traditions and customs we want to uphold and which we want to leave behind.

Few people object to the idea of rejecting certain traditions because of convenience or modernity, but when ethics are the driving force, people tend to react differently. Vegans have been accused of everything from being unpatriotic (for not consuming good old-fashioned American fare such as hot dogs and hamburgers) to "denying our evolutionary heritage" and "sacrificing our [human] identity" (favorite assertions of writer Michael Pollan), simply for not wanting to consume animals and their products.

Nobody wants to be seen as contributing to cruelty, but participating in cultural customs? Carrying out tradition? That doesn't sound so bad. To shroud our violence against animals in the sanctity of tradition is to romanticize our exploitation of them.

The tight grip of our meat-eating habit reminds me of Shirley Jackson's 1948 haunting short story, "The Lottery," about the annual selection of a sacrificial victim in a small American town. In it, Shirley Jackson sheds light on humanity's tendency to cling blindly to meaningless rituals and participate in pointless violence.

"There's always been a lottery," one of the townspeople in Jackson's story declares, when he hears that a neighboring village has given up this empty, violent ritual. We justify our use of animals in a similar way. But just because we *always have* done something doesn't mean we *always have to.*

ONCE WE KNOW BETTER, WE CAN MAKE BETTER CHOICES, MORE COMPASSIONATE CHOICES. THAT'S WHAT IT MEANS TO BE HUMAN. THAT'S WHAT IT MEANS TO GROW.

## RECLAIMING FOOD TRADITIONS

Eating compassionately and honoring tradition don't contradict each other. In fact, one is strengthened by the other, as our holiday foods and rituals are often *symbols* for something much deeper. In being attached to the *form* (turkeys at Thanksgiving, eggs at Passover, ham at Easter), we risk losing the true *meaning* of whatever we are celebrating or honoring, whether it be gratitude, abundance, renewal, rebirth, freedom, generosity, or mercy. If we uncover the *meaning* of these symbols, we may find that a plant-based menu better reflects the values and significance of these holidays.

The great humanitarian Albert Schweitzer wrote, "The thinking [person] must oppose all cruel customs, no matter how deeply rooted in tradition and surrounded by a halo. When we have a choice, we must avoid bringing torment and injury into the life of another."

With a little creativity and a lot of sensitivity, we will find that we can indeed adhere to traditions while honoring our values. We need not sacrifice one for the other.

# SUGGESTED SEASONAL MENUS

To round out these menus, consult *The Joy of Vegan Baking* for an array of holiday desserts.

## ☂ SPRING / ☀ SUMMER

### THE WILD BRUNCH, PAGE 200
Asian-Inspired Lettuce Wraps
Chili-Oil-Infused Soba Noodles
Lavender Lemonade
Monkey Bread

### WHEN IRISH EYES ARE SMILING, PAGE 204
Irish Soda Bread
Hearty Stew
Tempeh and Eggplant Pot Pies
Irish Coffee

### A PASSOVER SEDER, PAGE 209
Charoset
Passover Pizza
Matzoh Ball Soup
Homemade Vegetable Stock
Traditional Vegetable Soup
Matzoh Chocolate Brittle

## 🍃 AUTUMN / ❄ WINTER

### IT'S A WONDERFUL LIFE, PAGE 216
Savory Tofu Spread
Borscht (Beet Soup)
Old-Fashioned Lentil Loaf
Mashed Potatoes with Caramelized Onions
Golden Mushroom Gravy
Broccoli with Garlic Butter and Cashews
Decadent Chocolate Truffles

### HOME FOR THE HOLIDAYS, PAGE 224
Mushroom Walnut Pâté
Mashed Yukon Gold and Sweet Potatoes
Potato Latkes
Moroccan Phyllo with Curried Golden Tomato Sauce
Roasted Brussels Sprouts with Caramelized Onions and Toasted Pistachios
Benne Cakes (Kwanzaa Cookies)

### WINTER WONDERLAND, PAGE 233
Mexican Champurrado (Thick Hot Chocolate)
Harvest-Stuffed Acorn Squash *or* Butternut Squash Timbales
Mashed Root Vegetables with Fresh Herb Infusion
Sensational Stuffing with Nuts
Holiday Cranberry Relish
Garlic-Glazed Green Beans

# ASIAN-INSPIRED LETTUCE WRAPS

*Oil-free, wheat-free*

This recipe was inspired by a favorite dish at a local vegetarian Chinese restaurant. Serve as an appetizer or as a main dish, along with spring rolls and a bowl of miso soup!

- 4 tablespoons (60 ml) water, divided
- 2 tablespoons (20 g) minced garlic
- 1 tablespoon (6 g) grated or finely minced fresh ginger
- 1 red bell pepper, seeded and finely chopped
- 1 large carrot, peeled and finely chopped
- 1 package (16 ounces, or 455 g) extra-firm tofu
- 1 tablespoon (16 g) chili paste
- 2 tablespoons (30 g) light brown sugar
- 2 tablespoons (32 g) light miso paste
- 2 teaspoons (5 g) sesame seeds
- 10 Boston bibb or butter lettuce leaves, rinsed and patted dry
- 10 basil leaves
- 2 small cucumbers, peeled and julienned

## DIRECTIONS

Heat 2 tablespoons (30 ml) water in a sauté pan over medium heat. Add garlic and ginger, and cook for 2 minutes, until they soften. Add red pepper and carrot, and cook for another minute.

Meanwhile, crumble tofu in a separate bowl until pretty small, resembling bread crumbs. Add to sauté pan, and cook for 10 minutes, thoroughly combining with vegetables. Add chili paste, and stir to combine.

To make miso sauce, place brown sugar and remaining 2 tablespoons (30 ml) water in a saucepan, and dissolve over low-medium heat. Remove from heat, and stir in miso paste and sesame seeds. Add to tofu mixture, and thoroughly combine.

To make wraps, trim edges of lettuce leaves to make them uniformly circular. Add a basil leaf and some julienned cucumber to each "cup." Add tofu mixture, and enjoy!

**YIELD:** 10 servings

## SERVING SUGGESTIONS AND VARIATIONS

Some finely chopped, sautéed shiitake mushrooms would be a fantastic addition to the tofu mixture.

Per serving: 72 calories; 3g fat; 5g protein; 8g carbohydrate; 2g dietary fiber; 0mg cholesterol; 144mg sodium.

Advanced Preparation Required

# CHILI-OIL-INFUSED SOBA NOODLES

Japanese soba noodles are marinated in tamari, sesame oil, vinegar, sugar, and chili oil, then tossed with julienned carrots and red bell peppers for a delicious cold salad with an Asian flair. A favorite of mine.

- 16 ounces (455 g) dried soba noodles
- ¼ cup (60 ml) tamari soy sauce
- 3 tablespoons (45 ml) sesame oil
- 2 tablespoons (30 ml) seasoned rice vinegar
- 1 to 2 tablespoons (15 to 30 ml) chili oil
- 1 red bell pepper, thinly sliced
- 1 cup (100 g) chopped scallions
- 2 carrots, peeled and cut into matchsticks
- 2 tablespoons (16 g) toasted sesame seeds

## DIRECTIONS

In a large-size stockpot, cook pasta in boiling salted water until al dente. Rinse with cool water, drain well, and transfer to a large-size bowl.

In a small-size bowl, combine tamari, sesame oil, rice vinegar, and chili oil. Pour over noodles. Using tongs, toss noodles with sauce to coat well. Marinate in a covered bowl for at least 1 hour or up to 24 hours, tossing occasionally.

Before serving, stir in red pepper, scallions, and carrots. Taste, and add more tamari, sesame oil, vinegar, or chili oil, as needed. Sprinkle with toasted sesame seeds.

**YIELD:** 6 to 8 servings, as a side dish

## DID YOU KNOW?

The "seasoning" in "seasoned rice vinegar" is sugar. It adds a little sweetness. You can also find lite seasoned vinegar, which has less sugar. Be sure to look for seasoned rice vinegar that uses sugar, not corn syrup.

## COMPASSIONATE COOKS' TIP

If using regular unseasoned rice vinegar, add 1 tablespoon (13 g) granulated sugar to give the dish a little sweetness. For a beautiful color contrast, use black sesame seeds.

Per serving: 299 calories; 9g fat; 10g protein; 49g carbohydrate; 2g dietary fiber; 0mg cholesterol; 968mg sodium.

# LAVENDER LEMONADE

*Oil-free, wheat-free, soy-free*

Using the lavender from our garden, my husband makes this delightful drink on a regular basis during the summer months.

- 5 cups (1175 ml) filtered water, divided
- 1 ½ cups (300 g) sugar (or less, to your liking)
- ¼ cup (8 g) chopped lavender leaves
- 1 cup (235 ml) freshly squeezed lemon juice (4 lemons)
- Ice cubes

## DIRECTIONS

In a pot over low-medium heat, bring 2 ½ cups (590 ml) water to a boil, along with sugar, and heat until the sugar dissolves. Remove from heat. Add lavender and let mixture cool to room temperature. The longer you allow the lavender to infuse the water, the more flavorful it will be. A minimum of 30 minutes is ideal. Strain out lavender.

In a pitcher (preferably glass), add lavender infusion to remaining 2 ½ cups (590 ml) water, along with lemon juice.

Stir and add sugar to taste. Chill and serve over ice.

**YIELD:** 6 to 8 glasses, or servings

Per serving: 153 calories; 0g fat; trace protein; 41g carbohydrate; trace dietary fiber; 0mg cholesterol; 1mg sodium.

## CELEBRATING THE ESSENCE OF EASTER WITHOUT THE EGGS

The symbols of spring—life, birth, and renewal—are everywhere we look this time of year, but they are most definitely not in the eggs of chickens.

Growing up, I relished my family's annual egg-decorating ritual and the egg hunts that followed. But my fond memories have less to do with the eggs themselves and more to do with having the whole family together. We, the children, were given full license to be creative, and we participated in an exciting quest with all of our neighbors.

Painting wooden eggs or any wooden figures with a hole in the top (rather than chicken eggs) enables you to enjoy the artwork year-round or during the winter holidays, when you can hang them on the tree. Other items such as plastic eggs filled with treats, for example, allow for the same effect without contributing to unnecessary cruelty.

Know the facts about chickens and eggs. Hens from "free-range" or "cage-free" operations fare no better than their conventional counterparts. They are confined and crowded indoors, suffer debeaking, are purchased from the same hatcheries where 250 million male chicks are killed, and are all sent to slaughter when their production/profitability wanes.

## DID YOU KNOW?

The word *lavender* comes from the Latin word *lavare*, meaning "to wash." In Roman times, lavender was used to scent washed fabrics and as a bath perfume.

Advanced Preparation Required

# MONKEY BREAD

This is the easiest, most delightful bread recipe to make, and though it's elegant enough for a sophisticated brunch, children also love it.

- ¾ cup (150 g) granulated sugar
- ¾ cup (170 g) packed light brown sugar
- 2 teaspoons (4 g) ground cinnamon
- ½ cup (112 g) nondairy, nonhydrogenated butter (such as Earth Balance), melted
- 1 recipe risen sweet dough (see page 287)

## FOOD LORE

The exact etymology is uncertain and no theory is definitive. Feel free to make up your own reason for the name. The practice of baking little balls of dough in one pan was popular in the mid-19th century, and sweet gooey breads with cinnamon, like this one, date back to ancient Middle Eastern cooks.

## DIRECTIONS

Heavily grease a 10-inch (23 cm) tube or Bundt cake pan.

Combine granulated sugar, brown sugar, and cinnamon in a bowl. Mix well. In a separate bowl place melted butter, and set aside.

With flour-dusted hands, tear off pieces of risen dough (that you've already prepared), about 1 ½ inches (4 cm) in diameter. Roll each piece into a round ball.

Dip each dough ball into melted butter first, then into cinnamon sugar, until completely covered. Continue process until all balls are coated. Place each ball in prepared pan, about ½ inch (1 cm) apart. Add another layer of balls on top of the first, until you use all your dough. Cover with a dish towel, and let stand in a warm, dark spot for 30 minutes. The dough will rise more.

Preheat oven to 350°F (180°C, or gas mark 4).

Place pan in oven. Bake until a wooden skewer or toothpick inserted into the dough comes out clean, 30 to 40 minutes.

Remove from oven and let cool for 5 to 10 minutes, then unmold. Serve warm. Guests will delight in pulling off their own fluffy bread balls.

**YIELD:** 15 servings

## SERVING SUGGESTIONS AND VARIATIONS

For a little variety, while assembling, brush melted nondairy butter and sprinkle raisins or chopped nuts between the layers of dough balls.

Per serving: 240 calories; 7g fat; 4g protein; 40g carbohydrate; trace dietary fiber; 0mg cholesterol; 146mg sodium.

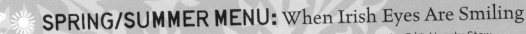
# IRISH SODA BREAD

This recipe, included in *The Joy of Vegan Baking*, cried out to be repeated here in honor of St. Patrick's Day. Add it to your Irish menu, and enjoy a tradition that just happened to be vegan long before I got my hands on it.

- 2 cups (470 ml) nondairy milk (soy, rice, almond, hazelnut, hemp, or oat)
- 2 teaspoons (10 ml) white distilled vinegar
- 4 cups (500 g) unbleached, all-purpose flour
- 1 teaspoon (5 g) baking soda
- 1 teaspoon (6 g) salt
- 4 tablespoons (50 g) nondairy, nonhydrogenated butter (such as Earth Balance)

## DIRECTIONS

Preheat oven to 425°F (220°C, or gas mark 7). Lightly grease a round 9- or 10-inch (23 or 25 cm) cake pan.

In a small-size bowl, combine milk and vinegar. Let stand for 5 minutes. By adding an acidic agent, you essentially just created buttermilk.

In a large-size bowl, combine flour, baking soda, and salt. Add milk and vinegar mixture and nondairy butter, and mix until you have a sticky dough. Knead dough in bowl or on a floured surface for 10 to 12 strokes.

Place dough in prepared pan, and cut a cross in the top. Bake for 40 to 45 minutes, or until the bottom sounds hollow when thumped. Cool slightly before serving.

**YIELD:** 20 servings

## SERVING SUGGESTIONS AND VARIATIONS

Add 1 ½ cups (220 g) raisins or 1 cup (145 g) various nuts for a little variety.

Per serving: 119 calories; 3g fat; 3g protein; 20g carbohydrate; 1g dietary fiber; 0mg cholesterol; 173mg sodium.

## FOOD LORE

Soda bread dates back to approximately 1840, when bicarbonate of soda was introduced to Ireland and replaced yeast as the leavening agent. It eventually became a staple of the Irish diet and is still used as an accompaniment to a meal.

There are several theories as to the significance of the cross in soda bread. Some believe that the cross was placed on each loaf to ward off evil, but it is more likely that the cross was used to help with cooking time or to serve as a guide for cutting even slices.

## COMPASSIONATE COOKS' TIP

Soda bread can dry out quickly and is typically good for 2 or 3 days. It is best when served warm or toasted with nondairy butter.

# HEARTY STEW

*Oil-free, wheat-free

The tempeh in this delicious and hearty stew provides a wonderful texture.
The veggies provide many essential nutrients. The thick sauce makes it perfect
for dipping bread and for serving as a main dish for St. Patrick's Day.

- 4 cups (940 ml) vegetable stock (store-bought or homemade, page 213)
- 1 package (8 ounces, or 225 g) tempeh, cubed
- 4 carrots, chopped (peeling optional)
- 3 yellow potatoes, cut into bite-size chunks (peeling optional)
- 1 medium-size yellow onion, coarsely chopped
- 2 garlic cloves, minced
- 2 tablespoons (32 g) tomato paste
- 3 tablespoons (45 ml) tamari soy sauce
- 2 bay leaves
- 1 teaspoon (1 g) dried marjoram
- 1 teaspoon (1 g) dried tarragon
- 1 teaspoon (1 g) dried thyme
- ¼ teaspoon ground black pepper
- Dash of liquid smoke or ½ teaspoon smoked paprika (optional)
- Salt, to taste
- 2 tablespoons (8 g) fresh parsley, minced, for garnish (optional)

## DIRECTIONS

In a large-size soup pot, combine stock, tempeh, carrots, potatoes, onion, garlic, tomato paste, tamari, bay leaves, marjoram, tarragon, thyme, and black pepper. Bring stew to a boil. Cover, and reduce heat to low. Simmer stew until vegetables are tender, about 25 minutes, stirring occasionally.

Add liquid smoke, and stir to combine. This will add a smoky, robust flavor to the stew, but you may consider it an optional ingredient.

Remove bay leaves, add salt to taste, and serve in individual soup bowls. Garnish each serving with minced parsley, if desired.

**YIELD:** 6 servings

## SERVING SUGGESTIONS AND VARIATIONS

Use vegetarian "beef" in place of tempeh.

Per serving: 260 calories; 6g fat; 14g protein; 40g carbohydrate; 5g dietary fiber; 0mg cholesterol; 1653mg sodium.

## COMPASSIONATE COOKS' TIP

Because tempeh is fermented with rice, it expands when it cooks, so consider that when cutting tempeh. Make the chunks smaller or larger, depending on your preference.

# TEMPEH AND EGGPLANT POT PIES

Use any combination of vegetables for the filling here. The dough is perfect for making drop biscuits (a recipe found in *The Joy of Vegan Baking*) and the topping is perfect for fruit-based cobblers.

## FOR FILLING:

- 2 cups (165 g) diced eggplant (1 small globe eggplant or 2 Asian eggplants)
- 1 package (8 ounces, or 225 g) tempeh, cut into ½-inch (1 cm) cubes
- 2 tablespoons (30 ml) water or olive oil
- 1 small-size yellow onion, chopped
- 1 celery stalk, chopped
- 1 teaspoon (2 g) fennel seeds
- 1 to 2 tablespoons (8 to 16 g) capers, rinsed
- 2 tablespoons (30 ml) balsamic vinegar
- 1 can or jar ( 15 ounces, or 420 g) tomato sauce
- ½ teaspoon red pepper flakes or hot sauce
- Salt and pepper, to taste

## FOR BISCUIT DOUGH:

- 1 ⅔ cups (210 g) all-purpose flour
- 1 tablespoon (15 g) baking powder (look for aluminum-free)
- ½ teaspoon salt
- ⅔ cup (160 ml) nondairy milk (soy, rice, almond, hazelnut, hemp, or oat)
- ⅓ cup (80 ml) canola oil or nondairy, nonhydrogenated butter (such as Earth Balance), melted

## DIRECTIONS

Preheat oven to 425°F (220°C, or gas mark 7). Coat 4 or 6 individual ramekins with oil, and set aside. You also can use a 9-inch (23 cm) square pan or a rectangular pan.

To make filling, steam eggplant and tempeh for 10 to 15 minutes, until eggplant is soft and translucent. At the same time, add water or oil to a large-size sauté pan and cook onion and celery until soft. Add fennel seeds, capers, and vinegar, and sauté for 1 minute. Add tomato sauce, red pepper flakes, and cooked tempeh and eggplant. Simmer for 10 minutes, stirring occasionally.

Meanwhile, prepare biscuit dough. Place flour, baking powder, and salt in a mixing bowl, and stir together. Pour in nondairy milk and butter or oil, and mix just until dry ingredients are evenly moistened. The dough should be lumpy and sticky, not smooth like cake batter.

Remove sauté pan from heat, and season filling with salt and pepper, to taste.

Divide filling evenly among prepared ramekins. Drop dough by small spoonfuls on top of each ramekin. Carefully spread dough with back of spoon so it evenly covers filling. Bake pot pies until crust is golden, about 15 minutes. Serve hot.

**YIELD:** 4 to 6 servings

Per serving: 358 calories; 16g fat; 13g protein; 44g carbohydrate; 3g dietary fiber; 0mg cholesterol; 889mg sodium.

# IRISH COFFEE

*Oil-free, wheat-free*

This Irish mainstay is a variation of a "hot toddy" generally comprised of a hot beverage (tea, coffee, or cocoa), an alcoholic spirit (rum, whiskey, or brandy), and a sweetener. It may well be the most famous export from a chilly land that knows the secret to staying warm.

- 1 ½ cups (355 ml) hot coffee, divided
- 2 tablespoons (30 g) brown or granulated sugar, divided
- 3 ounces (90 ml) Irish whiskey, divided
- Nondairy whipped cream (see Resources and Recommendations)

## DIRECTIONS

Rinse two 8-ounce (235 ml) glasses with hot water to warm them up. The most practical type to use is a glass mug with a handle.

Fill one glass two-thirds full with half of the coffee. Add 1 tablespoon (15 g) sugar and stir. Add 1 ½ ounces (45 ml) whiskey. Repeat with second glass.

Gently place fresh whipped cream on top of coffee in each glass. Use a spoon to float cream on top of coffee so it doesn't sink. Do not stir cream into coffee. Traditionally, the cream remains on top.

If you are making several, do one first and taste it to see whether you need to adjust proportions. The strength of the coffee, the type of whiskey you use, and the way you add the cream will all determine the final taste.

**YIELD:** 2 servings

Per serving: 158 calories; 0g fat; trace protein; 13g carbohydrate; 0g dietary fiber; 0mg cholesterol; 4mg sodium.

## FOOD LORE

Irish coffee was created in 1942 by Joe Sheridan, a chef in a restaurant in a major port in southwest Ireland that received travelers from Europe and the United States, who arrived exhausted and cold from their journeys. Sheridan devised a drink to warm their hearts and their bodies. It made its way to the United States through San Francisco in the early 1950s.

## IRISH TOAST

"May your heart be light and happy,
May your smile be big and wide,
And may your pockets always have
a coin or two inside!"

**SPRING/SUMMER MENU:** A Passover Seder

🐛/✳ Charoset   🐛/✳ Passover Pizza
🐛/✳ Matzoh Ball Soup   🐛/✳ Homemade Vegetable Stock
🐛/✳ Traditional Vegetable Soup   🐛/✳ Matzoh Chocolate Brittle

# CHAROSET

*\*Oil-free, wheat-free, soy-free*

Also called *charoses* or *haroset*, this dish is an integral part of every Passover Seder. An Eastern European recipe that combines apples, almonds, spices, and red wine, charoset can also include a variety of other ingredients, such as bananas, apricots, coconut, oranges, dates, exotic nuts, and a wide variety of spices.

- 6 apples, chopped (peeling optional)
- 1 cup (145 g) raisins
- ¾ cup (110 g) chopped toasted almonds
- Freshly grated zest of 1 large-size orange
- 3 tablespoons (45 ml) freshly squeezed orange juice
- 3 tablespoons (40 g) granulated sugar or agave nectar
- 2 tablespoons (30 ml) red wine
- 1 teaspoon (2 g) ground cinnamon
- Pinch of ground ginger

### DIRECTIONS

Combine all ingredients. For a coarse, chunky mixture, refrigerate until ready to serve. For a smoother more "mortarlike" mixture, blend well by hand, or pulse in a food processor or blender. Chill until ready to serve, or serve at room temperature.

**YIELD:** 6 to 8 servings

### SERVING SUGGESTIONS AND VARIATIONS

During Passover, charoset is one of the essential elements found on the Seder plate (see Creating a Traditional Vegan Passover Seder on page 212). Charoset also is served throughout the Passover meal and spread on matzoh. The rest of the year, this dish is a simple and refreshing no-bake snack or dessert.

## DID YOU KNOW?

The color and texture of charoset are meant to recall the mortar with which the Israelites bonded bricks when they were enslaved in ancient Egypt. The word comes from the Hebrew word *cheres*—which means "clay."

Per serving: 219 calories; 7g fat; 4g protein; 39g carbohydrate; 5g dietary fiber; 0mg cholesterol; 6mg sodium.

## COMPASSIONATE COOKS' TIP

Don't refrigerate for more than 2 hours before serving or the charoset will become too wet.

# PASSOVER PIZZA

*Oil-free*

This is a variation of my English Muffin Pizzas (page 178), made appropriate for Passover. A perfect fusion of Jewish and Italian cuisine, it's a breeze for kids to make.

- 12 slices matzoh
- 1 jar (25 ounces, or 700 g) pasta or pizza sauce
- Toppings such as vegetarian pepperoni, fresh tomato slices, red onion, mushrooms, or bell peppers
- 1 package (10 ounces, or 280 g) nondairy mozzarella cheese (such as Follow Your Heart brand), grated
- 2 tablespoons (6 g) dried oregano

Per serving (excluding toppings): 187 calories; 7g fat; 4g protein; 27g carbohydrate; 3g dietary fiber; 0mg cholesterol; 225mg sodium.

## FOOD LORE

This cracker-like flatbread has a variety of spellings, depending on the language: matza, matzah, or matzoh in Hebrew, matzo or matzoh in Ashkenazi, and matze in Yiddish.

## DIRECTIONS

Preheat oven to 425°F (220°C, or gas mark 7).

Place the matzoh slices in a single layer on a cookie sheet or baking pan.

Spread a few tablespoons of sauce over each matzoh, followed by any toppings you might be using. Distribute the cheese evenly on top. Sprinkle with oregano.

Bake for 8 to 9 minutes, until cheese is melted. If you watch it very closely, you can also bake the pizzas under the broiler, which will take about 2 to 3 minutes for the cheese to melt.

**YIELD:** 12 servings

## SERVING SUGGESTIONS AND VARIATIONS

* Make a Peanut Butter Pizza! [Please note, however, that peanut butter is made from legumes and therefore is not kosher for Passover for all Jews.]
* Instead of tomato sauce, spread creamy peanut butter onto each matzoh, top with thinly sliced bananas, and drizzle with agave nectar. Eat as is, warm it up for a couple of minutes in a 350°F (180°C, or gas mark 4) oven, or cook under the broiler for 1 to 2 minutes (watch it closely).
* You can also make grilled peanut butter matzoh sandwiches. Make the peanut butter pizza as directed, then spread a little more peanut butter on a second matzoh and place it on top of the first. Melt a spoonful of nondairy butter in a medium sauté pan, and place the matzoh sandwich in the pan. Cook over medium heat until golden brown (about 2 or 3 minutes), gently pressing down with a spatula every 30 seconds or so. Carefully turn it over and cook for another 2 to 3 minutes. Serve hot.

Advanced Preparation Required

# MATZOH BALL SOUP
*Soy-free*

Thanks to my friend Danielle Puller, who helped me perfect this essential Passover recipe.

- 3 tablespoons (20 g) ground flaxseed (equivalent of 3 "flax eggs")
- 6 tablespoons (90 ml) water
- 1 tablespoon (15 ml) olive oil
- ½ yellow onion, minced
- ½ cup (55 g) matzoh meal
- ½ teaspoon kosher salt (or to taste)
- 1 ½ tablespoons (6 g) minced fresh parsley
- 6 cups (1410 ml) Homemade Vegetable Stock, page 213
- 1 carrot, peeled and finely shredded, for garnish (optional)
- 1 tablespoon (4 g) chopped dill, for garnish (optional)

## COMPASSIONATE COOKS' TIP

The matzoh balls may have a nutty flavor and flecks of flax. To keep the color neutral, look for golden (instead of brown) flaxseeds. Bottom line is that the balls are delicious, nutritious, and cruelty-free!

## DID YOU KNOW?

Keeping kosher for Passover is a whole different ball-game than keeping kosher the rest of the year. There is some debate as to whether tofu (or any legume!) is kosher for Passover (an Ashkenazi versus Sephardic thing), so I was thrilled to veganize this staple without using legumes or tofu.

## DIRECTIONS

Whip flaxseed and water in a food processor for 2 to 3 minutes, until a very thick, creamy, almost yogurtlike consistency.

In a sauté pan, warm oil and sauté onion until golden brown, about 10 minutes. Combine "flax eggs," sautéed onion, matzoh meal, salt, and parsley in a bowl. Cover, and place in the refrigerator for at least 2 hours or even overnight.

When ready to assemble, fill a large soup pot with vegetable stock and bring to a boil. Remove matzoh batter from fridge, and form into tight, walnut-size balls (about 1 inch [2.5 cm] round). Make sure they are tightly packed. To help you form the balls, dip your hands in water before scooping batter and rolling each one. You should be able to make 10 or 12 balls.

Once the broth has boiled, reduce heat to a rapid simmer, and carefully drop in balls. Cover and cook for 30 minutes. (They're ready to eat after 15 minutes, but you can cook them longer to absorb more flavor.)

When ready to serve, ladle stock evenly into 5 or 6 bowls. Place 2 matzoh balls in each. Just before serving, sprinkle each bowl with shredded carrot and chopped dill, if desired.

**YIELD:** 5 to 6 soup servings, 2 matzoh balls per serving

Per serving: 187 calories; 7g fat; 6g protein; 28g carbohydrate; 8g dietary fiber; 0mg cholesterol; 590mg sodium.

# CREATING A TRADITIONAL VEGAN PASSOVER SEDER

Passover (*Pesach*), a Jewish holiday observed by most Jews, commemorates their Exodus out of Egypt, from slavery to freedom. A vegan Seder is not only traditional in its own right, but it also reflects the principles of freedom and mercy that embody this holiday.

## MATZOH

The most significant observance involves the removal of leavened foods and the serving of matzoh to commemorate the fact that Jews leaving Egypt didn't have time to let their bread rise.

Matzoh, an unleavened cracker made from flour and water, can be used as flour (for cookies and cakes), meal (for bread crumbs), farfel (a noodle or bread cube substitute), and full-size matzohs (as bread). Matzoh is eaten three times during the Seder.

## SEDER PLATE

The Seder plate contains six symbolic foods used to retell the story of the Exodus.

1. Charoset. Charoset, a mixture of fruit and ground nuts soaked in wine, represents the mortar used to cement bricks when the Jews were slaves in Egypt. (See page 209 for a recipe.)

2. Greens. Parsley, celery, or other green herbs dipped in saltwater symbolize spring and new life, as well as the tears of the Jewish slaves.

3. Horseradish. Freshly grated horseradish, sometimes mixed with cooked beets and sugar, symbolizes the harshness of slavery.

4. Bitter herbs. Bitter herbs, such as the bitter-tasting roots of romaine lettuce, are also used to signify the bitterness of slavery.

5. Roasted egg. Jewish vegans replace the egg, a symbol of fertility and new creation, with a flower or roasted nuts. Some even use a miniature white egg-size eggplant with the stem removed.

6. Shank bone. Jewish vegans replace the shank bone, meant to symbolize the sacrificial lamb, with roasted beets. In fact, the Talmud explicitly allows for roasted beets to be used instead.

## MAKE YOUR OWN SEDER PLATE

You can purchase decorative Seder plates, with sections for the various elements, which are named in Hebrew and sometimes in English as well. Vegan versions are not yet available, so a friend of mine went to one of those paint-it-yourself pottery stores and created her own vegan Seder plate, designating a place for the charoset, parsley (or "greens"), horseradish, bitter herbs, beetroot, and eggplant.

# HOMEMADE VEGETABLE STOCK

*Soy-free, wheat-free, oil-free if sautéed in water*

I admit to using store-bought organic vegetable bouillon cubes to add flavor to many dishes, but nothing beats a good homemade stock, especially for something like Matzoh Ball Soup (page 211).

- 1 tablespoon (15 ml) olive oil or water
- 1 large-size yellow onion, roughly chopped
- 2 celery stalks, including some leaves, roughly chopped
- 2 large-size carrots, peeled and roughly chopped
- 3 to 5 scallions, roughly chopped
- 8 garlic cloves, minced
- 8 sprigs fresh parsley
- 6 sprigs fresh thyme
- 2 bay leaves
- 1 teaspoon (6 g) salt (or more, to taste)
- 2 quarts (2.3 L) water

## DIRECTIONS

Heat oil or water in a large soup pot. Add onion, celery, carrots, scallions, garlic, parsley, thyme, and bay leaves. Cook over high heat for 5 to 10 minutes, stirring frequently.

Add salt and water, and bring to a boil. Lower heat and simmer, uncovered, for 30 minutes. Strain. Compost vegetables.

**YIELD:** 6 servings

## SERVING SUGGESTIONS AND VARIATIONS

So many vegetables work well for stock. Try mushrooms, asparagus, corn, fennel (stalks and trimmings), bell peppers (green or red), pea pods, chard (stems and leaves), marjoram (stems and leaves), basil, or tomatoes. For another twist, try roasting the veggies first!

Per serving: 90 calories; 3g fat; 4g protein; 15g carbohydrate; 6g dietary fiber; 0mg cholesterol; 426mg sodium.

# TRADITIONAL VEGETABLE SOUP

*Soy-free, wheat-free, oil-free if sautéed in water*

Although you'd think everyone has this standard in his or her repertoire, I have found that to be a hasty assumption. Fresh herbs are wonderful in this soup, but dried work well in a pinch.

- 1 tablespoon (15 ml) oil or water, for sautéing
- 1 yellow onion, chopped
- 2 carrots, chopped
- 2 celery stalks, sliced
- 1 can (16 ounces, or 455 g) diced tomatoes or 2 fresh tomatoes, diced
- 1 ½ teaspoons (1.5 g) minced fresh basil or 1 teaspoon (1.5 g) dried basil
- 1 ½ teaspoons (2 g) minced fresh parsley or 1 teaspoon (1 g) dried parsley
- 1 ½ teaspoons (2 g) minced fresh oregano or marjoram or 1 teaspoon (1 g) dried oregano or marjoram
- 6 cups (1410 ml) Homemade Vegetable Stock (page 213) or 6 cups (1410 ml) water and 1 veggie bouillon cube
- 2 zucchinis, sliced
- 1 bunch broccoli, chopped into florets
- Salt and ground black pepper, to taste

## DIRECTIONS

Heat oil in a large soup pot over medium-high heat. Sauté onion, carrots, and celery until onion is translucent and vegetables are tender, 5 to 7 minutes. Stir in tomatoes and herbs, and cook for 5 minutes longer, stirring frequently.

Add stock, adjust heat to a medium, and simmer for approximately 10 minutes. Add zucchini and broccoli, and cook until tender, 5 to 10 minutes longer. Adjust seasoning with salt and pepper, and serve.

**YIELD:** 6 servings

## SERVING SUGGESTIONS AND VARIATIONS

Add 1 can (15 ounces, or 420 g) cannellini or kidney beans, drained and rinsed, or 1 cup (160 g) cooked barley at the same time you add the zucchini and broccoli.

Per serving: 250 calories; 7g fat; 11g protein; 40g carbohydrate; 9g dietary fiber; 0mg cholesterol; 1680mg sodium.

## COMPASSIONATE COOKS' TIP

Soak 10 dried shiitake mushrooms in some tamari and water for 20 minutes, drain, slice, and add to this soup.

Advanced Preparation Required

# MATZOH CHOCOLATE BRITTLE

This decadent (and addictive) dessert is good for all ages and any time of the year, but I concocted it with Passover in mind.

- 5 to 6 matzoh crackers
- ³/₄ cup (170 g) nondairy, nonhydrogenated butter (such as Earth Balance)
- ¹/₂ to ³/₄ cup (115 to 170 g) packed brown sugar
- ³/₄ to 1 cup (130 to 175 g) nondairy semisweet chocolate chips

## DID YOU KNOW?

Depending on how it's processed, sugar from cane comes in several forms:

- Sucanat, which is an acronym for "Sugar Cane Natural." The molasses and fiber is in tact, and it has a full flavor.

- Turbinado sugar is rinsed in turbines and thus loses some of the molasses and fiber.

- White sugar is completely stripped and processed.

- Brown sugar is white sugar with molasses added back on. If you can grind Sucanat down to a fine substance like brown sugar, you get the same effect.

## DIRECTIONS

Preheat oven to 375°F (190°C, or gas mark 5). Cover a cookie sheet with aluminum foil, for easy cleanup.

Line cookie sheet with matzoh crackers, filling in gaps with broken matzoh and overlapping, if necessary.

In a small saucepan, melt butter and brown sugar until barely simmering. Turn off heat. (Alternatively, you can melt butter in the microwave, and stir in sugar until it dissolves.) Pour butter mixture over matzoh, spreading with a rubber spatula to completely cover all crackers. Don't worry if it drips to the underside of the crackers. It just means more toffee goodness on the bottom!

Bake for 7 minutes. Remove from oven, and turn off heat. Distribute chips evenly over matzoh crackers. Return to hot oven for just a minute or two, to accelerate melting of chips.

Using a rubber spatula, spread chocolate over crackers, covering them completely. Place in the refrigerator for at least 1 hour. Once chocolate has hardened, break chocolate-covered crackers into pieces, and serve as brittle.

**YIELD:** 48 pieces, or servings

Per serving: 48 calories; 32g fat; 5g protein; 59g carbohydrate; trace dietary fiber; 0mg cholesterol; 31mg sodium.

**AUTUMN/WINTER MENU:** It's A Wonderful Life

🌿/✳ Savory Tofu Spread   🌿/✳ Borscht (Beet Soup)   🌿/✳ Old-Fashioned Lentil Loaf
🌿/✳ Mashed Potatoes with Caramelized Onions   🌿/✳ Golden Mushroom Gravy
🌿/✳ Broccoli with Garlic Butter and Cashews   🌿/✳ Decadent Chocolate Truffles

# SAVORY TOFU SPREAD

*Oil-free, wheat-free*

This recipe is based on the Millennium Restaurant's famous tofu spread that accompanies the bread you receive when you sit down to dine. Just scrumptious.

- 1 medium-size yellow onion, roughly chopped
- 3 whole garlic cloves, peeled
- 1 teaspoon (6 g) salt
- ¾ cup (180 ml) vegetable stock (store-bought or homemade, page 213) or dry white wine, divided
- ½ teaspoon dried thyme
- ½ teaspoon dried sage
- ½ teaspoon minced fresh rosemary
- ½ teaspoon dried basil
- ½ teaspoon dried oregano
- ½ teaspoon freshly ground black pepper
- ¼ teaspoon ground nutmeg
- 12 ounces (340 g) extra-firm tofu (not silken)
- ¼ cup (65 g) light or white miso paste

## DIRECTIONS

In a sauté pan, combine onion, garlic, salt, and ¼ cup (60 ml) vegetable stock until onion starts to soften and turn translucent, about 5 minutes. Add thyme, sage, rosemary, basil, oregano, pepper, nutmeg, and remaining ½ cup (120 ml) vegetable stock. Cover and cook until liquid evaporates and onion and garlic are very soft and light brown, about 20 minutes. Remove from heat, and let cool to room temperature.

Add the tofu, miso, and cooled onion mixture to a food processor or blender, and blend until smooth.

Serve at room temperature or chilled.

**YIELD:** 2 ½ cups (565 g), or 40 (2-tablespoon [30 g]) servings

## SERVING SUGGESTIONS AND VARIATIONS

The heartiness of this spread deems it appropriate to accompany a hearty bread, preferably a sliced baguette, which you can serve fresh or toasted.

Per serving: 19 calories; 1g fat; 1g protein; 3g carbohydrate; 1g dietary fiber; 0mg cholesterol; 293mg sodium.

# BORSCHT (BEET SOUP)

*Wheat-free, oil-free if sautéing in water, soy-free depending on milk*

Originating in Ukraine, borscht is very popular in Russian and Polish cuisines. A version from the latter is served as the first course during the Christmas Eve feast. This favorite recipe of mine takes advantage of the healthful beet greens and adds them to the soup.

- 3 medium-size beets, plus greens
- 6 cups (1410 ml) water
- 1 ½ teaspoons (9 g) salt
- ½ cup (65 g) finely chopped carrots
- 5 yellow potatoes such as Yukon gold, (3 peeled and quartered; 2 diced and peeled, if desired)
- 2 tablespoons (28 g) nondairy, nonhydrogenated butter (such as Earth Balance) or olive oil
- 1 yellow onion, finely chopped
- 1 ½ cups (270 g) chopped fresh tomatoes or 1 can (15 ounces, or 420 g) diced tomatoes
- ¼ cup (60 ml) nondairy milk (soy, rice, almond, hazelnut, hemp, or oat) or soy creamer
- 1 ½ cups (105) finely shredded red or green cabbage
- 1 tablespoon (4 g) fresh dill
- Salt and freshly ground black pepper, to taste
- 1 large-size bunch fresh dill, snipped with scissors

## DIRECTIONS

Using a sharp knife, carefully cut off skin of beets, without taking too much beet flesh. Cut peeled beets into quarters. Wash beet greens to remove any soil and roughly chop. Set aside.

Place water, salt, carrots, the 3 quartered potatoes, beets, and beet greens in a large soup pot over high heat. Bring to a boil.

Meanwhile, in a separate sauté pan over medium heat, melt nondairy butter. Sauté onion until tender, approximately 5 minutes. Stir in tomatoes, reduce heat to medium-low, and simmer for 10 minutes. Set aside.

When beets are tender, about 30 minutes later, use a slotted spoon or tongs to remove them from pot, along with potatoes. Chop up half of these beets into bite-size pieces, and place the other half in a blender or food processor, along with potatoes. Add milk, and blend until smooth. (You can also mash them by hand.) Return bite-size beets and mashed beets/potatoes back to soup pot.

At the same time, add remaining 2 diced potatoes, shredded cabbage, dill, and tomato/onion mixture to the soup pot. Simmer stew until potatoes are just tender, 10 to 15 minutes. Season with salt and pepper to taste.

Spoon into individual serving bowls, and top with a generous amount of dill. Fresh dill is key to this dish, so don't be stingy with it!

**YIELD:** 8 servings

Per serving: 126 calories; 3g fat; 3g protein; 22g carbohydrate; 4g dietary fiber; 0mg cholesterol; 441mg sodium.

## FOOD LORE

The original base of this soup was the "cow parsnip" or *borsch* in Russian.

# OLD-FASHIONED LENTIL LOAF

*Oil-free*

Providing heartiness, protein, and lots of familiar flavor, this loaf makes a great main dish, accompanied by a side of potatoes and green veggies.

- 4 cups (940 ml) water, plus more for sautéing
- 2 cups (385 g) brown lentils, picked over and rinsed
- 1 to 2 yellow onions, chopped
- 3 garlic cloves, minced
- ³⁄₄ cup (180 g) ketchup, divided
- ¹⁄₂ cup (55 g) bread crumbs, Italian-style or plain
- ¹⁄₄ cup (30 g) finely chopped raw walnuts
- ¹⁄₂ cup (30 g) finely chopped fresh parsley
- 2 teaspoons (1 to 2 g) finely chopped fresh thyme or 1 teaspoon (1 g) dried thyme
- 1 to 2 tablespoons (15 to 30 ml) tamari soy sauce (or to taste)
- 1 to 2 tablespoons (15 to 30 ml) vegetarian Worcestershire sauce (no anchovies)
- ¹⁄₂ teaspoon freshly ground black pepper

## DIRECTIONS

Preheat oven to 350°F (180°C, or gas mark 4). Lightly oil a 4 x 8-inch (10 x 20 cm) loaf pan.

Place 4 cups (940 ml) water and lentils in a large-size saucepan. Cover and bring to a boil over medium-high heat, then immediately reduce heat and simmer until water is absorbed, 50 to 60 minutes. Check lentils after 30 minutes; add more water, if necessary. You want the result to be thick but with lentils cooked down to a soft texture, so add water sparingly.

Meanwhile, sauté onions and garlic in enough water to coat vegetables so they don't stick to the pan. Cook for 5 minutes, until onion is soft. Transfer to a large-size bowl.

When lentils are done, remove from heat, and let stand for at least 30 minutes. They will thicken up even more. When completely cool, combine with onion/garlic mixture, and add ¹⁄₄ cup (60 g) ketchup, bread crumbs, walnuts, parsley, thyme, tamari, Worcestershire sauce, and pepper. Thoroughly combine all ingredients. Adjust seasoning as necessary.

Press mixture firmly into prepared pan, and spread remaining ¹⁄₂ cup (120 g) ketchup on top. Bake for 45 minutes. Let cool for 10 minutes before slicing.

**YIELD:** 12 servings

## COMPASSIONATE COOKS' TIP

This dish is even better the next day!

Per serving: 173 calories; 2g fat; 11g protein; 29g carbohydrate; 11g dietary fiber; 0mg cholesterol; 428mg sodium.

# MASHED POTATOES WITH CARAMELIZED ONIONS

*Wheat-free, oil-free, soy-free depending on milk*

Mashed potatoes are my absolute favorite dish during the holidays. I never thought I'd modify the standard, but the addition of the caramelized onions makes it heavenly.

- 2 tablespoons (28 g) nondairy, nonhydrogenated butter (such as Earth Balance), plus more for individual servings
- 4 large-size yellow onions, thinly sliced
- 1 teaspoon (4 g) granulated sugar
- 3 to 4 pounds (1365 to 1820 g) yellow potatoes, peeled and quartered
- ¼ to ½ cup (60 to 120 ml) nondairy milk (soy, rice, almond, hazelnut, hemp, or oat)
- 1 teaspoon (6 g) salt
- ½ teaspoon ground black pepper

## COMPASSIONATE COOKS' TIP

To make your prep go faster, slice onions using the slicing blade of your food processor or a mandolin, a vegetable-slicing tool with adjustable blades.

## DIRECTIONS

In a large-size sauté pan, melt butter over medium-high heat. Add onions and sugar; cook, stirring occasionally, until onions turn dark golden brown, about 30 minutes.

Place potatoes in a 4-quart (4.5 L) saucepan. Cover with water. Cook potatoes over medium-high heat until soft, about 25 minutes. Drain them and place them in bowl for mashing.

Using a potato masher or an electric hand mixer on medium speed, blend together potatoes, milk (start with ¼ cup), salt, and pepper until well combined and fluffy. Fold in caramelized onions by hand using a rubber spatula.

**YIELD:** 4 to 6 servings

## SERVING SUGGESTIONS AND VARIATIONS

* When caramelizing the onions, don't overstir. Give them time to brown on one side before tossing them around the pan.
* The best potatoes to use are waxy yellow potatoes, such as yellow fin or Yukon gold.
* For more rustic mashed potatoes, don't peel them.
* Add roasted garlic instead of, or in addition to, caramelized onions.
* Use oil for caramelizing onions if you cannot find Earth Balance.

Per serving: 91 calories; 4g fat; 2g protein; 12g carbohydrate; 2g dietary fiber; 0mg cholesterol; 361mg sodium.

# GOLDEN MUSHROOM GRAVY

*Oil-free if sautéing in water*

This gravy is perfect for mashed potatoes, stuffed squash, or biscuits and gravy! Purée it to make a smooth, creamy concoction, or leave it chunky. As the latter, this gravy is fantastic as a side dish, served over quinoa, or as a topping for Salisbury tofu or tempeh.

- 2 teaspoons (28 g) nondairy, nonhydrogenated butter (such as Earth Balance)
- 1 yellow onion, chopped
- 1 pound (455 g) cremini mushrooms (about 20 mushrooms), thinly sliced
- 3 tablespoons (25 g) flour or other thickener
- 2 cups (470 ml) vegetable stock (store-bought or homemade, page 213)
- 2 to 3 tablespoons (30 to 45 ml) tamari soy sauce
- ½ teaspoon dried thyme
- Freshly ground black pepper, to taste

## DIRECTIONS

Heat butter in a large-size skillet and sauté onion and mushrooms over high heat, stirring frequently, until they turn translucent and a little golden brown and mushrooms soften, about 15 minutes.

In the meantime, in a separate bowl, whisk flour into stock along with tamari, thyme, and black pepper. When there appear to be no lumps, add to onion mixture and cook over low-medium heat, stirring constantly until thickened.

For smooth gravy, purée in a blender or food processor. You may want to play with the flavor a little by adding more tamari or pepper. If necessary, reheat mixture on low heat in a saucepan.

**YIELD:** 2 cups (235 ml), or 18 (2-tablespoon [30 ml]) servings

## SERVING SUGGESTIONS AND VARIATIONS

* Instead of nondairy butter, use olive or toasted sesame oil.
* If you want to eliminate oil altogether, sauté the onions in stock or water. It might just take a little longer (though, to be honest, in this case, I think the flavor is better when you use oil or nondairy butter).
* To aid the process, cover the mushrooms to help them "sweat."

## COMPASSIONATE COOKS' TIP

Shiitake, oyster, and other exotic mushrooms, though more expensive, are great candidates for this gravy.

## DID YOU KNOW?

Cremini mushrooms, which are related to white mushrooms but more flavorful, are the same as brown or baby portobello mushrooms.

Per serving: 28 calories; 1g fat; 1g protein; 4g carbohydrate; 1g dietary fiber; 0mg cholesterol; 263mg sodium.

# BROCCOLI WITH GARLIC BUTTER AND CASHEWS

*Wheat-free*

This is a fantastic side dish that touches almost all the flavors of our taste buds: sweet, salty, and tangy.

- 1 1/2 pounds (685 g) fresh broccoli, cut into bite-size florets
- 3 tablespoons (42 g) nondairy, nonhydrogenated butter (such as Earth Balance)
- 2 garlic cloves, minced
- 1 tablespoon (15 g) brown sugar
- 2 to 3 tablespoons (30 to 45 ml) tamari soy sauce
- 2 teaspoons (10 ml) rice vinegar
- 1/4 teaspoon freshly ground black pepper
- 1/3 cup (50 g) chopped salted cashews

## DIRECTIONS

In a medium-size pot with a steamer basket, steam broccoli until crisp-tender, about 10 minutes.

Meanwhile, in a small skillet over medium heat, melt nondairy butter. Stir in garlic, brown sugar, tamari, vinegar, and pepper. Bring to a boil, allowing it to thicken up a bit. Remove from heat, and stir in cashews.

When broccoli is finished cooking, transfer to a pretty serving bowl, pour sauce over, and toss gently. Serve immediately.

**YIELD:** 6 servings

Per serving: 138 calories; 9g fat; 6g protein; 11g carbohydrate; 4g dietary fiber; 0mg cholesterol; 583mg sodium.

## FOOD LORE

Cashews are never sold in their shell because between the outer and inner shells is an extremely caustic oil. The outer shell must be roasted or burned off with the oil. The kernels are then boiled or roasted again, and the second shell is removed.

Advanced Preparation Required

# DECADENT CHOCOLATE TRUFFLES

*Wheat-free, oil-free*

These are so much fun to make (kids can get involved), and when you coat the truffles in a variety of ingredients, they become a beautiful, delicious dessert.

- 1 container (8 ounces, or 225 g) nondairy cream cheese (see Resources and Recommendations)
- 3 cups (300 g) confectioners' sugar
- 3 cups (525 g) nondairy semisweet or dark chocolate chips (or any high-quality chocolate), melted
- 1 ½ teaspoons (8 ml) vanilla extract
- Ingredients for coating truffles (see below)

## DIRECTIONS

In the large bowl of a food processor, beat cream cheese until smooth. Add confectioners' sugar, 1 cup (100 g) at a time, until well blended. Add melted chocolate and vanilla and stir until thoroughly combined.

Cover and refrigerate for at least 1 hour or as long as overnight. The longer you refrigerate the batter, the easier it will be to roll into perfect balls. However, it will definitely require elbow grease to scoop them out.

Shape into 1-inch (2.5 cm) balls. Refrigerate again if the batter is too soft, especially if your kitchen is warm. Use a strong spoon or melon baller to create uniform balls.

Once rolled, either send balls back to fridge or coat in any of the following:

- Finely ground nuts (pecans, hazelnuts, walnuts, almonds)
- Sifted cocoa powder
- Toasted or raw coconut
- Sifted confectioners' sugar
- Candy sprinkles (the sparkly kind)

**YIELD:** 50 to 60 truffles, or servings

## SERVING SUGGESTIONS AND VARIATIONS

* To create a hard chocolate shell, refrigerate rolled truffle balls for at least 30 minutes (longer is fine, too). Melt some nondairy chocolate, either a good-quality chocolate bar or chocolate chips, and dip each ball into the chocolate. Return to the refrigerator and let set for at least 1 hour.
* To change the truffle flavor, omit the vanilla and replace it with 1 tablespoon (15 ml) of another flavor. You can even get several flavors out of one batch by dividing the truffle "batter" into thirds when you first combine the ingredients, and then adding 1 teaspoon (5 ml) of whatever flavor you want to each mixture.
* For an elegant dinner party, prepare the truffles with the melted dark chocolate coating, then buy some edible gold and silver powder from baking specialty shops and dust over.
* For grown-up parties, add 1 or 2 tablespoons (15 to 30 ml) Baileys Irish Cream, Kahlúa, Grand Marnier, cherry brandy, or another liqueur.

Per serving (excluding toppings): 310 calories; 17g fat; 2g protein; 38g carbohydrate; 4g dietary fiber; 0mg cholesterol; 308mg sodium.

# MAKE A TRUFFLE TREE

Being a grammar school teacher—and #1 aunt to our
nieces—my crafty sister-in-law comes up with all sorts
of wonderful ways to involve kids in food projects. Her
Truffle Tree is the most impressive I've seen, and it's
actually pretty easy to create. It makes a great presentation, and the older kids can help decorate it.

If you know you are going to make a tree out of your
truffles, perhaps you want to create larger and smaller
balls, so you'll have larger truffles for the bottom and
smaller truffles for the top. For this you will need:

- 9-inch (23 cm)-tall foam cone (from a craft supply
  store)

- 60 or more wooden toothpicks

- 60 refrigerated truffles (already rolled in their
  various ingredients)

## DIRECTIONS

Cover cone with foil.

Push a toothpick into a truffle, then push the other
end into the foam cone, making sure it is securely posi-
tioned. Start from the bottom (using larger truffles on
the bottom and working your way up). Repeat until tree
is complete. Refrigerate.

Because the presentation is so pretty, keep tree
tucked away until you're ready to serve dessert. Present
it on a pretty platter, along with confectioners' sugar
dusted on the plate to resemble snow. Serve with coffee
and tea.

Note, the tree will last for a couple of days in the
refrigerator, so you can prepare it in advance. Remove
from the refrigerator at least 30 minutes before serving
so the truffles aren't too cold.

**AUTUMN/WINTER MENU:** Home for the Holidays

/✱ Mushroom Walnut Pâté  /✱ Mashed Yukon Gold and Sweet Potatoes  /✱ Potato Latkes  /✱ Moroccan Phyllo with Curried Golden Tomato Sauce  /✱ Roasted Brussels Sprouts with Caramelized Onions and Toasted Pistachios  /✱ Benne Cakes (Kwanzaa Cookies)

# MUSHROOM WALNUT PÂTÉ

*Wheat-free*

This is a hearty, satisfying, elegant spread that coincidentally resembles one of my favorite spreads from the famous Millennium Restaurant in San Francisco.

- 2 tablespoons (30 ml) olive oil, divided
- 1 medium-size yellow onion, chopped
- 3 garlic cloves, minced
- 15 cremini or shiitake mushrooms, sliced
- 1 tablespoon (2 g) chopped fresh thyme or 2 teaspoons (2 g) dried
- 1 tablespoon (2 g) chopped fresh sage or 2 teaspoons (2 g) dried
- 2 tablespoons (25 g) nutritional yeast flakes
- 3 tablespoons (45 ml) tamari soy sauce, divided
- 2 tablespoons (30 ml) balsamic vinegar
- 2 cups (240 g) walnuts, toasted (see page 86)
- ½ teaspoon freshly ground pepper

## DIRECTIONS

Heat 1 tablespoon (15 ml) oil in a large-size sauté pan over medium heat. Add onion and garlic and sauté until onion becomes translucent, about 5 minutes. Add mushrooms, along with remaining 1 tablespoon (15 ml) oil, and cover; cook for 5 minutes longer, stirring occasionally. Uncover pan and allow them to cook for 10 minutes longer.

Add thyme, sage, nutritional yeast, 2 tablespoons (30 ml) tamari, and vinegar, and stir to combine. Cook for 1 minute and turn off heat. Transfer mushroom mixture and toasted walnuts to a food processor, adding freshly ground pepper and remaining 1 tablespoon (15 ml) tamari, if needed. Pulse until mixture becomes a creamy pâté. Taste and add more seasoning, if necessary.

Serve at room temperature with crackers, bread, or crostini.

**YIELD:** 1½ cups (340 g), or 12 (2-tablespoon [30 g]) servings

## WHAT'S THE DIFFERENCE? NUTRITIONAL YEAST VS. BREWER'S YEAST

Nutritional yeast is nonactive (not live) yeast fermented on molasses. Its cheesy flavor makes it great for popcorn or for creating nondairy cheese sauce. Brewer's yeast is nonactive (not live) yeast fermented on hops, hence the bitter (not cheesy) flavor.

Per serving: 45 calories; 3g fat; 2g protein; 4g carbohydrate; 1g dietary fiber; 0mg cholesterol; 253mg sodium.

# MASHED YUKON GOLD AND SWEET POTATOES

*Wheat-free*

The addition of sweet potatoes (or "yams") into this holiday classic imparts a sweet flavor and a beautiful color. Who says you can't improve on perfection?

- 2 pounds (910 g) large sweet potatoes or "yams" (see tip below), peeled and cut into 1-inch (2.5 cm) cubes
- 4 pounds (1820 g) Yukon gold potatoes, peeled and quartered
- ¼ to ½ cup (60 to 120 ml) nondairy milk (soy, rice, almond, hazelnut, hemp, or oat)
- 2 tablespoons (28 g) nondairy, nonhydrogenated butter (such as Earth Balance), plus more for serving
- Salt and freshly ground pepper, to taste

## DIRECTIONS

Place yams and potatoes in a large-size pot. Cover with water. Cook over medium-high heat until soft, about 25 minutes. Drain and transfer to a large bowl.

Using a potato masher or an electric hand mixer on low speed, mix potatoes, milk, butter, salt, and pepper until well combined.

Provide guests with extra nondairy butter to add to their individual servings.

**YIELD:** 6 to 8 servings

Per serving: 351 calories; 3g fat; 7g protein; 72g carbohydrate; 8g dietary fiber; 0mg cholesterol; 25mg sodium.

## COMPASSIONATE COOKS' TIP

What grocery stores call "yams" are actually a variety of sweet potatoes. True yams are not widely sold in North America, but are popular in South and Central America, the West Indies, and parts of Asia and Africa. For this recipe, use what are called garnet or jewel "yams" in the grocery stores.

# POTATO LATKES

*Soy-free if not serving nondairy sour cream*

Frying foods during Hanukkah is an ancient tradition, connected with the oil used to light the menorah during this "festival of lights."

- 2 tablespoons (14 g) ground flaxseed
- ¼ cup (60 ml) water
- 4 cups (440 g) peeled and shredded potatoes (about 5 medium-size potatoes)
- 6 scallions, finely chopped
- 1 tablespoon (8 g) all-purpose flour
- 1 teaspoon (6 g) salt (or to taste)
- Canola oil, for frying
- Nondairy sour cream and/or applesauce, for accompaniments
- Chopped chives, for garnish (optional)

## COMPASSIONATE COOKS' TIP

Shredded or grated potatoes will oxidize (turn a grayish brownish color) pretty quickly, so I recommend chopping your scallions and preparing your "flax egg" before shredding the potatoes. Prepare potatoes by hand, or use the special grating blade in your food processor, which is a lot easier and faster.

### DIRECTIONS

In a food processor or blender, whip flaxseed and water together, until mixture reaches a thick and creamy, almost gelatinous consistency, 1 to 2 minutes. Set aside.

Spread potatoes on a kitchen towel or cheesecloth, and roll up jelly-roll style. Twist towel tightly to wring out as much liquid as possible. You may need to do this again with a second towel to extract all the water. Transfer to a mixing bowl.

Add "flax egg" to potatoes, along with scallions, flour, and salt. Use your hands to combine ingredients and to get a feel for the mixture. You want it moist but not too wet.

Heat some oil in a large-size nonstick sauté pan over medium heat until hot but not smoking. Using a table spoon, scoop a large spoonful of potato mixture into hot oil, pressing down to form ¼- to ½-inch (6 mm to 1 cm)-thick patty. (To make a good medium-size patty, I use two tablespoons [32 g], but you can use one.) You are not trying to create dense patties, but the batter should stick together enough to be flipped without falling apart. Slide a spatula underneath latkes while they're cooking to make sure they don't stick to the pan.

Brown on one side, turn over, and brown on the other. You may need more oil as you add more latkes to pan. Transfer to a plate lined with paper towels to soak up excess oil. Season with salt.

Serve hot with nondairy sour cream and/or applesauce and sprinkled with chives, if desired.

**YIELD:** 15 to 20 latkes, or servings

Per serving: 31 calories; trace fat; 1g protein; 6g carbohydrate; 1g dietary fiber; 0mg cholesterol; 109mg sodium.

# MOROCCAN PHYLLO WITH CURRIED GOLDEN TOMATO SAUCE

*Oil-free, wheat-free*

This amazingly delicious dish is modified from *The Millennium Cookbook: Extraordinary Vegetarian Cuisine*, and extraordinary it is. Phyllo intimidates many people, but I can assure you, it's very forgiving. Don't fear the phyllo.

## FOR FILLING:

- 1 medium-size yellow onion, diced
- 4 garlic cloves, minced
- 2 red bell peppers, cut into ½-inch (1 cm) pieces
- 1 to 2 tablespoons (15 to 30 ml) water, for sautéing
- 2 Japanese eggplants (or 1 medium-size globe), cut into ½-inch (1 cm)-thick pieces
- 1 teaspoon (2 g) ground cumin
- 2 teaspoons (4 g) curry powder
- 2 teaspoons (1 g) minced fresh rosemary
- 1 teaspoon (2 g) minced fresh ginger
- ¼ teaspoon cayenne pepper
- 1 cup (245 g) tomato purée or mild tomato sauce
- 2 cups (60 g) packed fresh spinach leaves
- 2 tablespoons (30 ml) tamari soy sauce
- 12 ounces (340 g) extra-firm tofu, cut into ½-inch (1 cm) cubes
- 2 tablespoons (12 g) minced fresh mint leaves
- 1 cup (165 g) brown rice cooked in vegetable stock

## FOR PHYLLO:

- ½ cup (55 g) slivered almonds, toasted
- 2 tablespoons (25 g) granulated sugar
- 1 tablespoon (7 g) ground cinnamon
- 1 package (16 ounces, or 455 g) phyllo dough, thawed (be sure to thaw for at least 24 hours)
- ¼ cup (60 ml) canola oil, for brushing phyllo
- 1 recipe Curried Golden Tomato Sauce (recipe follows)
- Fresh sprigs rosemary, for garnish (optional)

### COMPASSIONATE COOKS' TIP

The Fillo Factory is a brand that makes organic phyllo dough. It is found in the frozen section of the grocery store.

## DIRECTIONS

To make the filling, in a large-size sauté pan, cook onion, garlic, and peppers in water over medium heat until onion is soft, about 10 minutes.

Add eggplants, cumin, curry powder, rosemary, ginger, and cayenne. Stir well and sauté for 2 minutes.

Stir in tomato purée, spinach, and tamari and simmer for 10 minutes, or until most liquid evaporates. You may cover the pan to accelerate this process and to ensure that the eggplant becomes tender. Remove from heat and stir in tofu and mint. Let cool to room temperature.

To make the phyllo, preheat oven to 400°F (200°C, or gas mark 6). Line a baking sheet with parchment paper.

In a blender or food processor, grind almonds, sugar, and cinnamon to a fine meal. Set aside.

Place 2 sheets of phyllo on a work surface. Keep remaining phyllo covered with a damp cloth. Brush phyllo with oil. Repeat process until 6 sheets of phyllo have been used. Cut the phyllo stack in half to make 2 roughly square stacks.

Place one-sixth rice 1 inch (2.5 cm) from nearest end of phyllo stack. Top with one-sixth filling. Roll phyllo into a log, tucking in sides as you roll, or create triangles by folding from the right corner to the left. Make sure edges are all sealed. (You can use a little more oil as "glue" to seal it at the end.)

Place wrapped phyllo on prepared pan. Repeat process until you have 6 filled logs or triangles. Brush top of logs/triangles with remaining oil and sprinkle with the almond mixture. Bake in center of oven for 15 to 20 minutes, until golden brown.

To serve, cover center of each serving plate with 1/4 cup (60 g) tomato sauce. Place 1 phyllo triangle over the sauce and garnish with rosemary sprigs, if desired.

**YIELD:** 6 servings

Per serving: 537 calories; 21g fat; 19g protein; 60g carbohydrate; 17g dietary fiber; 0mg cholesterol; 689mg sodium.

## CURRIED GOLDEN TOMATO SAUCE

- 1 medium-size yellow onion, cut lengthwise into thin crescents
- 1 tablespoon (15 ml) water, for sautéing
- 3 tablespoons (45 ml) dry sherry or nonalcoholic wine
- 1 tablespoon (6 g) curry powder
- 1 teaspoon (2 g) ground cumin
- 1/4 teaspoon ground cardamom
- 1/4 teaspoon ground cayenne pepper
- 2 medium-size ripe yellow tomatoes, cut into quarters
- 2 cups (470 ml) vegetable stock (store-bought or homemade, page 213)
- 1 teaspoon (6 g) salt (or to taste)

## DIRECTIONS

In a medium-size saucepan, sauté onion in water over medium heat until soft, about 10 minutes. Stir in sherry, reduce heat, and simmer until almost evaporated. Stir in curry powder, cumin, cardamom, and cayenne. Add tomatoes and stock.

Cover and simmer for 20 minutes, or until tomatoes are tender. Transfer to a blender and purée until smooth. Add salt to taste. Serve with phyllo.

**YIELD:** 2 1/2 cups (615 g), or 10 (1/4-cup [60 g]) servings

Per serving: 50 calories; 1g fat; 2g protein; 8g carbohydrate; 1g dietary fiber; 0mg cholesterol; 542mg sodium.

# ROASTED BRUSSELS SPROUTS WITH CARAMELIZED ONIONS AND TOASTED PISTACHIOS

*\*Wheat-free, soy-free if using oil and not Earth Balance*

The combination of roasted Brussels sprouts, sweet onions, and toasted pistachios puts this dish over the top in terms of flavor.

- 1 ¹/₂ pounds (685 g) Brussels sprouts (about 40), ends trimmed and cut in half, if large

- 3 tablespoons (45 ml) olive oil

- ¹/₂ teaspoon salt

- ¹/₂ teaspoon freshly ground black pepper

- 2 tablespoons (28 g) nondairy, nonhydrogenated butter (such as Earth Balance) or oil

- 4 small-medium yellow onions, thinly sliced

- 1 teaspoon (4 g) granulated sugar

- ¹/₂ cup (70 g) pistachios

## FOOD LORE

The word "onion" comes from the Latin word *unionem*, meaning "unity," referring to the connection of the layers of an onion.

## DIRECTIONS

Preheat oven to 425°F (220°C, or gas mark 7).

Place Brussels sprouts, olive oil, salt, and pepper in a large-size bowl. Toss to coat. Pour onto a baking sheet, and place on center rack in oven. Roast for 20 to 40 minutes, shaking pan every several minutes for even browning. Dark brown color signifies that the Brussels sprouts are done.

Meanwhile, in a large skillet or sauté pan, melt nondairy butter over low-medium heat. Add onions and sugar; cook, stirring occasionally, until onions turn dark golden brown and caramelize, about 30 minutes.

While onions and Brussels sprouts cook, toast pistachios in a 200°F (100°C) toaster oven for less than 4 minutes. Let cool, and coarsely chop.

Toss together onions, Brussels sprouts, and toasted pistachios. Serve hot or at room temperature in a pretty serving bowl.

**YIELD:** 4 to 6 servings

## SERVING SUGGESTIONS AND VARIATIONS

Use toasted pecans or walnuts instead of pistachios and tamari soy sauce instead of salt.

Per serving: 189 calories; 16g fat; 3g protein; 10g carbohydrate; 3g dietary fiber; 0mg cholesterol; 182mg sodium.

# BENNE CAKES (KWANZAA COOKIES)

Hailing from West Africa, these crispy thin cookies, characterized by the *benne*, or sesame seeds, are eaten for good luck!

- 1 ½ teaspoons Ener-G Egg Replacer
- 2 tablespoons (30 ml) water
- 1 cup (145 g) sesame seeds (I use a combination of black and white)
- 4 tablespoons (55 g) nondairy, nonhydrogenated butter (such as Earth Balance), softened
- 1 cup (225 g) firmly packed light brown sugar
- 1 teaspoon (5 ml) vanilla extract
- 1 teaspoon (5 ml) fresh lemon juice
- ½ cup (65 g) all-purpose flour
- ½ teaspoon baking powder (look for aluminum-free)
- Salt, to taste

## DIRECTIONS

Preheat oven to 325°F (170°C, or gas mark 3). Lightly oil 2 cookie sheets or line with parchment paper.

In a small food processor bowl or by hand, whip together egg replacer powder and water until mixture becomes thick and creamy. Set aside.

Place sesame seeds on an ungreased baking sheet and toast for 10 to 12 minutes, until light brown. Watch closely so they don't burn. You may use the toaster oven, but since you already have the oven preheating, it is easier—and more economical—to toast them in the oven.

In a large-size bowl, cream nondairy butter and brown sugar until light and fluffy. Beat in "egg" mixture, vanilla, and lemon juice. In a small-size bowl, whisk together flour, baking powder, and salt. Combine dry ingredients and butter mixture, then stir in sesame seeds.

Drop by rounded teaspoons onto prepared cookie sheets, about 2 inches (5 cm) apart. Pay attention to this, as the cookies spread out substantially. Make them smaller if you prefer.

Bake for 15 minutes, or until edges are lightly brown.

Let cookies cool for 2 minutes before transferring to a wire rack to cool completely.

**YIELD:** 3 dozen wafer cookies

## DID YOU KNOW?

The recipe actually originated in West Africa—brought over by slaves—and has become popular in the southern United States. The cookies are eaten and served during Kwanzaa, the African-American festival that lasts from December 26 through January 1.

Per serving (one cookie): 59 calories; 4g fat; 1g protein; 6g carbohydrate; 1g dietary fiber; 0mg cholesterol; 9mg sodium.

AUTUMN/WINTER MENU: Winter Wonderland

◢/✳ Mexican Champurrado (Thick Hot Chocolate)   ◢/✳ Harvest-Stuffed Acorn Squash
◢/✳ Butternut Squash Timbales   ◢/✳ Mashed Root Vegetables with Fresh Herb Infusion
◢/✳ Sensational Stuffing with Nuts   ◢/✳ Holiday Cranberry Relish   ◢/✳ Garlic-Glazed Green Beans

# MEXICAN CHAMPURRADO (THICK HOT CHOCOLATE)

*Oil-free, wheat-free, soy-free depending on milk*

Essentially a thick, spiced hot chocolate, this special drink is tasty hot or cold.

- ¼ cup (35 g) masa harina flour (see tip)
- 3 ½ cups (825 ml) cold water, divided
- 3 cups (705 ml) nondairy milk (soy, rice, almond, hazelnut, hemp, or oat)
- 1 tablet/disk (3 ounces, or 85 g) sweetened Mexican chocolate flavored with cinnamon
- ¼ cup (60 g) packed light or dark brown sugar
- ⅛ teaspoon salt
- Pinch of chili powder (optional)
- ¼ teaspoon ground aniseed

## DIRECTIONS

In a large-size pot, whisk together masa harina with ½ cup (120 ml) water until thoroughly combined. Add remaining 3 cups (705 ml) water. Bring to a boil. Reduce heat, and cook slowly for 20 minutes, stirring frequently (using a whisk), while mixture thickens.

Meanwhile, in another saucepan, bring milk to a boil. Add chocolate and cook for about 10 minutes, until it has completely dissolved. Add brown sugar, salt, and chili powder (if desired), and stir to combine. Pour chocolate into the masa harina mixture, stirring until well incorporated.

Whisk briskly for 3 minutes to create foam. Serve, hot or cold, in large mugs with a sprinkling of aniseed on top.

**YIELD:** 6 servings

## SERVING SUGGESTIONS AND VARIATIONS

Once everything finishes cooking, blend the mixture to make it nice and smooth. Instead of brown sugar, try *piloncillo*, a compressed cone of brown sugar found in Mexican groceries.

Per serving: 88 calories; 3g fat; 4g protein; 13g carbohydrate; 2g dietary fiber; 0mg cholesterol; 62mg sodium.

## FOOD LORE

Champurrado is a member of a group of Mexican corn-based drinks called *atoles*. It is somewhat filling, so consider serving as a late afternoon snack or even as part of breakfast. It is often a favorite around Christmastime and during the cold winter season.

## COMPASSIONATE COOKS' TIP

If you cannot find masa harina, use fine cornmeal or cornmeal flour, available in the bulk section of large natural food stores.

# HARVEST-STUFFED ACORN SQUASH

*Oil-free if using water for sautéing, wheat-free, soy-free*

The foundation of this dish is antioxidant-rich fruits and vegetables, whole grains, and nuts. The earthy colors make for a beautiful Thanksgiving dinner centerpiece. (Choose Butternut Squash Timbales, page 236, as an alternate main dish.)

- 4 acorn squash, halved lengthwise, seeds and membranes removed
- 1 tablespoon (15 ml) olive oil or 2 tablespoons (30 ml) water, for sautéing
- 2 medium-size onions, chopped
- 4 celery stalks, diced
- 1 1/2 cups (250 g) cooked brown rice
- 1 cup (165 g) cooked wild rice
- 1 cup (100 g) raw or toasted pecans, coarsely chopped (or walnuts, almonds, or chestnuts)
- 1/2 cup (65 g) dried diced apricots or raisins
- 2 teaspoons (4 g) ground ginger
- 1 teaspoon (2 g) ground cinnamon
- 1/2 teaspoon ground cardamom
- 1/4 teaspoon ground cloves
- 1/2 teaspoon salt (or to taste)
- Freshly ground pepper, to taste

## DIRECTIONS

Preheat oven to 375ºF (190ºC, or gas mark 5).

Place squash halves, cut side down, on 1 or 2 non-stick cookie or baking sheets. You don't need to oil the squash. Bake for 30 minutes. The squash may not be fully fork-tender, but don't worry. It will eventually go back in the oven to cook all the way through.

Meanwhile, in a sauté pan, heat olive oil and cook onions over medium heat until they become transparent. Add celery and sauté for several minutes. Remove from heat and add to a large-size mixing bowl, along with both cooked rices, pecans, apricots, ginger, cinnamon, cardamom, cloves, salt, and pepper. Adjust seasoning, as necessary.

Spoon out cooked squash, leaving some squash in the shells, with other ingredients. Press rice mixture into each squash cavity, mounding rice mixture as much as possible. (Any leftover rice mixture makes a great side dish by itself.) Cover with aluminum foil and bake for 30 minutes, or until squash flesh is thoroughly tender. Remove foil during the last 10 minutes of baking.

**YIELD:** 8 servings

## SERVING SUGGESTIONS AND VARIATIONS

Drizzle a little maple syrup on each squash half just before serving.

Per serving: 520 calories; 37g fat; 5g protein; 49g carbohydrate; 7g dietary fiber; 0mg cholesterol; 161mg sodium.

## COMPASSIONATE COOKS' TIP

You can cook the two varieties of rice in the same pot or look for rice mixtures that include brown, wild, and red rices.

# BUTTERNUT SQUASH TIMBALES

*Wheat-free, soy-free, oil-free if using water for sautéing*

Timbales (drum-shaped molds) look beautiful on a plate. The vegetable combination is molded in a round ramekin and unmolded on the dinner plate, resulting in a pretty presentation. (The Harvest-Stuffed Acorn Squash, page 235, is an alternate main dish for this menu.)

- 2 cups (255 g) ½-inch (1 cm) cubes butternut squash or any winter squash
- 2 ½ cups (590 ml) vegetable stock (store-bought or homemade, page 213)
- 1 cup (195 g) Arborio rice (do not rinse!)
- ¼ to ½ teaspoon salt (or to taste)
- 1 tablespoon (15 ml) olive oil or water, for sautéing
- 1 large-size yellow onion, finely chopped
- 1 teaspoon (3 g) minced garlic
- 2 tablespoons (8 g) finely chopped fresh parsley
- 1 teaspoon (1 g) finely chopped fresh thyme
- 2 to 3 tablespoons (7 to 14 g) finely chopped sun-dried tomatoes
- Freshly ground pepper, to taste
- ¼ cup (35 g) pine nuts, toasted, for garnish (optional; see page 135)

Per serving: 368 calories; 7g fat; 11g protein; 67g carbohydrate; 4g dietary fiber; 0mg cholesterol; 1345mg sodium.

## DIRECTIONS

Lightly oil four 1 ¼-cup (280 g) ramekins, custard cups, or mini loaf pans.

Steam squash until just tender, 10 to 12 minutes. Transfer to a bowl.

Bring stock and rice to a boil in a large-size saucepan. Add salt to taste. Reduce heat to low, cover, and cook until rice is tender but some liquid remains, stirring often, about 20 minutes. Uncover, stir, and remove from heat.

Heat oil or water in a large sauté pan over medium-high heat. Add onion, and sauté until translucent and turning golden brown, about 5 minutes. Add garlic, parsley, and thyme, and stir for 2 minutes. Add sun-dried tomatoes along with cooked squash. Stir, then remove from heat.

To assemble, place one-fourth veggie mixture into each ramekin, and press down with back of spoon to make compact. Top with rice and press down again, to make compact. Turn each timbale over, running a butter knife along the edge to unmold the beautiful rice/veggie mixture. Place 1 timbale per plate, preferably over a bed of sautéed kale. Grind fresh pepper over top, and sprinkle on toasted pine nuts, if desired.

**YIELD:** 4 servings

## SERVING SUGGESTIONS AND VARIATIONS

The Butternut Squash Soup recipe on page 88 has tips on cutting butternut squash. Also, try roasting the squash instead of steaming it.

# MASHED ROOT VEGETABLES WITH FRESH HERB INFUSION

*Wheat-free*

I would never, ever suggest that mashed potatoes be entirely replaced on the Thanksgiving table, so let's just say this is a variation to accompany the old standby.

- 4 to 5 cups (440 to 550 g) assorted root vegetables, such as yellow potatoes, carrots, parsnips, turnips, rutabaga, and celery root, coarsely chopped
- 1 teaspoon (6 g) salt (or to taste)
- 1 cup (235 ml) nondairy milk (soy, rice, almond, hazelnut, hemp, or oat) or soy creamer
- 4 garlic cloves, minced or pressed
- 5 tablespoons (70 g) nondairy, nonhydrogenated butter (such as Earth Balance)
- 3 sprigs fresh thyme
- 3 sprigs fresh rosemary
- 2 bay leaves
- Freshly ground black pepper, to taste
- 1 bunch fresh chives, chopped, for garnish (optional)

Per serving: 271 calories; 17g fat; 5g protein; 27g carbohydrate; 8g dietary fiber; 0mg cholesterol; 590mg sodium.

## DIRECTIONS

Place all vegetables in a large-size soup pot and fill with enough water to cover; season with salt. Bring to a boil over medium heat and simmer for about 30 minutes, until vegetables are very tender.

In the meantime, combine milk, garlic, butter, thyme, rosemary, and bay leaves in a pot and heat over low heat to melt butter and infuse herb flavor into milk. Simmer (but do not bring to a full boil) while root vegetables cook. Shut off heat, cover, and let steep until needed. Remove herb stems and bay leaves. (Some thyme and rosemary leaves may fall off into broth, which is fine. In fact, if you prefer a more rustic look, remove leaves from stems so they will be noticeable once you mash the vegetables. However, do remove bay leaves altogether.)

Drain root vegetables and put into large-size mixing bowl. Mash with a potato masher, an electric mixer, or an immersion blender. Stir in part of warm milk mixture and mix until liquid is absorbed and vegetables are smooth. Depending on the size of your root vegetables, you may use all or only some of the infused milk, so add a little at a time.

Season with salt and pepper. Place mashed root vegetables in a serving bowl, and garnish with chopped chives, if desired.

**YIELD:** 4 servings, as a side dish

# SENSATIONAL STUFFING WITH NUTS

Stuffing is my second favorite Thanksgiving dish (next to mashed potatoes, of course). This scrumptious bread stuffing leaves the bird out of it—or leaves the stuffing out of the bird!—but still satisfies with crunchy nuts and flavorful herbs.

- 6 cups (300 g) diced crusty Italian bread (day-old or fresh)
- 2 tablespoons (28 g) nondairy, nonhydrogenated butter (such as Earth Balance)
- 1 large-size onion, diced
- 4 celery stalks, diced
- 2 large-size carrots, peeled and thinly sliced
- ½ teaspoon fresh rosemary
- ½ teaspoon fresh thyme
- ½ teaspoon fresh sage
- ¼ cup (15 g) fresh parsley, chopped
- 3 tablespoon (30 g) raisins
- ½ cup (60 g) coarsely chopped walnuts
- ½ cup (60 g) coarsely chopped pecans
- 1½ to 2 cups (350 to 470 ml) vegetable stock (store-bought or homemade, page 213)
- Salt and freshly ground pepper, to taste

## DIRECTIONS

Preheat oven to 350°F (180°C, or gas mark 4).

Place diced bread in a 9 x 13-inch (23 x 33 cm) or 13 x 13-inch (33 x 33 cm) baking pan and place in oven for about 15 minutes, until bread is toasted and crisp.

Meanwhile, warm butter in a sauté pan and cook onion, celery, and carrots over medium heat until onion is translucent.

Remove bread from oven, and transfer to a large mixing bowl. Add onion mixture, rosemary, thyme, sage, parsley, raisins, walnuts, and pecans. Stir well. Carefully drizzle stuffing with vegetable stock and toss gently. Add salt to taste.

Bake bread stuffing in a casserole dish (or on baking sheet), uncovered, for 30 to 40 minutes. Season with black pepper, if desired.

**YIELD:** 4 to 6 servings, as a side dish

## SERVING SUGGESTIONS AND VARIATIONS

Although you can use any type of bread, including one that is wheat-free, a crusty Italian bread works great. My favorite is Pugliese, but any kind of bread will do, including sourdough. This is also the perfect time to use that day-old bread that would otherwise go to waste.

## DID YOU KNOW?

The word nut comes from the same root as the word nucleus, referring to the central core.

Per serving: 366 calories; 19g fat; 10g protein; 42g carbohydrate; 5g dietary fiber; 0mg cholesterol; 835mg sodium.

# HOLIDAY CRANBERRY RELISH

*Oil-free, wheat-free, soy-free*

This recipe makes a beautiful side dish, a spread for crackers, or, if you increase the sugar to 1 cup (200 g), a great pie or tart filling. If it's too sweet for you as directed, cut back on the amount of sugar recommended.

- 1 cup (235 ml) water
- ½ cup (100 g) granulated sugar
- ¼ cup (60 ml) freshly squeezed orange juice
- 1 package (12 ounces, or 340 g) fresh cranberries
- 1 apple, peeled and diced
- 1 pear, peeled and diced
- 1 cup (130 g) chopped dried mixed fruit
- 1 cup (110 g) chopped pecans
- ½ teaspoon salt
- 1 teaspoon (2 g) ground cinnamon
- ½ teaspoon ground nutmeg

## DIRECTIONS

In a medium-size saucepan, boil water and sugar until sugar dissolves. Reduce heat to a simmer, and stir in orange juice, cranberries, apple, pear, dried fruit, pecans, salt, cinnamon, and nutmeg. Cover, and simmer for 30 minutes, stirring occasionally, until cranberries burst. Remove from heat, and let cool to room temperature.

**YIELD:** 8 servings

Per serving: 229 calories; 10g fat; 2g protein; 38g carbohydrate; 5g dietary fiber; 0mg cholesterol; 137mg sodium.

## TOASTS FOR THE NEW YEAR

"Here's to the bright New Year
And a fond farewell to the old;
Here's to the things that are yet to come
And the memories that we hold."
—Anonymous

"Here's to the year that has gone
With its share of joy and sadness
And here's to the year to come
May it have a full measure of gladness."
—Anonymous

# GARLIC-GLAZED GREEN BEANS

*Wheat-free*

This is a staple in my house, and it's perfect any time of the year. Browning the beans in the beginning adds an interesting depth of flavor similar to searing, roasting, or grilling.

- 1 to 2 tablespoons (15 to 30 ml) olive oil
- 1 pound (455 g) green beans, tips removed
- 2 tablespoons (20 g) pressed or minced garlic
- 1 teaspoon (1 g) dried marjoram leaves
- 2 teaspoons (10 ml) tamari soy sauce
- 1 to 2 tablespoons (15 to 30 ml) real maple syrup
- ¼ cup (30 g) toasted walnuts or 2 tablespoons (18 g) toasted pine nuts or **sesame** seeds (optional)
- Pepper, to taste
- Lemon, to squeeze at end

## DIRECTIONS

Heat olive oil in a large-size sauté pan over medium-high heat. Add beans, and sauté until lightly golden, about 5 minutes. The amount of oil you use is up to you; some may want less, some may want more. The idea is to cook the green beans so they begin to brown.

Add garlic and marjoram, and sauté another minute or two. Add tamari, maple syrup, and walnuts, if using. Cover, reduce heat to medium, and cook for 10 to 15 minutes, or until beans are desired tenderness. In the last minute, add a dash of extra tamari, if needed, and toss. Season with pepper.

Squeeze fresh lemon juice on the beans and toss.

Serve immediately while hot, though they are also good at room temperature.

**YIELD:** 2 servings

## SERVING SUGGESTIONS AND VARIATIONS

In addition to, or in place of, the marjoram, try other fresh herbs, such as thyme, parsley, dill, or rosemary. Sauté a sliced yellow onion along with the green beans. Add a tablespoon of minced shallots along with the minced garlic or a dash of red pepper flakes during cooking, to add some heat.

## COMPASSIONATE COOKS' TIP

Don't let the garlic burn or it will become bitter tasting.

Per serving: 257 calories; 14g fat; 5g protein; 31g carbohydrate; 7g dietary fiber; 0mg cholesterol; 351mg sodium.

# THANKSGIVING IS FOR THE BIRDS

The roots of Thanksgiving, a North American holiday, are in autumn harvest festivals, similar to those that take place around the world. In the United States, this holiday meal has become so centered around the consumption of turkey that people have completely lost sight of its original meaning—if they ever knew it at all.

The first Thanksgiving took place in 1621, though it was not called Thanksgiving until many years later. In fact, much of what we associate with this holiday was contrived during the past few centuries.

Everything we know about the first Thanksgiving comes from two sources: a letter by Edward Winslow dated December 1621, and a book by William Bradford written twenty years after the actual events took place. His book was stolen during the Revolutionary War and didn't reappear until 1854.

In his letter, Edward Winslow wrote, "Our harvest being gotten in, our Governor sent four men on fowling, that so we might, after a more special manner, rejoice together, after we had gathered the fruit of our labors." He writes that the men hunted birds, not because they were starving but so that they might rejoice in the abundance of the fruits and vegetables with which they were blessed.

In his book, William Bradford mentions that the colonists killed wild turkeys during the autumn season; he doesn't say specifically that wild turkeys were killed for the first Thanksgiving. Although his book gives clues as to what was on this first menu, it disappeared until the mid-nineteenth century, so it didn't have any influence on how Thanksgiving was celebrated.

The animals killed for that first Thanksgiving were most likely ducks, geese, and various kinds of fish. If cranberries were served, they would have been used for their tartness or color—not in the sugary form we eat them today. Potatoes were not available, and because it is improbable that the colonists had flour for pie crust or an oven in which to bake it, pumpkin pie was most likely absent. They didn't use forks.

Does this mean we shouldn't serve mashed potatoes, pumpkin pie, sweet cranberry sauce, biscuits, or any of the things that were not on the table of the first Thanksgiving? Does that mean we shouldn't use forks? Of course not. I point this out to emphasize the fact that we selectively choose our traditions. Our emotional attachment to tradition is very powerful, so we justify our consumption of turkey at Thanksgiving by attempting to sanctify it in historical accuracy. The fact is that we eat turkeys because that's what we were taught and because of a woman named Sarah Josepha Hale.

Hale (1788–1879), the editor of a popular magazine, began, in 1827, a forty-year quest to make Thanksgiving a national holiday. She wrote romantic accounts of the first Thanksgiving, taking liberties to appeal to her readership and including recipes for roasted turkeys, stuffing, and pumpkin pies—none of the dishes that would have appeared on the table of the first Thanksgiving.

Although the holiday "traditions" Hale created share few similarities with the original feast, I think most of us would admit that we're not as interested in creating an exact replica of the first Thanksgiving as we are in having customs and traditions we can point to that connect us to something older than ourselves. We shape our traditions out of our ideals and pick and choose which ones we want to celebrate.

Even as the myths started by Hale began to permeate the culture's consciousness, "turkey" was still not widely accepted as the quintessential Thanksgiving dish until the mid-twentieth century. Wild turkeys—dark-feathered and thus dark-skinned—became unappetizing to consumers. To make turkey meat more appealing, the "Beltsville white" was bred in 1947 at the behest of the National Turkey Federation. Turkey consumption increased and has been increasing ever since.

Although Hale did a great disservice to turkeys—curious, playful, social birds—she did have noble ideas about the significance of this holiday. She envisioned that it would be about charity and generosity, writing, "Let us consecrate the day to benevolence of action, by sending good gifts to the poor and doing those deeds of charity that will, for one day, make every American home the place of plenty and of rejoicing."

As we prepare our feast of seasonal fare, may we recognize that we can celebrate tradition while honoring our own values of kindness and compassion, and may we rejoice in the plenty we have without causing harm to another.

# CHAPTER 6

EXCUSES TO PARTY:
# BUFFETS, HEAVY APPETIZERS, AND FINGER FOOD

If more than two months go by without my having thrown a party, friends usually start calling. I admit it: I like to host parties. If I didn't, I wouldn't have written this book. I've thrown every type and size, making mistakes and learning along the way, and I offer ideas and suggestions based on my own experience and lessons.

When I say I like to throw parties, I tend to be speaking for myself and not my husband, David. He loves spending time with our wonderful friends, but the process leading up to it stresses him out—even after all this time living with me. So I try to keep the planning as stress-free for him as possible. That was a lesson that took me years to grasp, but now that I have, we're each the happier for it.

# RECIPES

## SALADS, STARTERS, AND SIDES

## MAIN EVENT

## BEVERAGES AND DESSERTS

# THROWING PARTIES

Frankly, once you've gathered more than one person, you've got a party on your hands! (Hey, you could even party solo!) The bottom line is there are as many excuses to throw a party as there are spices on a spice rack, allowing for as much variety and color as you want to add.

## SURPRISE PARTIES

When we create surprises for our loved ones, it compels to think of the other person, be creative, and create anticipation and excitement around simply spending time together. The main tip I would offer about throwing a surprise party is to find out how the guest of honor feels about surprises. If she has expressed disdain for being surprised, then don't surprise her! It's important that the party you throw for someone reflects their personality and tastes—not just yours.

"Know thyself," said Shakespeare's Polonius. It took me a long time to heed this advice. For many years, I made the mistake of leaving the organization of my birthday celebration in David's capable hands. That was nothing short of torture for both of us. Being a natural organizer (organizer has a much nicer ring to it than control freak, don't you think?), I couldn't keep from sticking my nose in, demanding to know all the details of the "surprise," which, justifiably, drove David to distraction. Now, much to the delight of each of us, I organize my own birthday parties (with his help). Some people like giving surprises; some like getting them. I now know that I fall into the former category—not the latter.

## COSTUME PARTIES

Perhaps the most memorable party I've hosted was the surprise costume ball I threw for David's birthday (which falls near Halloween). Costume creativity ran high, and it was a great success.

Don't be afraid to ask friends to dress up (even for "theme parties" mentioned below), but always offer an "out" to those uncomfortable doing so. It's better to have them at the party sans costume than absent altogether.

## THEME PARTIES

I'm someone who can't help creating a theme for whatever party I'm throwing. Even if the mood and reason for the party are obvious (holidays, birthday, etc.), I am compulsively compelled to devise a celebration theme.

For example, this past year, in honor of our affinity for film noir, "Cold War, Hot Casseroles" became the theme for my birthday celebration. This required our friends to dress in attire from the 1940s and 50s. The food was reminiscent of (or at least an homage to) 1950s American cuisine, though it could just as easily have been appropriate for a 1970s

soiree: English muffin pizzas (page 178), creamy macaroni and cashew cheese (page 251), macaroni and tuna casserole (use the Better-Than-Tuna Salad on page 72 to create your own), and cocktails from that era.

We have thrown Oscar parties, a 1930s lawn party (women in floral dresses, men in white), Día de los Muertos fiestas, game nights, and several music "jam sessions." The options are only as endless as your imagination.

## PARTY FOR GOOD

If you just cannot help yourself and absolutely need an excuse to host a party, organize a fundraiser for a cause or nonprofit organization. It's a wonderful way to support a charity you care about or help a friend in need. The most strenuous element of this is soliciting donations for food, drinks, auction items, and location, but you can always ask friends to make food and ask local businesses to donate goods and services.

JUST USE YOUR IMAGINATION, KNOW YOUR LIMITATIONS (OR THE LIMITATIONS OF YOUR ACCOMPLICES), AND HAVE FUN. THAT IS THE WHOLE POINT, AFTER ALL.

# THEME MENUS

Many of these menus can be used interchangeably throughout the four seasons, so mix and match according to your party needs.

## A BIT OF SOUL, PAGE 250
Smokin' BBQ Tofu
Creamy Macaroni and Cashew Cheese
Hoppin' John (Black-Eyed Peas and Rice)
Sweet Potato Pie

## NOSTALGIA, PAGE 254
Zucchini Cakes
Swedish Meatballs (*Köttbullar*)
Ryan's Mushroom Poppers
Tofu Filet with Cornmeal Crust and Tartar Sauce
Pineapple Upside-Down Cake

## FOR THE LOVE OF THE GAME, PAGE 262
No Queso Nacho Dip
Scott Pepper's Mexican Beans
Three-Bean Chili
Grilled Vegetable Fajitas
Tempeh Sloppy Joes

## THE GREAT OUTDOORS, PAGE 271
Spicy Black Bean Burgers
Gado Gado Vegetable Skewers
Ensalada de Frijoles
Potato Salad in Radicchio Cups
Grilled Fruit

## THE LONG, HOT SUMMER, PAGE 277
Falafel Burgers
Tantalizing Thai Slaw (a.k.a. "Holy Slaw")
Grilled Corn on the Cob
Summer Fruit Bruschetta

## PICNIC FARE, PAGE 281
Roasted Red Pepper and Pine Nut Bruschetta
Tomato, Basil, and Arugula Bruschetta
Tempeh Reuben Sandwiches
Curried Better-Than-Chicken Salad

## MYSTIC PIZZA, PAGE 286
Basic Pizza Dough
Basic Tomato Sauce
Pizza Marinara
Basil Pesto Pizza
Artichoke, Red Onion, and Olive Pizza
Beet and Sweet Potato Pizza
Sun-Dried Tomato and Walnut Pesto
South of the Border Pizza

# SMOKIN' BBQ TOFU

*Wheat-free*

The fastest way to prepare this is to use a store-bought barbecue sauce, but I've also included a simple recipe for making your own.

- Olive or canola oil, for frying
- 1 package (16 ounces, or 455 g) extra-firm tofu, cut into ½-inch-thick (1 cm) cutlets
- 1 cup (250 g) barbecue sauce (store-bought or home-made, recipe follows)

## DIRECTIONS

Preheat oven to 350°F (180°C, or gas mark 4). Lightly oil 8 x 8-inch (20 x 20 cm) or 9 x 9-inch (23 x 23 cm) baking dish.

In a skillet coated with oil, sauté tofu until golden brown on both sides.

Once tofu is crispy, place in baking dish. Spoon barbecue sauce over tofu, cover dish, and bake for 30 minutes, checking occasionally to make sure sauce has not evaporated. Add more barbecue sauce, if necessary, and serve over sautéed greens or brown rice.

## BBQ SAUCE

- 1 onion, finely chopped
- 2 tablespoons (30 ml) olive or canola oil or water, for sautéing
- 2 tablespoons (30 ml) white vinegar
- 2 tablespoons (30 g) brown sugar
- ¼ cup (60 ml) lemon juice
- 1 cup (250 g) ketchup
- 3 tablespoons (45 ml) vegan Worcestershire sauce
- ½ cup (120 ml) water
- ½ teaspoon Tabasco sauce

## DIRECTIONS

Heat oil in a sauté pan and sauté onion until translucent, about 5 minutes. Add remaining ingredients, stir, and simmer over low heat for 10 minutes.

**YIELD:** 4 servings

## FOOD LORE

The tomato-based ketchup that we know today first appeared in American cookbooks during the early nineteenth century, but its origins are in eastern Asia. English and Dutch sailors brought the Asian-style condiment to Europe. From there, it made its way to the United States, where it was initially combined with mushrooms, tomatoes, and walnuts.

Per serving: 241 calories; 12g fat; 10g protein; 28g carbohydrate; 3g dietary fiber; 0mg cholesterol; 815mg sodium.

# CREAMY MACARONI AND CASHEW CHEESE

*Soy-free depending on milk*

Here is a fabulous cheese made from cashews based on the recipe in *The Real Food Daily Cookbook* by Ann Gentry. I modified it only slightly, as it is an absolutely delicious recipe.

- 1 ¼ cups (180 g) raw cashews
- ½ cup (100 g) nutritional yeast
- 2 teaspoons (4 g) onion powder
- 1 to 2 teaspoons (6 to 12 g) salt, to taste
- 1 teaspoon (2 g) garlic powder
- ⅛ teaspoon ground white pepper
- 3 ½ cups (825 ml) nondairy milk (soy, rice, almond, hazelnut, hemp, or oat)
- 3 tablespoons (25 g) thickener such as cornstarch or kudzu root (see note below)
- ½ cup (120 ml) canola oil
- ¼ cup (65 g) light (yellow or white) miso paste
- 2 tablespoons (30 ml) freshly squeezed lemon juice (about 1 lemon)
- 12 to 16 ounces (340 to 455 g) elbow macaroni noodles, cooked

## DIRECTIONS

Place cashews in large-size bowl of the food processor and finely grind. Don't, however, allow cashews to turn to paste. Add nutritional yeast, onion powder, salt, garlic powder, and white pepper. Pulse three more times to blend in spices.

In a heavy saucepan, combine milk, thickener, and oil. Bring to a simmer over high heat. Decrease heat to low-medium, cover, and simmer, stirring occasionally, for 10 minutes, or until thickener dissolves.

With the food processor running, gradually add milk/oil mixture to cashew/nutritional yeast mixture. Blend for 2 minutes, or until smooth and creamy. Next, blend in miso and lemon juice.

Combine cashew cheese with macaroni noodles and serve. You also may bake it (see below). If you have extra cheese, make more noodles, pour over broccoli, or serve as fondue dip. Cashew cheese will keep for 4 days, covered and refrigerated.

**YIELD:** 8 servings

## SERVING SUGGESTIONS AND VARIATIONS

The cashew cheese for this recipe will be creamy, perfect for macaroni and cheese or as a sauce for vegetables. To make a hard block of cheese, substitute thickener for 1 cup (about 2 ounces, or 55 g) agar flakes. Transfer creamy mixture to container you want to use for a mold (rectangular, square, round). Once it sets (after a few hours in the refrigerator), unmold, and slice or grate. Serve on crackers.

To make the baked version: Preheat oven to 325°F (170°C, or gas mark 3). Transfer macaroni mixture to an 8- or 9-inch (20 to 23 cm) square baking dish. Cover and bake for 20 minutes, or until heated through. Uncover dish, and sprinkle ½ cup (60 g) herbed bread crumbs on top. Continue baking, uncovered, for 15 to 25 minutes, or until topping is golden brown and crisp. Serve hot.

Per serving: 443 calories; 29g fat; 17g protein; 33g carbohydrate; 7g dietary fiber; 0mg cholesterol; 1025mg sodium.

# HOPPIN' JOHN
# (BLACK-EYED PEAS AND RICE)

*Oil-free if using water for sautéing, wheat-free, soy-free*

This dish originates from a time when slaves had to make their own food from scraps given to them by the slaveholders. For that reason, African-American dishes often call for a ham bone or some kind of pork flavoring. You'll find no flavor missing here, especially once you add that very same flavor (salt and liquid smoke) without using animal parts.

- 1 tablespoon (15 ml) olive oil or water, for sautéing
- 1 large-size yellow onion, finely diced
- 1 red bell pepper, finely diced
- 2 garlic cloves, finely chopped
- 2 cups (360 g) ripe tomatoes, chopped, or 1 can (15 ounces, or 420 g) diced tomatoes
- ¼ cup (60 ml) water
- ½ teaspoon dried basil
- ½ teaspoon dried thyme
- ½ teaspoon liquid smoke
- 3 cups (585 g) cooked brown rice
- 2 cups (360 g) cooked black-eyed peas
- Salt and freshly ground pepper, to taste
- Dash of hot sauce (optional)
- Any fresh herbs, finely chopped, for garnish (optional)

## DIRECTIONS

Heat oil in a large-size sauté pan over medium heat. Add onion, bell pepper, and garlic, and sauté, stirring constantly, for 2 minutes, or until onion becomes translucent.

Add tomatoes, water, basil, thyme, and liquid smoke, and cook for about 5 minutes. Add rice and peas, and season to taste with salt and pepper. Add hot sauce, if desired.

Stir together and simmer over low heat for 10 to 15 minutes. If mixture needs more moisture as it cooks, add a touch more water. Serve with a sprinkling of fresh herbs, if desired.

**YIELD:** 4 to 6 servings

Per serving: 223 calories; 4g fat; 8g protein; 41g carbohydrate; 7g dietary fiber; 0mg cholesterol; 12mg sodium.

## DID YOU KNOW?

This African-American dish is traditionally a high point of New Year's Day, when a shiny dime is buried among the black-eyed peas before serving. Whoever receives the coin in his or her portion is assured good luck for the entire year. To maximize good luck, eat this at the stroke of midnight on New Year's Eve. If you serve it with collard greens, which represent money, you might even get rich!

# SWEET POTATO PIE

This pie, a traditional staple around the winter holidays, is especially delicious chilled.

- 1 pound (455 g) sweet potatoes, peeled and quartered
- 2 tablespoons (16 g) cornstarch
- ¼ cup (60 ml) nondairy milk (soy, rice, almond, hazelnut, hemp, or oat)
- ½ cup (112 g) nondairy, nonhydrogenated butter (such as Earth Balance), softened
- ¾ cup (150 g) granulated sugar
- 12 ounces (340 g) firm silken tofu
- 2 tablespoons (30 g) nondairy sour cream (store-bought or Cashew Sour Cream, page 51)
- 1 teaspoon (2 g) ground cinnamon
- ½ teaspoon ground nutmeg
- ½ teaspoon ground ginger
- ¼ teaspoon ground cloves
- 1 teaspoon (5 ml) vanilla extract
- One 9-inch (23 cm) unbaked pie crust

## DIRECTIONS

Steam or boil sweet potatoes until soft and easily pierced with a fork. Transfer to a food processor.

Preheat oven to 350°F (180°C, or gas mark 4).

In a small-size bowl or measuring cup, dissolve cornstarch in milk, and add to food processor with sweet potato. Add remaining ingredients (except pie crust), and purée until completely smooth.

Pour filling into pie crust, and bake for 55 to 60 minutes. You will know it's done when the middle no longer jiggles. You may need to bake for 15 minutes longer to get it just right. Although you can serve it warm (or at room temperature), I find that it sets really well in the fridge for at least an hour or overnight. I love chilled pie!

**YIELD:** 10 to 12 servings

Per serving: 185 calories; 10g fat; 3g protein; 22g carbohydrate; 1g dietary fiber; 0mg cholesterol; 15mg sodium.

## COMPASSIONATE COOKS' TIP

If you're in a pinch, use one can of sweet potato purée instead of fresh sweet potatoes. Also, try the pie crust in *The Joy of Vegan Baking* or check out Resources and Recommendations on page 296 for a good store-bought pie crust.

# NOSTALGIA

- Zucchini Cakes ▪ Swedish Meatballs (*Köttbullar*)
- Ryan's Mushroom Poppers ▪ Tofu Filet with Cornmeal Crust and Tartar Sauce
- Pineapple Upside-Down Cake

# ZUCCHINI CAKES

*Soy-free*

With the use of Old Bay Seasoning, a classic herb mixture most often used for crab cakes, these little patties can justifiably be called Vegan Crab Cakes.

- 2 ½ cups (300 g) peeled and grated zucchini (about 5 small-size zucchini),
- 2 tablespoons (30 ml) nondairy, nonhydrogenated butter (such as Earth Balance), melted
- 1 cup (110 g) bread or cracker crumbs, seasoned or plain
- ¼ cup (40 g) minced yellow or red onion
- 1 teaspoon (2 g) Old Bay Seasoning
- ¼ teaspoon salt (or to taste)
- Freshly ground pepper, to taste
- ¼ cup (30 g) all-purpose flour
- Canola oil, for frying

## DIRECTIONS

Spread grated zucchini on a kitchen towel, and roll up jelly-roll style. Twist towel tightly to wring out as much liquid as possible. (You may even need to do this twice with two different towels.) If you fail to do this, your zucchini cakes will be too wet.

In a large-size bowl, combine zucchini and nondairy butter. Stir in bread crumbs, minced onion, Old Bay Seasoning, salt, and pepper. Mix thoroughly to combine.

Coat your hands in oil, and shape mixture into patties. Coat each patty in flour. In a skillet, heat oil over medium-high heat until hot. Fry patties until golden brown on both sides. (Reheat in toaster oven or skillet.)

**YIELD:** 8 servings

Per serving: 100 calories; 4g fat; 3g protein; 14g carbohydrate; 1g dietary fiber; 0mg cholesterol; 193mg sodium.

## FOOD LORE

Old Bay Seasoning is a blend of herbs and spices named for the Chesapeake Bay area, where it was developed by German immigrant Gustav Brunn in the 1940s. The seasoning mix includes celery salt, bay leaf, mustard seed, black and red pepper, cinnamon, and ginger.

## COMPASSIONATE COOKS' TIP

Grate zucchini with grating blade in food processor or with a grater or mandolin. (It will go much faster in the food processor.) The tester for this recipe wanted me to emphasize that even without using a food processor, she whipped up this recipe in 20 minutes. She also was very excited to have used crushed Saltine crackers as the cracker meal. Thanks Allison!

# SWEDISH MEATBALLS (KÖTTBULLAR)

Traditionally served with gravy, boiled potatoes, lingonberry jam, and sometimes fresh pickled cucumber, these treats were always on the smorgasbord at my mother's parties. This version improves on the original by leaving out the animals!

## FOR MEATBALLS:

- 1 cup (110 g) seasoned bread crumbs
- 1 cup (235 ml) unsweetened nondairy milk (there are unsweetened versions of soy and almond milk)
- 1 package (14 ounces, or 395 g) vegetarian sausage (such as LightLife Gimme Lean)
- 1 yellow onion, finely chopped
- 4 cloves garlic, minced
- ½ teaspoon salt
- ½ teaspoon ground allspice
- ¼ teaspoon ground nutmeg
- ¼ teaspoon cayenne pepper
- 3 tablespoons (45 ml) olive oil, divided

## FOR SAUCE:

- 2 tablespoons (28 g) nondairy, nonhydrogenated butter (such as Earth Balance)
- 1 cup (235 ml) vegetable stock (store-bought or homemade, page 213)
- 1 ½ cups (355 ml) unsweetened nondairy milk
- 2 tablespoons (16 g) all-purpose flour
- ¼ cup (60 ml) water
- ½ teaspoon salt (or to taste)

## DIRECTIONS

Soak bread crumbs in milk for 5 minutes.

Meanwhile, combine sausage, onion, garlic, salt, allspice, nutmeg, and cayenne in a large-size bowl. Add soaked bread crumbs, and mix well by hand, making sure you fully combine sausage with seasonings.

Form mixture into tiny meatballs, ¾ inch (2 cm) in diameter, and place on a platter.

Heat 1 tablespoon (15 ml) olive oil in a deep skillet over medium-high heat for 1 minute. When oil is hot, add one-third of meatballs, and brown on all sides. Transfer to a platter lined with paper towels to drain off excess oil. In 2 more batches, brown remaining meatballs in remaining oil, and drain on paper towels.

To make sauce, heat butter, stock, and milk in a saucepan over low-medium heat.

In a bowl, combine flour and water, and mix into a thin paste. (Make sure flour thoroughly dissolves.) Add water/flour blend to saucepan and mix thoroughly. Bring to a boil, reduce heat to low, and simmer until mixture thickens. Season with salt.

Add all meatballs back to skillet, along with sauce, cooking just until heated through, about 5 minutes. Transfer to a serving dish and serve immediately.

**YIELD:** 60 meatballs or servings

Per serving: 46 calories; 3g fat; 3g protein; 12g carbohydrate; 1g dietary fiber; 0mg cholesterol; 164mg sodium.

# RYAN'S MUSHROOM POPPERS

*Oil-free, wheat-free*

Two of my devoted podcast listeners, Ryan Thibodaux and Poppy Nguyen, brought these little goodies to a party we threw, and they were a huge hit. Guests gobbled them up fast, so I recommend doubling the batch!

- 15 to 20 white or brown mushrooms, stems removed
- 1 package (5 ounces, or 140 g) veggie bacon (about 12 strips)
- 1 container (8 ounces, or 225 g) nondairy cream cheese, at room temperature
- 3 garlic cloves, minced
- ½ bunch chives, finely chopped
- Pinch of salt and pepper

## DIRECTIONS

Preheat oven to 350°F (180°C, or gas mark 4).

Clean mushrooms using paper towels or mushroom brush. Follow package directions to heat up bacon. Chop into small pieces.

In a large-size bowl, combine cream cheese, chopped bacon, garlic, chives, salt, and pepper. With a small spoon, fill mushrooms with cream cheese mixture (not more than ½ inch [1 cm] above top of mushroom).

Place filled mushrooms on a cookie sheet and bake for 15 minutes, or until cream cheese starts to brown.

**YIELD:** 15 to 20 servings

Per serving: 98 calories; 6g fat; 2g protein; 9g carbohydrate; 2g dietary fiber; 0mg cholesterol; 216mg sodium.

# TOFU FILET WITH CORNMEAL CRUST AND TARTAR SAUCE

I modeled this dish after one I ate in a local vegetarian restaurant, reminding me of the not-so-vegetarian fish filets I ate growing up.

- 1 1/2 cups (190 g) unbleached all-purpose flour
- 1/2 cup (70 g) polenta (coarse cornmeal)
- 1 teaspoon (1 g) dried thyme
- 1 teaspoon (1 g) dried basil
- 1 teaspoon (1 g) dried oregano
- 1 teaspoon (2 g) paprika
- 1/2 teaspoon ground pepper
- 1 cup (235 ml) nondairy milk (soy, rice, almond, hazelnut, hemp, or oat)
- 2 tablespoons (30 g) Dijon mustard
- 1 package (16 ounces, or 455 g) extra-firm tofu (see note below)
- Canola oil, for frying

### DIRECTIONS

In a bowl, mix together flour, polenta, thyme, basil, oregano, paprika, and ground pepper. In a separate bowl, whisk together nondairy milk and mustard.

Cut tofu into eight 1/2-inch-thick (1 cm) slices. Heat oil in a sauté pan.

Dip tofu into milk mixture, then dredge in flour mixture. Add tofu to hot oil, and brown on each side. Transfer to a paper towel-lined plate to soak up any excess oil. Serve hot or at room temperature.

**YIELD:** 8 filets, or servings

### SERVING SUGGESTIONS AND VARIATIONS

* Serve on a roll with tartar sauce (recipe follows).
* Serve as a main dish with tartar sauce and oven-roasted veggies on the side.
* Substitute Old Bay Seasoning for the various herbs.

### TARTAR SAUCE

Mix together eggless mayonnaise (see Resources and Recommendations) and relish or a combination of finely chopped pickles, capers, and fresh parsley. Add vinegar for a sharper flavor, or horseradish for some extra bite!

## COMPASSIONATE COOKS' TIP

The more you cook with tofu, the more intuitive it becomes to figure out when you need firm, when you need extra-firm, and when you need super-firm (in the case of Wildwood brand). For these tofu filets, super-firm would make them too dense. I think a water-packed extra-firm is just the right texture, so they have a good "mouthfeel" while remaining tender.

Per serving (exluding tartar sauce): 204 calories; 4g fat; 9g protein; 34g carbohydrate; 4g dietary fiber; 0mg cholesterol; 55mg sodium.

# PINEAPPLE UPSIDE-DOWN CAKE

A real crowd-pleaser, this cake—somewhat retro—is perfect for a 1950s or 1970s theme party.

- 9 tablespoons (126 g) nondairy, nonhydrogenated butter (such as Earth Balance), melted, divided
- ¾ cup (170 g) firmly packed light or dark brown sugar
- ¾ cup (175 ml) unsweetened pineapple juice, divided
- 1 small-size pineapple, peeled, cored, and cut into rings, or 1 can sliced pineapple (20 ounces, or 560 g)
- ¼ cup (60 g) maraschino cherries (optional)
- 1 ½ cups (190 g) all-purpose flour
- 2 teaspoons (9 g) baking powder (look for aluminum-free)
- ½ teaspoon salt
- ½ cup (100 g) granulated sugar
- ¼ cup (60 ml) nondairy milk (soy, rice, almond, hazelnut, hemp, or oat)
- 1 container (6 ounces, or 170 g) nondairy yogurt, vanilla or plain
- ½ teaspoon vanilla extract

## DIRECTIONS

Preheat oven to 400°F (200°C, or gas mark 6). Lightly oil a 9 x 13-inch (23 x 33 cm) cake pan.

Mix 5 tablespoons (70 g) butter with brown sugar and ¼ cup (60 ml) pineapple juice. Place this mixture in bottom of cake pan. Arrange pineapple rings on top, in a decorative pattern. Be creative! If you're using maraschino cherries, fill the middle of each pineapple ring with a cherry. Set aside.

In a bowl, stir together flour, baking powder, salt, and sugar. Create a well in center of dry ingredients, and add remaining ½ cup (60 ml) pineapple juice, milk, yogurt, remaining 4 tablespoons (56 g) melted butter, and vanilla. Stir to combine, but do not overmix.

Pour cake batter over top of brown sugar and pineapple rings. (It may seem very wet, but it will all come together.)

Bake for 30 minutes, or until a toothpick inserted into the center comes out clean. After cake cools in the pan for 10 minutes, cover tightly with a serving dish and invert so pineapple rings are facing up.

**YIELD:** 10 to 12 servings

## COMPASSIONATE COOKS' TIP

If you use a springform cake pan, you might want to place a sheet of tinfoil on the bottom of the oven to catch any potential drippings. Also, one of my trusty testers said there was a shared consensus that using whole-wheat pastry flour made the cake taste more like pancakes, hence the call for all-purpose flour.

Per serving: 264 calories; 9g fat; 2g protein; 44g carbohydrate; 1g dietary fiber; 0mg cholesterol; 187mg sodium.

# SURVIVAL TIPS FOR VEGANS

Gatherings that revolve around food can be, to say the least, stressful for vegans. Navigating the tricky waters of family dynamics, traditions, and expectations is not easy, and can cause waves in an otherwise calm sea. Here are some tips for smoother sailing.

## BE PATIENT

Anyone who has transitioned from an animal-to a plant-based diet knows that it is so much more profound than simply making new food choices. It's about questioning assumptions, reexamining values, aligning behavior with principles, and shifting the paradigms with which we grew up. All of this seems to happen spontaneously once you've had a consciousness shift, and it can be a little unnerving—not only to ourselves but also to those closest to us.

As we go through this transition, we are at once incredibly excited to see the world through a different lens and devastated to recognize the dauntingly huge scale of meat, dairy, and egg consumption in our society. It is a painful awareness for those who know the suffering that animals endure.

But vegans have to remember that as much as we have experienced a transformation, not everyone around us has. Even though we may feel completely changed, we must remember to look at how our changes affect those around us, especially our parents, no matter how old we are.

Most likely, they have cooked the same food night after night, year after year, holiday after holiday. They have gone through our picky phases, cut the crusts off our bread, toiled over our favorite holiday roast, and now we tell them that it has all changed.

On a practical level, their less-than-enthusiastic reaction may be because they have absolutely no idea what to feed you. (This is when you slip them a copy of this cookbook!) Short of that, provide them with recipes, help them create a menu, and offer to cook with them, or even for them. And all the while, let them have their reactions. Give them time to process it, just as you had to do.

## BE SENSITIVE

One reason parents take our transition to veganism so personally is because from the day we're born, food is used as a way for our parents to express their love for us. They've used it to nurture us and be close to us. When we reject what they have fed us, it may feel like we're rejecting them.

Use holiday meals as an opportunity to demonstrate that you are not rejecting their traditions but rather embracing your values. Be clear that it has nothing to do with them. Holidays are also a wonderful opportunity to show your parents that nothing need be sacrificed—not a beautiful centerpiece, not a filling meal with all the traditional fixings, not the true meaning of the gathering. How?

- Offer to host the holiday dinner. By hosting, you can show off the endless array of options and treat your family to a vegan feast.

- Offer to make the main dish and bring it to the meal.

- Communicate with the person hosting the event, and introduce some easy ways to "veganize" the standards: Earth Balance instead of dairy-based butter, nondairy milk instead of cow's milk, vegetable broth instead of animal-based broth. You get the idea.

- Don't expect family members to bend over backwards to accommodate you without any help from you.

- Be true to yourself. Although we need to weigh the consequences of our decisions, if you are uncomfortable attending an event where a turkey is displayed on the table, you do not have to go.

## BE GRACIOUS

Time and again, I hear from people who panic around the holidays because they think their families won't understand, that they will have nothing to eat. If that is our expectation, then that will be our experience. But time and again, I see the opposite take place. When you stand up for what you believe in, with grace and humility, incredible things can happen.

As much as we want our family members to be understanding and compassionate, we have to provide the same compassion and understanding. By giving compassion, understanding, respect, and patience, that's what we receive.

# NO-QUESO NACHO DIP

*Wheat-free depending on flour*

Another winner from my friend Tami Wall, this is perfect for pouring over tortillas and serving at a festive football game party!

- ½ cup (100 g) nutritional yeast flakes
- ½ cup (65 g) all-purpose flour
- 1 teaspoon (2 g) paprika
- ½ teaspoon garlic powder
- ½ teaspoon chili powder (optional)
- ⅛ teaspoon salt
- 2 cups (470 ml) water
- 3 tablespoons (36 g) nondairy, nonhydrogenated butter (such as Earth Balance)
- Tortilla chips

## DIRECTIONS

Combine nutritional yeast, flour, paprika, garlic powder, chili powder, and salt in a saucepan. Add water, and whisk constantly over medium heat until thick and bubbly. Remove from heat, add butter, and stir until butter melts.

Return to low heat to serve warm (or when reheating it). Pour over tortilla chips to make nachos, or serve as a dip along with salsa.

**YIELD:** 2 cups (450 g), or 16 (2-tablespoon [30 g]) servings

## SERVING SUGGESTIONS AND VARIATIONS

Add finely diced tomatoes and peppers (hot, if that's your preference!). Tami's original recipe called for adding 1 can (10 ounces, or 280 g) diced tomatoes and chile peppers (a brand called RO*TEL offers such a combination).

## COMPASSIONATE COOKS' TIP

Because the nondairy butter already has salt, I have virtually eliminated it. I recommend tasting it first before serving, and adding salt if necessary. This dip can easily be made in advance. Simply reheat it on the stove over low heat before serving, or better yet, pour it into a fondue pot, and keep it warm while you dip!

Per serving: 62 calories; 2g fat; 4g protein; 6g carbohydrate; 2g dietary fiber; 0mg cholesterol; 18mg sodium.

Advanced Preparation Required

# SCOTT PEPPER'S MEXICAN BEANS

*Oil-free, wheat-free, soy-free*

It is an absolute pleasure to share this famous recipe with you, known the world over (well, at least known to anyone who knows Scott Pepper). Thanks to Scott for sharing his secret, and thanks to my dearest friend, Kenda Swartz, who married this awesome guy!

- 4 pounds (1820 g) dried pinto or black beans (or 2 pounds [910 g] of each)
- ½ head garlic (6 to 8 cloves), peeled and finely chopped
- 6 chile peppers (Anaheim green if you want it mild), finely chopped
- 2 large-size yellow onions, finely chopped
- ¼ cup (30 g) chili powder
- ¼ cup (28 g) ground cumin
- 1 tablespoon (18 g) salt (or to taste)

## DIRECTIONS

Rinse beans repeatedly, and soak overnight in a large-size stockpot with plenty of extra water to cover beans.

The next morning, drain beans, and rinse repeatedly. Fill pot with fresh water that reaches 2 inches (5 cm) over top of beans. Place on stove over medium heat.

Add garlic, chile peppers, onions, chili powder, and cumin. Do not add salt yet.

Cover, and bring to a boil, stirring occasionally. Lower heat, and simmer for 2 hours with the lid off ("so the house smells good," Scott says). Stir thoroughly every 30 minutes.

Every 15 minutes or so, test for doneness. When the beans are done, add a little salt, stir, and taste. Add more salt, if desired. Serve right away or let cool.

This makes a huge quantity, perfect for a large party. The beans can be enjoyed alone, with rice, or on a tortilla or tostada. See note at left about freezing.

**YIELD:** 48 servings

## COMPASSIONATE COOKS' (WELL, SCOTT PEPPER'S) TIP

Store beans in quart (liter) containers and freeze until needed. Keep as much liquid in with beans as possible, to keep them tender when reheated.

Per serving: 116 calories; 1g fat; 7g protein; 21g carbohydrate; 5g dietary fiber; 0mg cholesterol; 145mg sodium.

# THREE-BEAN CHILI

*Oil-free, wheat-free, soy-free*

Delectable and dramatic, this dish—with its many vegetables—is a mosaic of colors. It also makes a delicious filling for burritos. Make it a one-, two-, or three-bean chili, depending on the type of beans you have on hand.

- 3 to 4 tablespoons (45 to 60 ml) water, for sautéing
- 3 bell peppers (red, orange, yellow), seeded and cut into ½-inch (1 cm) squares
- 1 medium-size yellow onion, coarsely chopped
- 2 or 3 garlic cloves, minced
- 2 tablespoons (15 g) chili powder
- 1 teaspoon (2 g) ground coriander
- 1 teaspoon (2 g) ground cumin
- 1 teaspoon (1 g) dried oregano
- ¼ teaspoon cayenne pepper
- 1 can (16 ounces, or 455 g) diced tomatoes (or fresh tomatoes, see serving suggestions)
- 1 can (15 ounces, or 420 g) corn, drained (or 1 ½ cups fresh or frozen corn, thawed)
- 1 can (15 ounces, or 420 g) kidney beans, drained and rinsed
- 1 can (15 ounces, or 420 g) black beans, drained and rinsed
- 1 can (15 ounces, or 420 g) pinto beans, drained and rinsed
- Salt and freshly ground pepper, to taste
- ½ cup chopped (8 g) fresh cilantro leaves or fresh parsley (optional)

## DIRECTIONS

Heat water in a soup pot over medium heat. The water replaces the oil that is often used for sautéing, and you won't know the difference. Use enough water to coat vegetables so they don't stick to the bottom of the pot.

Add peppers, onion, garlic, chili powder, coriander, cumin, oregano, and cayenne, and cook for 5 minutes, stirring, until onion becomes translucent. Stir in tomatoes, corn, and all the beans.

Lower heat and simmer for 30 minutes. Season with salt and black pepper, and turn off heat. Serve in shallow bowls, topped with chopped cilantro, if desired.

**YIELD:** 4 to 6 servings

## SERVING SUGGESTIONS AND VARIATIONS

* If you use fresh tomatoes (3 diced tomatoes would be sufficient), be sure to add ¼ to ½ cup (60 to 120 ml) water. Canned tomatoes have enough liquid of their own, so no additional water is necessary.
* You also can add a dollop of nondairy sour cream or guacamole on top of the chili once it's plated, or serve it with different color tortilla chips such as white, red, or black/blue.
* To change the temperature of your chili, add more or less cayenne and chili powder.

Per serving: 268 calories; 2g fat; 14g protein; 52g carbohydrate; 13g dietary fiber; 0mg cholesterol; 1050mg sodium.

# GRILLED VEGETABLE FAJITAS

*Wheat-free depending on tortillas, soy-free*

Although you can make these based only on vegetables, add some meatless
chicken strips or grilled tofu for a different flavor.

- Juice from 2 limes
- ¼ cup (60 ml) olive oil
- 1 teaspoon (1.8 g) dried oregano
- 1 teaspoon (2 g) ground cumin
- ¼ to ½ teaspoon chili powder, depending on your heat preference
- ¼ cup (4 g) chopped fresh cilantro
- Salt and pepper, to taste
- 1 large-size red onion, cut into wedges
- 3 bell peppers (red, orange, yellow, or green), cut into ½-inch (1 cm) strips
- 2 yellow or zucchini squash, halved and cut into ½-inch (1 cm) strips
- 4 garlic cloves, cut in half lengthwise
- 12 (8-inch, or 20-cm) flour or corn tortillas
- 1 cup (260 g) your favorite salsa
- Variation, Chipotle Cashew Sour Cream, (page 51)
- Guacamole

## DIRECTIONS

In a large-size bowl, stir together lime juice, olive oil, oregano, cumin, chili powder, cilantro, salt, and pepper. Add onion, bell peppers, yellow squash, and garlic and toss to combine. Set aside.

Prepare your grill or roasting pan. The vegetables can be made in a large grill pan, grilled outdoors, grilled on a tabletop electric grill, broiled, or roasted. It's up to you. Grilling, broiling, or roasting will yield the most flavor. Cook vegetables until desired doneness, 7 to 15 minutes, turning occasionally to char each side. Brush on marinade as the vegetables cook. Reserve in a large-size bowl.

Grill the tortillas, about 1 minute on each side, or microwave them on high, wrapped in a paper towel, for 20 seconds. Once warm, keep them in a low oven or wrapped in a kitchen towel to retain heat.

To serve, place vegetables, tortillas, salsa, cashew sour cream, and guacamole on a table or buffet-style on kitchen counter. Each person can assemble his or her fajita, as desired.

**YIELD:** 12 servings

Per serving: 70 calories; 5g fat; 1g protein; 7g carbohydrate; 2g dietary fiber; 0mg cholesterol; 98mg sodium.

## COMPASSIONATE COOKS' TIP

If you plan to make the cashew sour cream, consider doing it the night before so you don't spend too much time prepping all at once.

GRILLED VEGETABLE FAJITAS,
(page 265) WITH CHIPOTLE CASHEW
SOUR CREAM (page 51)

# TEMPEH SLOPPY JOES

*Oil-free if using water for sautéing, wheat-free depending on buns*

Here's another way to use tempeh instead of tofu, although the latter is perfectly acceptable. This is a hearty dish that can be a main event or a sandwich.

- 1 package (8 ounces, or 225 g) tempeh, cubed
- 1 tablespoon (15 ml) olive oil or water
- 1 onion, finely chopped
- 1 bell pepper (red, yellow, or orange), finely chopped
- 1 can (15 ounces, or 420 g) tomato sauce
- 1 tablespoon (8 g) chili powder (or to taste)
- 1/2 teaspoon salt
- 1/4 teaspoon ground pepper
- 2 tablespoons (30 ml) vegetarian Worcestershire sauce
- 1 teaspoon (5 ml) hot sauce (optional)
- 4 buns, toasted

## DIRECTIONS

Steam tempeh for 10 minutes in a steamer basket placed in a pot filled with 2 to 3 inches (5 to 7.5 cm) water. Once your kitchen fills with tempeh's nutty aroma, the tempeh is done. (It really takes only 10 minutes.) Transfer to a bowl, and crumble with your hands (if it's not too hot) or mash with a fork or potato masher.

In a large-size saucepan over medium heat, heat oil and sauté onion until translucent. Add bell pepper and tempeh, and sauté for a few minutes more, stirring constantly to prevent sticking. Add tomato sauce, chili powder, salt, pepper, Worcestershire sauce, and hot sauce (if using). Cover, reduce heat, and simmer for 10 minutes or longer. Serve on toasted buns.

**YIELD:** 4 servings

## SERVING SUGGESTIONS AND VARIATIONS

Add 1 cup (225 g) black or white beans for more texture.

## DID YOU KNOW?

Many versions of Worcestershire sauce contain anchovies. Look for one without.

Per serving: 199 calories; 8g fat; 13g protein; 23g carbohydrate; 3g dietary fiber; 0mg cholesterol; 1025mg sodium.

# SURVIVAL TIPS FOR FRIENDS AND FAMILY OF VEGANS

However much we like to think we are open-minded, flexible creatures, the truth is we are incredibly habit-oriented. Most of us crave routine and appreciate predictability. We like to feel comfortable. We seek out the familiar. We want to feel connected and safe.

This is what we attempt to create during the holidays, with our many rituals and traditions. Sometimes we succeed, but sometimes situations out of our control sneak in and rock our boats. Enter the vegan.

### YOU PANIC
"What am I going to *feed* you?" "How are you going to *survive*?"

### YOU TAKE IT PERSONALLY
"What's wrong with the way I raised you?" "You've always *loved* my chicken pot pie!" "Why are you doing this to *me*?"

### YOU LOSE REASON
"Eating chicken *broth* is not the same thing as eating the *chicken*!" "Just pick around the pieces of meat."

### YOU GET PASSIVE-AGGRESSIVE
"If animals weren't meant to be eaten, why do they taste so good?"

These may sound like exaggerated responses, but I'm sure many of us can find our own voices in one or two of them. And we feel justified in reacting this way. Because food plays such a huge role at family gatherings, we feel this change will upset the order that's taken years to establish.

It may be helpful to understand that even for the vegan, who may be viewed as the upstart, everything has changed. What was once a normal part of everyday life is now a viscerally painful reminder of immense suffering and pain. This acute awareness is the by-product of becoming awake.

Recognizing that someone's decision to be vegan is not a personal attack can go a long way toward creating harmony. In fact, families should be proud that they have raised a conscious, sensitive, compassionate person who wants to do everything he or she can to reduce suffering and promote kindness.

With a little communication, a few dashes of humility, a sprinkling of understanding, and an abstention from unnecessary or hurtful jokes directed toward the vegan, holiday gatherings can be enjoyable for everyone—vegan and non-vegan alike.

## THE GREAT OUTDOORS

- Spicy Black Bean Burgers
- Gado Gado Vegetable Skewers  ■ Ensalada de Frijoles
- Potato Salad in Radicchio Cups  ■ Grilled Fruit

# SPICY BLACK BEAN BURGERS

*Soy-free*

Depending on how much heat you prefer, you can make these burgers super spicy or mild. The recipe below is just right for any spice preference. Feel free to modify it according to your own tastes.

- ¼ cup (30 g) all-purpose, unbleached flour
- ¼ cup (35 g) coarse cornmeal or polenta
- Olive or canola oil, for sautéing
- 1 yellow onion, diced
- 1 small hot or jalapeño pepper, minced (seeds removed, optional)
- 1 red bell pepper, diced
- 2 garlic cloves, minced
- ½ teaspoon dried oregano
- 2 cups (340 g) cooked or canned black beans drained and rinsed
- ½ cup (65 g) organic corn kernels
- ½ cup (55 g) bread crumbs
- 2 teaspoons (5 g) chili powder
- ¼ teaspoon cumin
- ½ teaspoon salt
- 2 tablespoons (8 g) minced fresh parsley

## DIRECTIONS

On a shallow plate, combine flour and cornmeal, and set aside for coating later.

In a saucepan over medium heat, heat oil and sauté onion, hot and bell peppers, garlic, and oregano, until onion becomes translucent. Set aside.

In a large-size bowl, mash black beans with a potato masher or fork. Stir in onion/pepper mixture, along with corn, bread crumbs, chili powder, cumin, salt, and parsley. Mix well.

Shape into patties. Coat each with flour mixture.

Fry in a lightly oiled sauté pan over medium heat for 5 to 10 minutes, or until browned on both sides. There's a chance these burgers could fall through the slats on a grill, so if you want to grill them, use a special pan made for grilling more delicate foods.

**YIELD:** 8 patties, or servings

## SERVING SUGGESTIONS AND VARIATIONS

Melt nondairy cheese on each patty or top each with salsa and fresh avocado. Serve on a fresh bun. Freeze any uneaten patties.

Per serving: 151 calories; 1g fat; 7g protein; 30g carbohydrate; 6g dietary fiber; 0mg cholesterol; 201mg sodium.

Advanced Preparation Required

# GADO GADO VEGETABLE SKEWERS

*Oil-free, wheat-free*

Gado Gado, a traditional Indonesian dish, is comprised of a vegetable salad with a peanut sauce dressing. I thought it would be fun to serve them on vegetable skewers, which is great as finger food.

- 2 cups (140 g) broccoli florets
- 2 cups (200 g) cauliflower florets
- 1 cup (150 g) 1-inch-square (2.5 cm) bell pepper (red or yellow)
- ⅓ cup (85 g) natural peanut butter (or more, to taste)
- ¼ cup (60 ml) water
- ¼ cup (60 ml) nondairy milk (soy, rice, almond, hazelnut, hemp, oat, or coconut!)
- 2 tablespoons (30 ml) lemon juice
- 2 to 3 tablespoons (30 to 45 ml) tamari soy sauce
- 1 tablespoon (15 g) brown sugar
- ½ teaspoon red pepper flakes (or to taste)
- 1 package (16 ounces, or 455 g) tofu, cut into ½-inch (1 cm) cubes, pan-fried or grilled (optional)

## DIRECTIONS

Add a steamer basket to a large saucepan, and bring water to a boil over high heat. Add broccoli, cauliflower, and bell pepper, and cook until tender-crisp, about 3 minutes. Drain, and rinse under cold water.

In a small-size bowl or measuring cup, stir together peanut butter and water, just to thin out peanut butter to make it easier for combining with other ingredients. Add to a large-size bowl, along with milk, lemon juice, tamari, brown sugar, and red pepper flakes. Whisk until thoroughly combined. Taste, and adjust seasonings, if necessary.

Add cooked veggies, and gently toss to coat. Let marinate at room temperature for at least 2 hours or cover and refrigerate for up to 1 day.

To serve, thread 2 broccoli florets, 2 cauliflower florets, 2 pepper squares, and 2 tofu squares (if using) onto each of 9 skewers, alternating to make a pretty presentation. Do not discard marinade. Arrange skewers on a platter in a single layer and drizzle with extra marinade.

**YIELD:** 9 skewers, or servings

## DID YOU KNOW?

A typical Gado Gado salad includes mostly raw vegetables, such as shredded cabbage, cauliflower, green beans, tomatoes, watercress, and bean sprouts. Any of these veggies can be blanched (cooked quickly). Sliced, boiled potatoes and tempeh are great options as well.

Per serving: 120 calories; 8g fat; 8g protein; 8g carbohydrate; 3g dietary fiber; 0mg cholesterol; 396mg sodium.

# ENSALADA DE FRIJOLES

*Oil-free, wheat-free, soy-free*

As you have no doubt guessed, "bean salad" is the English translation of this delightful dish, perfect for a summer picnic, as a dip for tortilla chips at a party, or for combining with mixed greens for a hearty salad.

- 3 cups (495 g) cooked brown rice (recipe follows)
- 2 carrots, peeled and chopped or grated
- ½ cup (80 g) chopped red onion
- ¼ teaspoon chili powder
- 3 tablespoons (45 ml) seasoned rice vinegar
- 1 can (15 ounces, or 420 g) black beans, drained and rinsed
- 2 tomatoes, chopped
- 1 can (15 ounces, or 420 g) corn, drained (or 1 ½ cups [200 g] fresh or frozen)
- 1 cup (260 g) your favorite salsa (or more to taste)
- 1 garlic clove, chopped or pressed
- ½ cup (8 g) chopped fresh cilantro or parsley leaves
- 10 to 12 pitted black olives, sliced (optional)

## DIRECTIONS

Combine all ingredients in a large-size bowl and serve.

**YIELD:** 4 to 8 servings

## SERVING SUGGESTIONS AND VARIATIONS

To serve as a salad, top a bed of mixed greens with the bean dish and serve as a full meal or as a side. I find that the salsa really determines the ultimate flavor of this dish. Choose a fresh or homemade version.

## BROWN RICE

Here is a simple, surefire recipe for brown rice.

- 3 cups (705 ml) water
- 1 ½ cups (285 g) short or long grain brown rice
- ¼ teaspoon salt

## DIRECTIONS

In a medium-size pot with a tight-fitting lid, bring water to a boil, then add rice and salt. Cover and simmer until the rice is tender, about 40 minutes. Add a vegetable bouillon cube for flavor.

**YIELD:** 12 servings

Per serving: 86 calories; 1g fat; 2g protein; 18g carbohydrate; trace dietary fiber; 0mg cholesterol; 45mg sodium.

# POTATO SALAD IN RADICCHIO CUPS

*Wheat-free, soy-free*

This recipe, perfect as a side dish, lunchtime snack, or picnic-basket staple, can be easily modified to include your favorite potato salad ingredients.

- 8 medium-size creamy yellow potatoes, quartered (peeling optional)
- ½ cup (115 g) eggless mayonnaise (see Resources and Reccommendations)
- 4 scallions (white and green parts), finely chopped
- 2 small-size carrots, peeled and finely chopped
- 2 tablespoons (8 g) finely chopped fresh parsley
- 2 celery stalks, finely chopped
- 1 small-size red onion, finely chopped
- 1 tablespoon (15 ml) lemon juice
- 1 teaspoon (6 g) salt (or to taste)
- Black pepper, to taste
- 24 small-size radicchio, Boston lettuce, or endive leaves

## DIRECTIONS

Steam or boil potatoes until tender but not too soft. Drain, cool, and cut into cubes.

In a large-size bowl, combine cooled potatoes with mayonnaise, scallions, carrots, parsley, celery, onion, lemon juice, and salt. Add more mayonnaise, if necessary. Season with pepper, and mix well.

To serve, place 2 tablespoons (60 g) potato salad in each radicchio (or lettuce or endive) leaf.

**YIELD:** 24 servings

## SERVING SUGGESTIONS AND VARIATIONS

* Add something special to this dish, such as curry powder, to give it a unique flavor.
* Cover and refrigerate for several hours or overnight. After storing for a day or two, you may need to add more mayonnaise before serving.

Per serving: 44 calories; 1g fat; 1g protein; 7g carbohydrate; 1g dietary fiber; 0mg cholesterol; 98mg sodium.

## FOOD LORE

Variations of potato salad abound throughout the world. Some are made only with a vinegar dressing; some include tomatoes and green beans; some are more sour and tangy; some include apples. Let your imagination—and taste buds—soar!

# GRILLED FRUIT

*Wheat-free, soy-free, oil-free*

Imagine the best piece of fruit you've ever had. Now imagine it even better. Grilling extracts a fruit's natural sugar, making for a heavenly and healthful treat! Here is a guide to grilling various fruits. Most fruits take about 10 minutes to prepare this way.

## FIRM FRUITS

Cantaloupe, honeydew melon, watermelon, pineapple, apples, and pears grill well because of their firmness, and are best grilled on skewers (see below). Before serving, add a drizzle of coconut milk and a sprinkling of chopped macadamia nuts.

## SOFT FRUITS

Figs, apricots, mangos, papayas, peaches, and nectarines need to be watched more closely on the grill. Cut them in half and remove pit (where applicable). Brush with some melted nondairy butter (such as Earth Balance) or light oil, and place facedown on the grill for 5 to 7 minutes. Serve hot with vanilla nondairy ice cream.

## BANANAS

Brush peeled whole bananas with melted nondairy butter and cook, turning once, just until fruit turns golden and dark grill marks appear, about 5 minutes per side. Sprinkle on some cinnamon, drizzle on some agave nectar, and enjoy.

## SERVING SUGGESTIONS AND VARIATIONS

Although the grilled fruit is perfect as is, you can flavor it with any number of herbs, spices, or sauces before, during, or after grilling. Sprinkle with cinnamon, ginger, cardamom, nutmeg, or brown sugar, for example. Or create a spicy fruit salsa to serve as a complement to the fruit. Brush fruit with a glaze made from orange juice, lime juice, apple cider vinegar, and fresh mint.

## MAKING FRUIT SKEWERS

Fruit skewers work best for firmer fruits. Submerge wooden skewers in water for 15 minutes. (This prevents them from burning when grilled.) Cut similar-textured fruit into chunks. Thread onto skewer, filling only halfway so you have enough empty skewer to grab.

Using a pastry brush, paint fruit with a light coating of melted nondairy butter. Place skewers, a few at a time, on a hot grill. Turn occasionally until fruit has grill marks on all sides, about 5 minutes on each side.

## THE LONG, HOT SUMMER

- Falafel Burgers ■ Tantalizing Thai Slaw (a.k.a. "Holy Slaw")
- Grilled Corn on the Cob
- Summer Fruit Bruschetta

# FALAFEL BURGERS

*Oil-free, soy-free (patties); oil-free, wheat-free (sauce)*

Although a ball shape is traditional for falafel, I love making them as patties,
which bake well and fit better on a bun or in a pita pocket with all the fixings.

## FOR FALAFEL PATTIES:

- 1 can (15 ounces, or 420 g) chickpeas, drained and rinsed
- 1 yellow onion, diced
- 3 garlic cloves, minced
- ¼ cup (15 g) chopped fresh parsley
- 2 tablespoons (30 g) tahini
- 1½ to 2 teaspoons (3 to 4 g) ground cumin
- 1 teaspoon (2 g) ground coriander
- ½ teaspoon salt
- ⅛ teaspoon freshly ground black pepper
- ¼ teaspoon cayenne pepper
- 1 teaspoon (5 ml) lemon juice
- 1 teaspoon (4.5 g) baking powder (look for aluminum-free)
- 1 cup (110 g) plain bread crumbs

## FOR FALAFEL SAUCE:

- 1 container (6 ounces, or 170 g) plain nondairy yogurt
- 1 to 2 tablespoons (15 to 30 g) tahini
- ½ cucumber, peeled, seeded, and finely chopped
- 1 to 2 teaspoons (5 to 10 ml) lemon juice
- 1 teaspoon (1 g) dried dill

## DIRECTIONS

Preheat oven to 400°F (200°C, or gas mark 6).

Pulse chickpeas in a food processor until thick and pasty. (You can do this by hand with a potato masher) Transfer to a medium-size bowl.

Add onion, garlic, parsley, tahini, cumin, coriander, salt, black pepper, cayenne pepper, lemon juice, and baking powder. Slowly add bread crumbs until mixture holds together. Add more or less bread crumbs, as needed. One cup should work well. Shape into patties.

Place on a nonstick cookie sheet, and bake for 10 to 12 minutes, until golden brown on the bottom. Flip over each patty, and cook for 10 to 12 minutes longer, until the other side is golden brown. Remove from oven. (You can also fry these in a little oil in a sauté pan.)

Meanwhile, make the sauce. In a small bowl, combine yogurt, tahini, cucumber, lemon juice, dill, and salt and pepper to taste. Chill for at least 30 minutes. It is best if cold when added to the falafel burger. Serve with lettuce and tomato in a pita pocket, along with tahini sauce.

**YIELD:** 8 to 10 patties, each with 2 tablespoons (30 g) sauce

Per serving for patties: 186 calories; 3g fat; 6g protein; 33g carbohydrate; 3g dietary fiber; 0mg cholesterol; 510mg sodium.

Per serving for sauce: 34 calories; 2g fat; 1g protein; 3g carbohydrate; trace dietary fiber; 0mg cholesterol; 12mg sodium.

# TANTALIZING THAI SLAW (A.K.A. "HOLY SLAW")

*Oil-free, wheat-free, soy-free if omitting tofu*

I call this "Holy Slaw" because it tastes so darn good. This is a real crowd-pleaser, pleasing to the eyes—and to the tummy.

## FOR THAI SLAW:

- 1 small-size head green cabbage, shredded
- ½ to 1 head red cabbage, shredded
- 1 cup (110 g) peeled and shredded carrot
- 1 red onion, thinly sliced
- 1 cup (145 g) roasted, unsalted peanuts
- ½ cup (50 g) chopped scallion
- ¼ teaspoon red pepper flakes (or more, if you like it spicy)
- 1 to 2 teaspoons (3 to 6 g) black sesame seeds
- ½ cup (30 g) chopped parsley or cilantro
- 1 package (16 ounces, or 455 g) extra-firm tofu, cubed and fried in sesame oil (optional)

## FOR ORANGE GINGER VINAIGRETTE:

- ¼ cup (60 ml) orange juice
- ¼ to ½ cup (60 to 120 ml) seasoned rice vinegar
- 3 tablespoons (45 ml) real maple syrup
- 2 tablespoons (12 g) minced ginger
- 2 teaspoons (6 g) minced garlic

## DIRECTIONS

To make the slaw, mix together all slaw ingredients in a large-size bowl.

To prepare vinaigrette, combine all vinaigrette ingredients in a small-size bowl.

Pour vinaigrette over veggies and stir well.

**YIELD:** 6 to 10 servings

## SERVING SUGGESTIONS AND VARIATIONS

The tofu is optional, as this delicious salad is perfect on its own. Tofu (sautéed in sesame oil) can give the dish added flavor and texture. To prepare golden brown tofu with no oil, place cubed or sliced tofu directly in a non-stick skillet. Let it brown and crisp before turning over. Don't fuss with it; let it get brown on each side before turning it. Cool before adding to slaw. Toss to coat with vinaigrette.

## COMPASSIONATE COOKS' TIP

If you are serving this at a party, bringing it to a potluck, or just preparing it in advance, I suggest readying the veggies and storing them in a bowl in the fridge *without* the dressing. About 15 to 30 minutes before serving, add vinaigrette. Otherwise, it becomes too soggy.

Per serving: 167 calories; 10g fat; 8g protein; 14g carbohydrate; 3g dietary fiber; 0mg cholesterol; 15mg sodium.

# GRILLED CORN ON THE COB

*Wheat-free, soy-free if not using Earth Balance*

A fabulous way to prepare this favorite summer vegetable, grilling brings out the sweetness, while adding a smoky flavor. It simply can't be beat.

- 6 to 8 ears of corn, in husks
- Olive oil, for brushing
- Seasoning such as garlic powder, salt, black pepper, or fresh or dried herbs, such as basil, cilantro, or oregano (optional)
- Twine, for tying ears
- Nondairy, nonhydrogenated butter (such as Earth Balance), for serving (optional)

Per serving (excluding butter or seasonings): 77 calories; 1g fat; 3g protein; 17g carbohydrate; 2g dietary fiber; 0mg cholesterol; 14mg sodium.

## FOOD LORE

What is called "grilling" in the U.K. is actually "broiling" in the U.S. What is called "grilling" in the U.S. is actually "barbecuing" in the U.K.

## DIRECTIONS

If ears of corn have several layers of husk, peel off only the first few, leaving a few layers for protection. Pull remaining husks away from corn, but do not remove them altogether. Remove and discard silky, stringy fibers inside.

Soak whole cobs (ears with remaining husk pulled back) in a pot of cold water for 15 minutes, making sure they are completely immersed. This provides extra moisture, essentially steaming the corn inside the husks.

While corn is soaking, preheat grill to a medium temperature.

Remove corn from water and shake off any excess. Brush corn kernels with olive oil. Add seasonings, if desired.

Reposition husks back over kernels and tie each ear with a piece of loose husk or twine. To prevent burning when grilled, soak twine in water first.

Place prepared ears on grill, rotating as needed to prevent any single side from getting too charred.

After a few turns, place corn husk on top shelf of grill, and close cover. Allow corn to slowly roast for 15 minutes. Remove from grill with oven mitts, a pot holder, or tongs.

Grasping one end with a pot holder, peel down husk (as if peeling a banana), and remove remaining silk. It should come off pretty easily. Serve with nondairy butter, salt, and freshly ground black pepper, if desired.

**YIELD:** 6 to 8 ears or servings

# SUMMER FRUIT BRUSCHETTA

This normally savory dish turned sweet dessert is a real conversation piece.

- 1 baguette, cut into 24 1/4-inch (6 mm) slices
- 4 tablespoons (56 g) nondairy, nonhydrogenated butter (such as Earth Balance), softened
- 6 tablespoons (90 g) light brown sugar, divided
- 1/4 teaspoon ground cinnamon
- 2 medium-size peaches or nectarines, chopped
- 2 medium-size plums, chopped
- 2 tablespoons (30 ml) fresh lime juice (from 1 medium-size lime)
- 2 tablespoons (15 g) chopped walnuts
- 2 tablespoons (12 g) finely chopped (or chiffonade) mint leaves (optional)

### DIRECTIONS

Preheat oven to broil.

Place baguette slices in a single layer on a large baking sheet.

Stir together butter, 4 tablespoons (60 g) brown sugar, and cinnamon, and spread on top side of each baguette slice. Broil for 2 minutes, or until bread lightly browns on edges and butter starts bubbling.

Combine remaining 2 tablespoons (30 g) brown sugar, peaches, plums, lime juice, and walnuts in a small bowl. Spoon equal amounts over bread slices, and sprinkle with mint, if desired.

**YIELD:** 24 bruschetta, or servings

### SERVING SUGGESTIONS AND VARIATIONS

This recipe features summer fruits, but you can also prepare it with finely chopped banana, apricots, apples, or any favorite fruit. See pages 281 and 283 for savory bruschetta recipes.

Per serving: 88 calories; 3g fat; 2g protein; 14g carbohydrate; 1g dietary fiber; 0mg cholesterol; 116mg sodium.

## PICNIC FARE

- Roasted Red Pepper and Pine Nut Bruschetta
- Tomato, Basil, and Arugula Bruschetta ■ Tempeh Reuben Sandwiches
- Curried Better-Than-Chicken Salad

# ROASTED RED PEPPER AND PINE NUT BRUSCHETTA

*Soy-free*

Another variation of traditional bruschetta calls for roasted red peppers. You can certainly roast the red peppers yourself, but you have my permission to take a shortcut and use jarred peppers.

- 1 loaf fresh Italian bread or baguette
- Olive oil, for brushing
- 2 garlic cloves (1 peeled and whole, 1 peeled and minced)
- 1 jar (12 ounces, or 340 g) roasted red peppers, chopped (about 2 peppers if done from scratch)
- 1/4 cup (15 g) finely chopped basil
- 2 tablespoons (18 g) pine nuts, toasted (see page 135)
- Salt and freshly ground pepper, to taste

## DIRECTIONS

Preheat oven to broil.

Cut bread into 1/2-inch-thick (1 cm) slices. Brush each side of each slice with olive oil. Broil for 2 to 3 minutes on one side (being careful not to burn), turn, and broil on other side for 2 minutes longer. Alternatively, you can grill or toast bread. If you toast bread, you do not need to add oil.

Once you remove bread from oven, rub whole peeled garlic clove on each slice. Place on a serving platter, and set aside.

In a bowl, combine remaining minced garlic clove, roasted red peppers, basil, pine nuts, and salt and pepper. Toss to combine.

Top each bread slice with veggie mixture, and sprinkle on extra basil or pine nuts, if desired.

**YIELD:** 20 to 25 servings

Per serving: 57 calories; 1g fat; 2g protein; 10g carbohydrate; 1g dietary fiber; 0mg cholesterol; 106mg sodium.

## DID YOU KNOW?

To roast peppers: Turn flame on burner to high, and coat pepper lightly with oil. Using metal tongs, hold pepper directly in flame of burner or as close to heat source as possible. Rotate pepper to blacken and blister skin.

Remove pepper when it has blackened completely. Place in a closed paper bag to allow it to steam for 15 to 20 minutes. Peel off and discard the blackened skin, and remove and discard seeds, stem, and inner ribs before using.

# TOMATO, BASIL, AND ARUGULA BRUSCHETTA

*Soy-free*

Traditional bruschetta consists of grilled bread rubbed with garlic and topped with extra-virgin olive oil, salt, and pepper. This variation is oh-so-satisfying and pretty!

- 1 loaf fresh Italian bread or baguette
- 2 tablespoons (30 ml) olive oil, plus more for brushing on bread
- 3 large-size garlic cloves (1 peeled and left whole, 2 peeled and minced or pressed)
- 1 pint (300 g) cherry tomatoes, sliced
- 4 cups (80 g) chopped arugula
- 1 cup (40 g) finely chopped fresh basil, divided
- 2 teaspoons (10 ml) balsamic vinegar
- Salt and freshly ground pepper, to taste

## DIRECTIONS

Preheat oven to broil.

Cut bread into ½-inch-thick (1 cm) slices. Brush each side of each slice with olive oil. Broil for 2 to 3 minutes on one side (being careful not to burn), turn, and broil on other side for 2 minutes longer. Alternatively, you can grill or toast bread. If you toast bread, you do not need to add oil.

Once you remove bread from oven, rub whole peeled garlic clove on each slice. Place on serving platter and set aside.

In a small bowl, combine remaining minced or pressed garlic, tomatoes, arugula, ½ cup (20 g) basil, 2 tablespoons (30 ml) oil, and vinegar. Toss to coat greens with dressing.

Divide mixture among broiled bread slices, add salt and freshly ground pepper, sprinkle with remaining ½ cup (20 g) chopped basil, and serve.

**YIELD:** 20 to 25 servings

## DID YOU KNOW?

Arugula is also known as "rocket lettuce," "roquette," and "rucola."

Per serving: 70 calories; 2g fat; 2g protein; 12g carbohydrate; 2g dietary fiber; 0mg cholesterol; 114mg sodium.

# TEMPEH REUBEN SANDWICHES

This highly flavorful sandwich has great texture and crunch and is easy to make. Tempeh is a traditional Indonesian food made from fermented soybeans combined with rice.

- 8 slices rye bread, toasted
- ¼ cup (60 g) eggless mayonnaise
- 4 teaspoons (20 g) Dijon mustard
- 1 cup (140 g) sauerkraut, drained
- 4 lettuce leaves
- 4 tomato slices
- 12 to 14 slices Tempeh Bacon (page 29)

## DIRECTIONS

Separate bread into pairs. Spread mayonnaise and mustard on each slice. Add sauerkraut, lettuce, and tomato slices on 1 bread slice per pair. Add tempeh, assemble sandwiches, and cut into small triangle or squares.

**YIELD:** 4 large sandwiches or 16 finger sandwiches

Per serving for one large sandwich: 276 calories; 8g fat; 10g protein; 41g carbohydrate; 6g dietary fiber; 0mg cholesterol; 1169mg sodium.

## FOOD LORE

An alternative to the "Reuben", the "Rachel" substitutes coleslaw for the sauerkraut.

## DID YOU KNOW?

Rye is one of the grains used to make whiskey. Other varieties include barley, wheat, or corn.

# CURRIED BETTER-THAN-CHICKEN SALAD

*Wheat-free*

This is a surefire crowd-pleaser. The eggless mayonnaise adds creaminess, the apples and raisins add sweetness, and the tempeh provides a satisfying texture.

- 2 packages (8 ounces each, or 225 g each) tempeh, diced into ¼-inch (6 mm) cubes
- 3 celery stalks, chopped
- 1 apple, diced (peeled optional)
- 2 tablespoons (18 g) raisins
- ¼ cup (28 g) coarsely chopped raw pecans or walnuts
- 2 teaspoons (4 g) curry powder
- ½ teaspoon salt
- ½ teaspoon freshly ground black pepper
- ¼ teaspoon ground cayenne pepper
- 1 cup (225 g) eggless mayonnaise, or to taste (see Resources & Recommendations)

## DIRECTIONS

Steam tempeh for 10 minutes in a steamer basket placed in a pot filled with 2 to 3 inches (5 to 7.5 cm) water. Let cool completely.

Combine tempeh with celery, apple, raisins, pecans, curry powder, salt, black pepper, cayenne pepper, and mayonnaise in a large bowl, adding more or less mayonnaise to moisten according to your taste. Cover and refrigerate until ready to serve, at which point you may need to add more mayonnaise.

**YIELD:** 8 servings

## SERVING SUGGESTIONS AND VARIATIONS

Add some chopped pineapple for a tropical flair. Try coarsely chopped water chestnuts in place of walnuts and pecans.

Per serving: 227 calories; 14g fat; 11g protein, 16g carbohydrate; 1g dietary fiber; 0mg cholesterol; 150mg sodium.

## DID YOU KNOW?

Because it's a fermented food, tempeh tends to contain vitamin B12. The nutrients we need are plant-based and, in the case of B12, bacteria-based.

## MYSTIC PIZZA

- Basic Pizza Dough ▪ Basic Tomato Sauce ▪ Pizza Marinara ▪ Basil Pesto Pizza
- Artichoke, Red Onion, and Olive Pizza ▪ Beet and Sweet Potato Pizza
- Sun-Dried Tomato and Walnut Pesto ▪ South of the Border Pizza

Advanced Preparation Required

# BASIC PIZZA DOUGH
*Soy-free*

Make any type of pizza with this basic dough. If you're entertaining a crowd or just want to prepare extra dough for freezing, double the recipe.

- 1 cup (235 ml) warm water
- 1 envelope (2 ½ teaspoons) active dry yeast
- 1 tablespoon (13 g) granulated sugar
- 3 ¼ cups (405 g) unbleached all-purpose, semolina, or bread flour, or a combination
- 1 teaspoon (6 g) salt
- 1 tablespoon (15 ml) olive oil, plus extra for greasing bowl

## DIRECTIONS

In a measuring cup, place warm water. The water should be warm to the touch but not too hot, the temperature of a comfortable bath. Water that is too hot will kill the yeast; water that is too cold will not activate it.

Sprinkle yeast into water, add sugar, and stir gently until both ingredients dissolve, about 1 minute. When yeast is mixed with water at the proper temperature, a smooth, beige mixture results.

Let stand for 5 minutes, until a thin layer of creamy foam covers surface, indicating that the yeast is effective. (If bubbles have not formed within 5 minutes, discard mixture and start over with a fresh package of yeast.)

For the next steps, you can mix by hand or use a stand mixer. Directions for each are below.

## MIXING YOUR DOUGH BY HAND:

Combine 3 cups (375 g) flour with salt in a large-size mixing bowl. Make a well in center and pour in yeast mixture and oil. Using a wooden spoon, vigorously stir flour into well, beginning in center and working toward sides of bowl, until flour is incorporated and soft dough just begins to hold together.

Turn dough out onto a lightly floured surface. Dust your hands with flour and knead gently, pressing down on dough with the heels of your hands, pushing it away from you, then partially fold it back over itself. Shift a quarter turn and repeat.

While kneading, gradually add just enough of remaining ¼ cup (30 g) flour until dough is no longer sticky or tacky; this should take about 5 minutes. As you work, use a metal dough scraper to pry up bits of dough that stick to your work surface. Continue kneading until dough is smooth, elastic, and shiny, 10 to 15 minutes longer. Knead dough only until it feels smooth and springy; too much kneading overdevelops the gluten in the flour and results in a tough crust.

## MIXING YOUR DOUGH WITH A STAND MIXER:

Combine 3 cups (375 g) flour, salt, yeast mixture, and oil in large mixer bowl. Attach dough hook, turn machine to low speed, and beat until well mixed, about 1 minute. Switch to medium speed and mix until dough is smooth and elastic, about 5 minutes. Continue kneading while gradually adding just enough of remaining 1/4 cup (30 g) flour for dough to lose its stickiness. If dough is dry and crumbly, add warm water, 1 tablespoon (15 ml) at a time, until dough is smooth and elastic.

After mixing and kneading dough, shape into a ball and place in a well-oiled bowl, turning to coat completely on all sides. (This oiling prevents a hard surface from forming that would inhibit rising.) Cover bowl tightly with plastic wrap and drape a dish towel over top.

Set aside to rise in a draft-free, warm place until doubled in bulk, about 45 minutes for quick-rising flour or 1 1/2 to 2 hours for regular flour.

Once dough has doubled in bulk, use your fist to punch it down, to prevent over-rising. Squeeze dough into a ball, pressing out air bubbles. If you cannot bake pizza dough within 2 hours of rising, punch it down, turn it in an oiled bowl to coat once more, cover the bowl tightly with plastic wrap, and refrigerate. (Dough can be kept refrigerated for up to 36 hours before the yeast is exhausted and the dough unusable.) Let chilled dough come to room temperature before proceeding.

To make one 15- to 16-inch (38 to 40.5 cm) pizza, keep dough in a single ball. To make two 12-inch (30.5 cm) pizzas or two 9-inch (23 cm) deep-dish pizzas, divide dough into 2 pieces. To make individual 9-inch (23 cm) pizzas, divide dough into 4 to 6 equal-sized portions. To make appetizer-sized pizzas, divide dough into 12 to 18 equal-sized portions.

To freeze dough for later use, wrap pieces tightly in plastic wrap or seal in airtight plastic containers and freeze for up to 4 months. Before using, thaw in refrigerator for 1 to 2 days or for a few hours at room temperature.

**YIELD:** Dough for 2 pizzas, or 16 slices/servings

## SERVING SUGGESTIONS AND VARIATIONS

Cornmeal dough: Substitute 1 cup (140 g) yellow cornmeal or polenta (coarse cornmeal) for an equal amount of flour. Stir cornmeal, flour, and salt together before adding yeast mixture.

Whole-wheat dough: Substitute 1 cup (125 g) whole-wheat flour for an equal amount of white flour. Stir flours and salt together before adding yeast mixture.

Cracked pepper dough: Add 3 tablespoons (18 g) freshly cracked black pepper while kneading dough.

Herbed dough: Add 3 tablespoons (8 g) minced fresh herbs or 1 tablespoon (2 g) crumbled dried herbs while kneading dough.

Sweet dough: Add 2 to 3 tablespoons (25 to 30 g) granulated sugar with flour, reduce salt to 1/2 teaspoon, and replace olive oil with 2 to 3 tablespoons (28 to 42 g) nondairy, nonhydrogenated butter, such as Earth Balance. This is the dough called for in the Monkey Bread recipe, page 203.

Seeded dough: Add 1/4 cup (36 g) sesame seeds, lightly toasted, or 1/4 cup (25 g) poppy seeds while kneading dough.

Per serving: 104 calories; 1g fat; 3g protein; 20g carbohydrate; 1g dietary fiber; 0mg cholesterol; 134mg sodium.

# BASIC TOMATO SAUCE

*Oil-free if using water for sautéing, wheat-free, soy-free*

Consider making this sauce in quantity during the summer tomato season and freezing it for year-round pizza or pasta topping.

- 1 tablespoon (15 ml) olive oil or water
- 1 medium-size yellow onion, finely chopped
- 2 carrots, peeled and finely chopped
- 2 celery stalks, finely chopped
- 4 garlic cloves, minced or pressed
- 3 cups (540 g) peeled, seeded, chopped tomatoes or 1 can (24 ounces, or 680 g) diced tomatoes
- 1 tablespoon (15 ml) balsamic vinegar
- 2 tablespoons (2.5 g) minced fresh basil
- 1 tablespoon (3 g) dried oregano
- Salt and freshly ground black pepper, to taste

## DIRECTIONS

In a saucepan, heat olive oil or water over medium heat. Add onion, carrots, and celery and cook, stirring frequently, until vegetables are soft, about 5 minutes.

Stir in garlic, tomatoes, and vinegar. Increase heat to high and bring to a boil, then reduce heat to medium and cook until thickened, about 10 minutes.

Stir in basil and oregano about 5 minutes before sauce is done. Season to taste with salt and pepper.

Leave sauce chunky, or transfer to a food processor or blender. Process to a purée. Use immediately, or cover and refrigerate for up to 4 or 5 days.

**YIELD:** 4 servings

Per serving: 96 calories; 4g fat; 2g protein; 15g carbohydrate; 4g dietary fiber; 0mg cholesterol; 44mg sodium.

## FOOD LORE

We often think of the tomato as a quintessential Italian food. Its origins, however, have been traced back to the Aztecs around 700 AD, making it native to the Americas. It wasn't until the 16th century that the tomato made its way to Europe.

Advanced Preparation Required

# PIZZA MARINARA

*Soy-free*

This is the most basic (and most authentic) Italian pizza you can make.

- Cornmeal or flour, for dusting pizza peel and stone
- ½ recipe Basic Pizza Dough or herbed variation (page 286)
- ½ cup (125 g) Basic Tomato Sauce (page 288)
- 3 or 4 Roma tomatoes, sliced
- 2 tablespoons (8 g) chopped fresh oregano
- 2 tablespoons (5 g) chopped fresh basil
- 2 fresh garlic cloves, thinly sliced
- Salt and freshly ground black pepper, to taste
- Olive oil, for brushing crust and drizzling on top of pizza

## DIRECTIONS

Preheat oven to 500°F (250°C, or gas mark 10). At least 30 minutes before baking pizza, place a pizza stone in oven on a rack in the lowest position. Dust your pizza peel (see note below) with cornmeal, and set aside.

On a floured surface, roll out dough and shape as directed on page 287. Fold dough over once or twice, place on prepared peel, and unfold. Jerk peel once or twice to make sure dough will easily slide off. If it sticks, lift dough, sprinkle more cornmeal underneath it, and replace.

Spread tomato sauce on dough, leaving a ½-inch (1 cm) border. Distribute tomatoes over sauce, sprinkle with oregano, basil, garlic, salt, and pepper, and drizzle evenly with olive oil. Brush sauce-free rim with olive oil.

Line up far edge of peel with far edge of baking stone, and tilt peel toward stone, jerking gently to encourage dough to slide off. Carefully pull back peel, completely transferring pizza to the stone.

Bake pizza for 7 to 10 minutes, or until dough is crisp and golden brown. Slide cooked pizza back onto peel, and transfer to a cutting board. Cut pizza into wedges and serve immediately.

**YIELD:** 8 slices, or servings

## FOOD LORE

Pizza purists consider the "Marinara" to be one of the two only *true* pizzas (along with the "Margherita," which is similar but has mozzarella cheese, which is easy to veganize). Although both hail from Naples, pizza marinara is the older of the two.

## DID YOU KNOW?

A peel is a long-handled, wide wooden or metal spatula-like implement that slides quickly and easily under a pizza, making for a smooth transfer to the pizza stone. A pizza stone is a flat stone or piece of ceramic or earthenware that allows for the pizza to cook more evenly in the oven. It also helps absorb moisture, giving the pizza a crisper crust.

Per serving: 175 calories; 4g fat; 5g protein; 32g carbohydrate; 3g dietary fiber; 0mg cholesterol; 162mg sodium.

Advanced Preparation Required

# BASIL PESTO PIZZA

*Soy-free, depending on cheese*

A delightful pizza for the summer months, this pizza's simplicity matches
its delicious flavor.

- Cornmeal or flour, for dusting pizza peel and stone
- ½ recipe Basic Pizza Dough (page 286)
- 1 recipe Basil Pesto (page 75)
- 3 fresh tomatoes (any kind in season), seeded and diced
- 2 garlic cloves, minced
- 2 tablespoons (18 g) pine nuts
- Olive oil, for brushing crust and drizzling on pizza
- Nondairy mozzarella cheese, shredded (optional)
- Salt, to taste

## DIRECTIONS

Preheat oven to 500°F (250°C, or gas mark 10). At least
30 minutes before baking pizza, place a pizza stone in
oven on a rack in the lowest position. Dust your pizza
peel with cornmeal, and set aside.

On a floured surface, roll out dough and shape it as
directed on page 287. Fold dough over once or twice,
place on prepared peel, and unfold. Jerk peel once or
twice to make sure dough will easily slide off. If it sticks,
lift dough, sprinkle more cornmeal underneath, and
replace.

Spread pesto on dough, leaving a ½-inch (1 cm) border. Distribute tomatoes, garlic, pine nuts, and shredded
mozzarella (if using) over the pesto. Drizzle evenly with
olive oil, and sprinkle on a little salt. Brush pesto-free
rim with olive oil.

Line up far edge of peel with far edge of baking
stone, and tilt peel toward the stone, jerking it gently
to encourage the dough to slide off. Carefully pull back
peel, completely transferring pizza to the stone.

Bake pizza for 7 to 10 minutes, or until dough is crisp
and golden brown. Slide cooked pizza back onto peel,
and transfer to a cutting board. Cut pizza into wedges
and serve immediately.

**YIELD:** 8 slices, or servings

Per serving (excluding cheese): 210 calories; 10g fat; 6g
protein; 25g carbohydrate; 2g dietary fiber; 0mg cholesterol; 206mg sodium.

These pizzas have been staples in the Patrick-Goudreau household for many years and are just a few of the variations you can create when you use your taste buds as a guide. If you are preparing these for a pizza party, have all the fixings out for people to make their own personal pizzas.

Advanced Preparation Required

# ARTICHOKE, RED ONION, AND OLIVE PIZZA

A favorite of my husband's for many years, this recipe has followed us from New Jersey to California.

- ½ recipe Basic Pizza Dough, herbed variation (page 287)
- Cornmeal or flour, for dusting pizza peel and stone
- ½ cup (85 g) marinated artichokes, drained and sliced
- 1 red onion, thinly sliced
- ¼ cup (25 g) chopped Kalamata olives
- 2 tablespoons (8 g) chopped fresh thyme
- Nondairy mozzarella cheese, shredded (optional)

## COMPASSIONATE COOKS' TIP

Have fun with different olives for this recipe and in general. I love trying a variety at my favorite olive bar, using some for cooking, some for baking, and some for eating.

## DIRECTIONS

Preheat oven to 500°F (250°C, or gas mark 10). At least 30 minutes before baking pizza, place a pizza stone in oven on a rack in the lowest position. Dust your pizza peel with cornmeal, and set aside.

On a floured surface, roll out dough and shape as directed on page 287. Fold dough over once or twice, place on prepared peel, and unfold. Jerk the peel once or twice to make sure dough will easily slide off. If it sticks, lift dough, sprinkle more cornmeal underneath it, and replace.

Top pizza dough with artichokes, red onion, kalamata olives, fresh thyme, and nondairy mozzarella cheese, if desired. Use as much of a certain ingredient as you like, just be careful not to pile your fixings on too heavy.

Line up far edge of peel with far edge of baking stone, and tilt peel toward the stone, jerking it gently to encourage the dough to slide off. Carefully pull back peel, completely transferring pizza to the stone.

Bake in oven for 10 to 12 minutes, until golden brown. When the pizza comes out of the oven, transfer to a cutting board and slice into wedges and serve.

**YIELD:** 8 slices, or servings

Per serving: 145 calories; 4g fat: 4g protein; 24g carbohydrate; 2g dietary fiber; 0mg cholesterol; 300mg sodium.

# BEET AND SWEET POTATO PIZZA

I modeled this recipe after a favorite version served at a café in San Francisco. I must confess, I am thrilled to be able to enjoy this at home and not have to travel 40 minutes to enjoy this delicious pizza!

- 2 red beets

- 1 or 2 small sweet potatoes (garnet or jewel yams)

- 1 package (16 ounces, or 455 g) extra-firm tofu

- Olive oil, for brushing

- Salt, to taste

- 1 recipe Basic Pizza Dough (page 286) or cornmeal variation (page 287)

- Cornmeal or flour, for dusting pizza peel and stone

- 1 recipe Sun-Dried Tomato and Walnut Pesto (recipe follows)

## DIRECTIONS

Preheat broiler.

Peel and cube beets and potatoes. Steam or roast until tender.

Cut tofu into slices, brush slices with olive oil, and broil for 3 minutes. Flip the slices over, and broil for 3 minutes more. Sprinkle with salt.

Preheat oven to 500°F (250°C, or gas mark 10). At least 30 minutes before baking pizza, place a pizza stone in oven on a rack in the lowest position. Dust your pizza peel with cornmeal, and set aside.

On a floured surface, roll out dough and shape as directed on page 287. Fold dough over once or twice, place on prepared peel, and unfold. Jerk the peel once or twice to make sure dough will easily slide off. If it sticks, lift dough, sprinkle more cornmeal underneath it, and replace.

Spread half of the pesto on 1 pizza dough, and half on another, to make 2 pizzas. Top with steamed or roasted beets and sweet potatoes, and broiled tofu.

Bake in oven for 10 to 12 minutes, until golden brown. When the pizza comes out of the oven, transfer to a cutting board and slice into wedges and serve.

**YIELD:** 16 slices, or servings

Per serving: 204 calories; 8g fat; 7g protein; 28g carbohydrate; 3g dietary fiber; 0mg cholesterol; 186mg sodium.

# SUN-DRIED TOMATO AND WALNUT PESTO

*Wheat-free, soy-free*

A fine topping for crostini, this pesto also is outstanding tossed with any pasta or atop roasted veggies! It can be thinned with pasta cooking liquid or vegetable stock.

- 1 cup (40 g) loosely packed fresh basil leaves
- 1 cup (60 g) packed fresh flat-leaf parsley
- $^3/_4$ cup (90 g) walnuts
- $^1/_4$ cup (30 g) oil-packed sun-dried tomatoes, drained and rinsed (5 or 6 individual sun-dried tomatoes)
- 3 whole garlic cloves, peeled
- Juice from $^1/_2$ lemon
- 1 to 2 tablespoons (15 to 30 ml) olive oil (or oil from sun-dried tomatoes jar)
- $^1/_4$ teaspoon salt (or to taste)

## DIRECTIONS

Combine basil, parsley, walnuts, sun-dried tomatoes, garlic, and lemon juice in a food processor, and blend until a smooth paste forms. Scrape down sides, drizzle in 1 tablespoon (15 ml) oil, and blend again. Add another drizzle of oil, if necessary, along with salt, and taste. Add more salt as necessary, a little at a time.

**YIELD:** 1 $^1/_2$ cups (390 g), or 12 (2-tablespoon [35 g]) servings

## SERVING SUGGESTIONS AND VARIATIONS

Toss pesto with roasted vegetables or use it as a pasta sauce, along with fresh tomatoes. Also, try using all basil instead of halving it with parsley.

Per serving: 76 calories; 7g fat; 2g protein; 2g carbohydrate; 1g dietary fiber; 0mg cholesterol; 54mg sodium.

# SOUTH OF THE BORDER PIZZA

One of the first pizzas my husband and I made together before we were married, this recipe has a special place in my heart.

- ½ recipe cornmeal variation of Basic Pizza Dough (page 287)
- Cornmeal or flour, for dusting pizza peel and stone
- Canola oil, for brushing dough
- ½ cup (60 g) nondairy Monterey Jack cheese, shredded
- 2 cups (360 g) cooked pinto beans
- 1 Jalapeño pepper, sliced
- ½ cup salsa (130 g) of your choosing
- ¼ cup (115 g) nondairy sour cream or Cashew Sour Cream (page 51)
- 1 whole avocado, diced or ½ cup (113 g) guacamole (optional)

## DIRECTIONS

Preheat oven to 500°F (250°C, or gas mark 10). At least 30 minutes before baking pizza, place a pizza stone in oven on a rack in the lowest position. Dust your pizza peel with cornmeal, and set aside.

On a floured surface, roll out dough and shape as directed on page 287. Fold dough over once or twice, place on prepared peel, and unfold. Jerk peel once or twice to make sure dough will easily slide off. If it sticks, lift dough, sprinkle more cornmeal underneath it, and replace.

Brush dough with oil. Add shredded nondairy cheese, pinto beans, and jalapeños.

Line up far edge of peel with far edge of baking stone, and tilt peel toward the stone, jerking it gently to encourage the dough to slide off. Carefully pull back peel, completely transferring pizza to the stone.

Bake in oven for 10 to 12 minutes, until golden brown. When pizza comes out of oven, transfer to a cutting board and slice into wedges, and top with salsa, nondairy sour cream, and avocado, if desired.

**YIELD:** 8 slices, or servings

Per serving: 288 calories; 8g fat; 8g protein; 49g carbohydrate; 6g dietary fiber; 0mg cholesterol; 333mg sodium.

# RESOURCES AND RECOMMENDATIONS FOR THE KITCHEN AND HOME

Here is a quick guide to some great foods and companies.
More suggestions can be found among the recipes themselves.

## EGGLESS MAYONNAISE

Wildwood Garlic Aioli: www.wildwoodfoods.com

Follow Your Heart Vegenaise:
www.followyourheart.com

NASOYA Nayonaise: www.nasoya.com

Spectrum Organics Eggless Mayo:
www.spectrumorganics.com

## NONDAIRY CHEESE

Follow Your Heart Vegan Gourmet:
www.imearthkind.com

Soymage Vegan Parmesan

Teese: www.teesecheese.com

Dr. Cow: www.dr-cow.com

## NONDAIRY SOUR CREAM AND CREAM CHEESE

Tofutti: www.tofutti.com
(choose the nonhydrogenated version)

## NONDAIRY YOGURT

Wildwood: www.wildwoodfoods.com

WholeSoy & Co.: www.wholesoyco.com

Trader Joe's Soy Yogurt

## NONDAIRY WHIPPED CREAM

Soya Too Whipped Soy Cream: www.soyatoo.com

## NONDAIRY BUTTER

Earth Balance: www.earthbalance.net

## MY FAVORITE TEA

Teance: www.teance.com

Samovar: www.samovartea.com

Numi: www.numi.com

## FROZEN PIE CRUST

Wholly Wholesome sells delicious organic vegan pies as well as organic vegan pie shells (white, whole wheat, and spelt). Look for the shells in the frozen section of large natural food stores.

## VEGETARIAN SAUSAGE

Gimme Lean: www.lightlife.com

Turtle Island Foods Tofurky: www.tofurky.com

Fieldroast: www.fieldroast.com

## NONSTICK COOKWARE WITHOUT TEFLON

There are times that I prefer to cook with nonstick pots and pans, though I try to limit my use of Teflon. I was thrilled to discover a new line of ceramic-based nonstick cookware by Xtrema. It's safe, green, and cleans like a charm! www.ceramcor.com

## ECO-FRIENDLY LOGS

Java logs: www.java-log.com

## CANDLES

I light candles every day in honor of the innocent victims in our society. Check out my favorite vegan-owned candlemakers:

A Scent of Scandal: www.ascentofscandal.com

Soy Candles by Phebes: www.soycandlesbyphebes.com

## ONLINE VEGAN STORES

www.veganessentials.com

www.veganstore.com

## COMPASSIONATE COOKS RESOURCES

Please visit www.compassionatecooks.com to become a member, listen to my *Food for Thought* podcast, sign up for my monthly newsletter, read articles and essays, shop for cookware and books, and access countless resources and recommendations for all things veg-related.

# ACKNOWLEDGMENTS

They say the second time is a charm, and that is definitely true in the case of working with the crew at Fair Winds Press. Their professionalism, sense of humor, and dedication has made the process for this book as enjoyable as the last. Thank you Jill Alexander and Will Kiester for your trust in me and my message, Amanda Waddell for your expertise and easy-going manner, Jen Grady for your careful and thoughtful editing, Nancy Bradham and Sylvia McArdle for your gorgeous design and Mary Aarons for all your support. Thank you Patti Breitman for being my number-one cheerleader and for guiding me with your experience and enthusiasm and *VegNews Magazine* for making me part of the family.

Each and every recipe in this book was tested by a number of people, who generously gave their time and feedback to make sure the recipes were perfect. The enthusiasm with which they took these recipes into their homes and the precision with which they combed them helped make this book what it is. I am very grateful to:

Mikko Alanne, Fred Branaman, Shad Clark, Mary Conway, Cheryl Crain, Michelle Cross, Jacqueline Dunn, Terri Elder, Angela Fortezza-Soto, Toni Ann Gestone, Jen Goudreau, Joanne Goudreau, Mary Jane Goudreau, Paul Goudreau, Mark Hawthorne, Meridith Hayden, Chessa Hickox, John Keathley, JoAnn Klassen, Stephen Kling, Cheri Larsh, Randy Lind, Connie Leonard, Sharon Lew, Bylle Manss, Amanda Mitchell, Elizabeth Montgomery, Cadry Nelson, Pamela Perkins, Jill Russell, Monica Sather, Allison Schwarz, Kristin Schwarz, Ari Solomon, Sandra Soto, Mike Stickel, Shannon Tervo, Charles Tsai, Monica Valencia, Leigh Wall, Brian Walsh, Trev Yoder, and Christine Zardecki. A very special thanks to Kathy Gamez, X-tine Goodreau, Krista Hiddema, Melissa Mills (aka Miss Millie), Jessica Olson, Danielle Puller, Marybeth Strack, Tami Wall, Madeline Woo, Abby Kaster and Mir Yaksich.

Thank you to everyone whose generosity and support help Compassionate Cooks to run smoothly and with integrity: Lori Patotzka, Matt Props, and Pam Webb, my committed cooking class assistants who help me conduct the classes without a hitch; Tami Wall and Melissa Mills for generously fulfilling merchandise orders; Nate Wall for printing my flyers, brochures, and recipes; Daneen Agecoutay, Tania Kac, Chris Marco, and Jennifer Tyson for beautifying Compassionate Cooks with their amazing creative powers; Ryan Andrews for providing helpful nutrition information; Amanda Mitchell for managing so many admin tasks; Krista Hiddema for her guidance and support; Eric Zamost for his generous replication services; Mark Arellano and Darcel Walker for their pro-bono video and audio services; Margo Vigo McMacken for her Spanish-language translations; and Carynne McIver and Asae Dean for taking the time and energy to manage my Facebook and MySpace pages.

In addition, the sponsorships from my podcast listeners have enabled me to use a very powerful medium to connect with people all around the world. Thanks to Marty and Wendy Beckers, whose sponsorship of my Podcast Sampler CD as well as my *Compassion in Action* CD, have made it possible for me to spread the message of compassion far and wide.

My friends and family are the foundation on which I stand, and I adore and love you all, especially my parents John and Arlene Patrick, my in-laws Paul and Mary Jane Goudreau, and my dear friends Stephanie Arthur, Antonia Fokken, Cheri Larsh, Diane Miller, Simone Olsen-Varela, Lauren Schneider, Kenda Swartz (aka Sunny K), and Cathleen Young. Everyone else I hold dear has either already been mentioned here or is in my heart.

Simon and Schuster, my feline boys of 15 years, bring me joy every single moment. They are everything that is perfect in this world.

And finally, clichéd though it is, everything I do is possible because of my husband, David Goudreau. He spends countless hours enhancing the technical aspects of Compassionate Cooks—even after working all day to bring home the veggie bacon—and is my cohort in living a compassionate life. Not only am I lucky enough to live with my CTO, but I get to live with my best friend, as well. After 14 years of his love and support, my only hope is that I can reciprocate with equal selflessness and devotion. *E non ho amato mai tanto la vita! Tanto la vita!*

# ABOUT THE AUTHOR

Raised on a typical American diet of meat, dairy, and eggs, Colleen Patrick-Goudreau was shocked by what she learned when she read *Diet for a New America* at age nineteen. No longer able to justify eating animals and their products, Colleen began a journey of discovery that continues to this day. Determined to raise awareness about animal suffering, she founded Compassionate Cooks to be a voice for the more than 45 billion land and sea animals killed every year in the United States for human consumption. Her work is dedicated to them.

Having earned a master's degree in English literature, Colleen uses her writing and communication skills to raise consciousness of the animal issues about which so many people are unaware. A sought-after and inspiring public speaker on the spiritual, social, and practical aspects of a vegan lifestyle, Colleen has appeared on the *Food Network*, is a columnist for *VegNews Magazine*, and is a contributor to *National Public Radio*. Her first book, *The Joy of Vegan Baking*, won *VegNews Magazine's* "Cookbook of the Year" award. She is grateful to have the opportunity to witness transformations taking place in people as they gain the tools and resources they need to reflect their values in their daily choices.

# INDEX